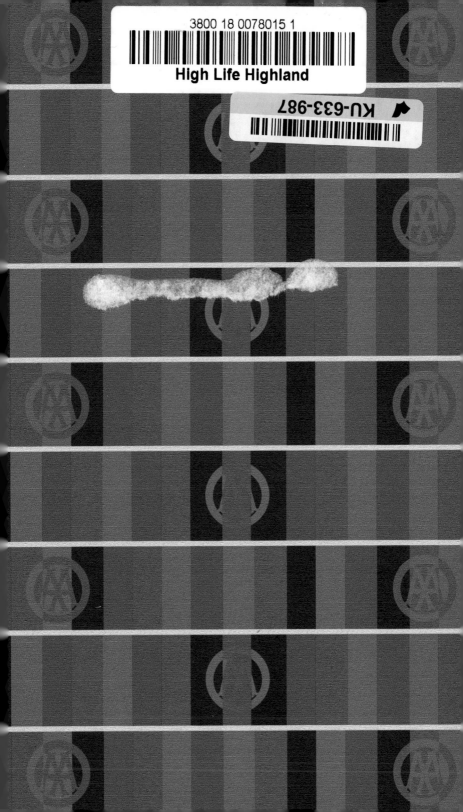

BUS FARE: WRITINGS ON LONDON'S MOST LOVED MEANS OF TRANSPORT

BUS FARE: WRITINGS ON LONDON'S MOST LOVED MEANS OF TRANSPORT

edited by Travis Elborough & Joe Kerr

Published by AA Publishing, a trading name of AA Media Limited,
Fanum House, Basing View, Basingstoke, Hampshire, RG21 4EA, UK.

theAA.com

First published in 2018

10 9 8 7 6 5 4 3 2 1

A CIP catalogue record for this book is available from the British Library.

ISBN: 978-0-7495-7928-9

Typeset in Komet Light 9pt

Managing Editor: Rebecca Needes
Art Director: James Tims
Designer: Tom Whitlock
Repro: Ian Little
Cover: David Wardle

Printed and bound by CPI Group (UK) Ltd, Croydon, CR0 4YY

A05556

In tribute to the late Colin Curtis OBE, who served London Transport for more than 40 years, and was the last survivor of the design team for the legendary Routemaster bus

Travis Elborough's books include *The Bus We Loved: London's Affair with the Routemaster.* He was the co-editor of *A London Year,* an anthology of diaries charting life in the capital over the last five hundred years.

Professor **Joe Kerr** is an architectural historian and co-editor of *London: From Punk to Blair.* He is also a bus driver at Tottenham garage.

CONTENTS

13 THE BORIS BUS

14 HOLD ON, SLEEP TIGHT, GOOD NIGHT BUS

APPENDIX: TRANSPORT TERMS AND LONDON BUS TIMELINE

END

INTRODUCTION

This anthology aims to capture something of the unique relationship that Londoners have with their most important mode of transport, the London bus. Citizens of this great metropolis have a complex relationship with the place they live in, complaining about many aspects of their daily life there, whilst simultaneously remaining staunch advocates of its greatness and uniqueness. And so it is with their buses, endlessly criticised for lateness, slowness and the overall quality of service, and yet relied upon by all, of whatever class or culture, to keep the city moving and working, and held in great affection by most (if not all) of their passengers.

London's bus network, which is comprised of 675 routes and operated by around 9,000 buses at peak times, is integral to the city. It functions as a vast distribution system for people, information and goods, and acts as a conduit for every kind of human feeling and emotion. But, equally, it is enigmatic and perverse — it serves the city whilst simultaneously helping to pollute it, and it works to keep the whole place moving whilst often being held responsible for jamming it up. It is reasonably clear and logical for its daily users, but often hopelessly complex and confusing for visitors to the city; it is convenient and easy to use for the nimble and able-bodied, but a daunting challenge for the elderly and less mobile, and a potential battleground for wheelchair users and for parents with pushchairs. But it is precisely its complexity and contrariness that provides such a rich seam of urban experience to dig into.

Like so many aspects of London life, to understand how London's buses operate in the present requires a knowledge of the network's long and eventful history. This book explores the origins and the development of the bus network over the last two centuries, from a single horse-drawn service introduced in 1829 to the complex and comprehensive service provided today. It is perhaps not well enough known that the core of the modern network has operated in a form that is recognisable to us today for over a hundred years. If you catch a No 2 on Baker Street, or a No 9 on the Strand, or a No 24 in Parliament Square then you are in effect repeating a journey that has been made on a daily basis since before World War I. We will consider the consequences for the city and for its citizens and schools and businesses, of running the same bus route down the same streets a hundred or more times a day for a hundred years.

But London's buses are not merely a vital component of the city's infrastructure; they are equally embedded in its culture: written about,

Crews in white boilersuit uniforms pose with an RT-type bus in 1950, prior to the official send-off of the goodwill continental tour to herald the Festival of Britain

sung about, joked about, filmed, painted (and painted on), advertised, and celebrated in myriad ways. And for the many thousands of people who have depended on them for a livelihood – drivers, conductors, cleaners, mechanics, inspectors – they are a world all of their own, complete with a distinct language, with uniforms, with places, and with men and women of every imaginable culture and ethnicity. London's buses have also travelled to many other parts of the world, both to carry troops to battle on the Western Front, and to advertise swinging London to audiences in San Francisco and Montreal; either way, they helped to establish the double-decker bus as the quintessential icon of the city they served.

We have aimed to illustrate something of this richness and diversity, by drawing on a range of sources from newspaper reports, technical and transport journals, guide books, diaries, letters, poems, novels and non-fiction pieces combined with freshly commissioned articles and interviews with leading Londoners of today. To the best of our knowledge, there has never been a comparable attempt to draw together the diversity of writing on the London omnibus between the covers of a single book. This is not altogether surprising, as buses have been justly described as the Cinderella service of London's various transport systems; despite carrying nearly twice as many passengers as the Underground, the bus network features far less prominently in public consciousness. Buses are just there, carrying their 2 billion passengers a year, generating little attention or fuss – unless, of course, something goes significantly wrong with the service.

The surprising revelation of this project, however, has been the realisation of quite how many writers, including those with considerable literary reputations, have been drawn to write about the humble bus. Who would have thought an anthology that embraces such exalted figures as Dickens, Woolf, Morton, Hardy, Kipling, Bennett, Self and Sinclair could possibly be directed at such a such a workaday subject? Indeed, these writers display such an expert knowledge of buses and their operation that they sometimes even play a significant role in narrative and plot, rather than merely featuring as background colour. For instance:

> [Virginia] Woolf knew the colours, routes, and fares of the omnibuses that formed a web across London. She would have been familiar with the constant accounts in The Times and elsewhere about omnibus-related traffic congestion, accidents, fares, and strikes (especially the 1926 strike). It is therefore not surprising that she would

have appropriated the omnibus as a constant symbol in
*her city novels**

It is perhaps typical that the same commentator notes that the role played by the omnibus in Woolf's writing is 'largely unexamined'. But what is equally revealing about collecting together this material is how richly and vividly it portrays the daily experiences and discomforts of bus passengers and bus crew alike, creating a seamless unity of experience across nearly two centuries of London life. For although buses have undergone so much change over their long history – from horse drawn to motorised; from open to roofed top decks and staircases; and from private operation through public ownership and back to private again – nonetheless to read these accounts is to be constantly surprised and delighted at how recognisable and familiar so many of the details are of a journey on a Victorian omnibus compared to today's version of the same. Who could not empathise with the trepidations of provincial women making their first excursion on a London bus in 1862, and suffering such familiar indignities as buses stopping too far from the kerb? And who could fail to recognise that number five of the twelve Omnibus Laws published by *The Times* in 1836 – 'Sit with your limbs straight, and do not let your legs describe an angle of 45 degrees, thereby occupying the room of two persons' – is responding to what is known today as *manspreading*?

This sense of a continuity of experience is particularly valuable for the light it sheds on the life of the bus in the era before London Transport, Routemaster buses, Cliff Richard, and all those other signifiers of the system that we all know and use today. It shows that buses were equally as important to those older iterations of the city beyond the reach of contemporary memories, and played as vivid a part in the culture and commerce of those older Londons as they have for more recent generations – if anything, even more so. It is also delightful to learn that the personal knowledge of bus routes and destinations and times that Dickens and Woolf and Bennett possessed a century and more ago were just as precious and hard-won an acquisition for the dedicated Londoner as they are for contemporary metropolitans.

So do please Hold Very Tight on this journey across 190 years of life, movement, congestion, joy, frustration and wonder in the company of the indefatigable London Bus.

---

* (Eleanor McNees, in Evans & Cornish, eds. *Woolf and the City: Selected Papers from the Nineteenth Annual Conference on Virginia Woolf* Clemson University Digital Press, 2010)

1 THE AGE OF THE OMNIBUS

London owes its buses to one man: George Shillibeer. A coach-builder with a livery stable in Bury Street, Bloomsbury, Shillibeer began operating an omnibus service modelled after those he'd seen in France on 4 July 1829. His horse-drawn omnibus 'on the Parisian mode' ran from Paddington to Bank along the New Road (now the Marylebone, Pentonville, Euston and City Roads) and was helmed by a uniform-wearing driver and conductor. A winning formula was born and the capital at a stroke transformed. The humble London omnibus and its routes, rules, and types, immediately became topics to be considered in worthy newspapers and journals, the efficacy of their operational methods pondered by Charles Dickens, their staff quizzed by proto-social anthropologists like Henry Mayhew and the vehicles themselves finding their way into Victorian works of fiction and verse.

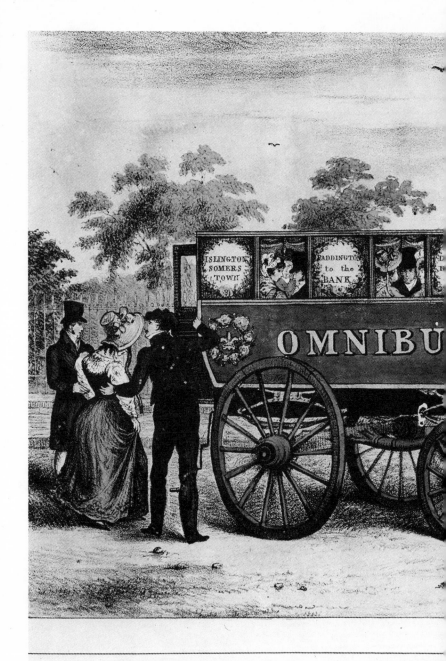

SHILLIBE

A New Carriage on the Parisian Mode, for the Con

Lithograph illustrating Shillibeer's Omnibus c.1829.

OMNIBUS.

Inside Passengers from PADDINGTON to the BANK.

OMNIBUS

G. SHILLIBEER, induced by the universal admiration the above vehicle called forth at Paris, has commenced running one upon the Parisian mode, from PADDINGTON TO BANK.

The superiority of the Carriage over the ordinary Stage Coaches, for comfort and safety, must be obvious, all the Passengers being Inside and the Fare charged from Paddington to the Bank being One Shilling, and from Islington to the Bank or Paddington, Sixpence.

The Proprietor begs to add, that a person of great respectability attends his Vehicle as Conductor; and every possible attention will be paid to the accommodation of Ladies and Children.

the first Omnibus advertisement,
published in The British Traveller, *4 July 1829*

GEORGE SHILLIBEER

The man who introduced the bus to London

Nick Rennison

The Yorkshire Stingo was a pub that once stood more or less where Edgware Road tube station now stands. It took its odd, memorable name from an 18th-century slang word for a particularly strong beer. On Saturday morning, 4 July 1829, anyone passing the Yorkshire Stingo would have witnessed an unusual sight. A weird kind of elongated stagecoach was about to set off on its maiden journey. More than 16 feet in length, it could, readily if not entirely comfortably, accommodate up to 22 passengers, all of whom had to clamber into it via steps and a door at the rear. Exciting considerable notice, 'both from the novel form of the carriage and the elegance with which it was fitted out', as one report put it, the vehicle had a green body with yellow wheels and neat red curtains for its windows. Its driver was dressed in a greatcoat of plum-coloured cloth, and sported both a rakish beaver hat and a green-and-blue cravat. Its conductor, a man supposed to attract clients, collect fares, and to give 'every possible attention to the accommodation of Ladies and Children', was 'a person of great respectability', suitably attired in white trousers, and a black jacket adorned with metal buttons. (The uniform was designed to mimic that of a Royal Navy midshipman.) The first conductor was said to be a French 'nautical friend' of the vehicle's inventor. In the words of one commentator at the time, this elegant individual 'captivated all the fair damsels of Paddington Green with his handsome figure and beautiful accent'.

Four times daily the new 'omnibus', as it was called, made its way from the Yorkshire Stingo to the Bank of England. Then it turned around and headed back to the tavern. Traversing the Marylebone, Euston, Pentonville Roads, and venturing further via City Road and Moorgate, it was following (and helping to establish) one of the first commuter routes into the City. For some weeks, until the novelty wore off, crowds assembled outside the Yorkshire Stingo to see it set off on its journey. It became the talk of the town and the subject of an outpouring of newspaper articles. Three days after its debut, the *Morning Post* newspaper heralded its arrival. 'Saturday the new vehicle, called the Omnibus, commenced running from Paddington to the City, and excited considerable notice... It was drawn by three beautiful bays abreast, after the French fashion. The Omnibus is a handsome machine, in the shape of a van. The width the horses occupy will render the vehicle rather inconvenient to be turned or driven through some of the streets of London.' The fare between Paddington and the Bank was 1s (five pence) and initially included the use of newspapers and magazines, although this had to be given up because too many inconsiderate passengers, in the words of one early conductor, 'boned the books' i.e. walked off with them.

The man behind this extraordinary addition to London's streets was George Shillibeer. Just about the only image of Shillibeer that exists today is a photograph which shows him in late middle age as a seemingly prosperous, paunchy Victorian, sitting for his portrait in an armchair as well-upholstered as he is and staring po-faced into the middle distance. In fact, of course, he was a product of the Georgian and Regency eras. He was born, probably in Marylebone, although some sources claim Tottenham Court Road, in 1797. His initial career was in the Navy but, by his early twenties, he was working for Hatchetts, one of the largest coach-making firms in Long Acre, then the centre of that industry. Once he had learned his trade, the adventurous Shillibeer decided that Paris offered him better opportunities than London and he moved to the French capital in the early 1820s.

Almost certainly, he had already heard of the new developments in public transport in Paris. In 1819, the banker and politician Jacques Laffitte had introduced super-sized coaches to the city's streets. Another Frenchman gave them their name. A retired soldier called Baudry also began operating giant coaches. Noticing a grocer by the name of Omnès who advertised his shop with the slogan 'Omnès Omnibus', a pun on the Latin words meaning 'Everything for Everybody', Baudry decided to dub his vehicle 'L'Omnibus'. The name caught on.

Meanwhile Shillibeer had made a success of his time in Paris. He was employed by Laffitte himself to build two of the new omnibuses and began to realise that what worked for Paris would work for his home city. Returning to London, he set up as a coach-builder and livery stable keeper in Bury Street, Bloomsbury. In 1827, he was commissioned by the newly established Newington Academy of Girls, a Quaker school in what is now Stoke Newington Church Street, to build another of the giant coaches which he had already constructed across the Channel. This one was intended to carry pupils from the school to the Quaker meeting house in Gracechurch Street. The first school bus trundled out of Stoke Newington that year and headed off to the City. A Quaker gentleman named Joseph Pease wrote a letter to a relative. It included a poem about the school which mentioned Shillibeer's coach:

> *The straight path of Truth the dear Girls keep their feet in,*
> *And ah! it would do your heart good, Cousin Anne,*
> *To see them arriving at Gracechurch Street Meeting,*
> *All snugly packed up, twenty-five in a van.*

(Judging by this example of his versifying skills, it is just as well that Pease had other talents with which to make his way through life. He was a pioneer of the railways, one of the first investors in the Stockton and Darlington Railway Company, and later became the first Quaker to take his seat in the House of Commons.)

The success of his school bus stimulated Shillibeer's ambitions to make more extensive use of his Parisian experience. At the beginning of April 1829, he wrote, 'I am engaged in building two vehicles after the recently established French omnibus, which when completed I propose starting on the Paddington Road.' Two months later the first of his new omnibuses left the Yorkshire Stingo and a new era in the history of London transport had begun. George Shillibeer originally wanted to call his carriages 'Economists' but the name never caught on. For a time, Londoners knew them as 'Shillibeers' but they ended up, like their Parisian counterparts, as 'Omnibuses'. (We could, in a parallel universe, be talking today about catching the 'beer' rather than the 'bus'.)

In order for the idea to be profitable, the new vehicles needed to be full. They were not aimed at the lower end of the transport market. In the 1980s, Margaret Thatcher allegedly said that any man over the age of 26 who found himself on a bus could count himself a failure in life. But Shillibeer's potential customers were not the financial flops of the era. They were the businessmen and bankers who worked in the City and lived in Paddington, then a leafy village on the very outskirts of urban development. A fare of one shilling does not seem much today but, at a time when a workman may not have been earning more than a pound a week, and some received much less, it excluded most people from travelling on the omnibus.

Despite this, the new omnibuses had at least three radically new features. First, they started at the time announced however many people were on board. If only a couple of the seats were filled, the bus still departed. Second, if you could pay the fare, there was no class distinction. Everybody travelled together. There was no first class, second class and third class as there was to be on the railways. Finally, there was no need to book in advance – you simply turned up and took what seat was available

The brilliance and timeliness of Shillibeer's ideas were clear from the speed with which competitors sprang up. For a short period of time,

Shillibeer was raking in the money. Takings were up to £100 a day. It was too good to last. Others eyed his success and thought they could match it. Within a couple of years there were dozens and dozens of rival omnibuses touting for trade between Paddington and the City. Shillibeer was obliged to emphasise his priority by painting 'Shillibeer's Original Omnibuses' on the sides of his vehicles in a desperate attempt to distinguish them from the multitude of competitors. It didn't work.

Two years after the maiden journey from the Yorkshire Stingo, Shillibeer was running 12 buses along the New Road but, between them, his rivals were running 78. The courtesy and efficiency of his conductors were initially praised — many were said to be the sons of naval officers — but, as other bus operators appeared and competition became fiercer, stories of conductors' courtesy became rarer. Instead, they grew notorious for their eagerness to cram as many passengers into their vehicles as possible. The four-mile route into the City became a devil-take-the-hindmost madhouse. Buses raced one another along the New Road at top speed, as customers clung to their seats. Bus drivers and conductors (and sometimes passengers) came to blows in their attempts to fill the seats of the vehicles. Accidents and disturbances of the peace became so frequent that in 1832 the 'omnibus nuisance' was mentioned in Parliament as a problem that needed a solution. Acts were passed for the regulation of the new buses. Drivers and conductors should be licensed. The job of Registrar of Licenses was promised to Shillibeer but it was given to somebody else with greater pull in the corridors of power. He was offered instead the consolation prize of assistant to the Registrar but declined it.

By this time, he was in trouble. He had persistent problems with dishonest employees. Henry Mayhew, who writes at some length about Shillibeer in his famous 1851 work *London Labour and the London Poor*, describes how drivers and conductors defrauded him of some of his takings. In an attempt to prevent this, Shillibeer hired an inventor to come up with a machine that fitted to the steps of an omnibus. Every time someone entered or left the vehicle, a plate was depressed and a counter triggered. The total number of passengers in a day was automatically recorded. The fraudsters were enraged by this attempt to thwart their scam. After a fortnight's trial on one omnibus, men wielding sledgehammers smashed the machine to smithereens. Shillibeer was obliged to revert to the less ingenious method of a meter which the conductor was supposed to operate every time anyone got on board. Obviously, this was open to cheating by any conductor who fancied doing so.

His finances went into freefall. He declared himself bankrupt in 1831 and was obliged to give up his New Road route. The Stage Carriages Act of the following year lifted restrictions on the new omnibuses operating in the

City. By the end of the decade there were 600 buses in London. A survey in 1839 gathered some early traffic statistics. Of 5,515 wheeled vehicles which passed a given point in 18 hours on Wednesday January 16, about one in six was an omnibus. Shillibeer, the man who started it all, bounced back from bankruptcy and set up a new route between Woolwich and Greenwich. Competition was stiff on that route, particularly from newly developed railway, and he went out of business again in 1835. This time he was obliged to catch the ferry for Boulogne with creditors in hot pursuit.

He returned to London some months later, hoping to evade attention, but was promptly arrested, tried in a debtors' court and sentenced to a spell in the Fleet Prison. He served his time but, soon after his release, dozens of cases of smuggled French brandy were found on premises he owned in Camden. Before he knew it, he was back in stir.

After his second experience of jail, Shillibeer seems to have decided that running omnibuses (and smuggling brandy) were too exciting for him. He chose instead to go into the funeral business. He invented a 'Patent Funeral Carriage, expanding and contracting at pleasure' which he displayed at the Great Exhibition in 1851. Advertised as combining in one vehicle 'the necessary funeral cortege of a hearse and a mourning coach' and being 'particularly adapted for the interment of children', it nonetheless failed to attract the attention his omnibus had. Shillibeer lived on for another 15 years after his expanding hearse had been one of the less publicised sights to be seen at the Crystal Palace. He died in Brighton in 1866 and was buried in the churchyard at Chigwell, the small Essex town where he had made his home in his final years.

Memories of the man himself have long faded. Few recognise his name today. Even the fabled 'man on the Clapham omnibus' probably has no idea who introduced to London the mode of transport on which he is travelling. There is no blue plaque to commemorate Shillibeer, although plenty exist to people who had far less influence on London than he did. Shillibeer Place in Marylebone recalls the site of the livery stables where the horses for his New Road buses were kept. Until recently there was a George Shillibeer pub in North London where the depot for an omnibus company once stood. Even that has now changed its name to the less evocative, indeed downright banal 'The Depot'. Those who want to celebrate George Shillibeer's unique contribution to London's history would do best to visit the London Transport Museum in Covent Garden. There in all its glory they can see a replica, built in the centenary year of 1929 by apprentices at London General Omnibus Company's Chiswick works, of the original omnibus which set off from the Yorkshire Stingo nearly two centuries ago.

OMNIBUSES, STREET SKETCHES NO 1

Charles Dickens

It is very generally allowed that public conveyances afford an extensive field for amusement and observation. Of all the public conveyances that have been constructed since the days of the Ark — we think that is the earliest on record — to the present time, commend us to an omnibus. A long stage is not to be despised, but there you have only six insides, and the chances are, that the same people go all the way with you — there is no change, no variety. Besides, after the first twelve hours or so, people get cross and sleepy, and when you have seen a man in his nightcap, you lose all respect for him; at least, that is the case with us. Then on smooth roads people frequently get prosy, and tell long stories, and even those who don't talk, may have very unpleasant predilections.

We once travelled four hundred miles, inside a stage-coach, with a stout man, who had a glass of rum-and-water, warm, handed in at the window at every place where we changed horses. This was decidedly unpleasant. We have also travelled occasionally, with a small boy of a pale aspect, with light hair, and no perceptible neck, coming up to town from school under the protection of the guard, and directed to be left at the Cross Keys till called for. This is, perhaps, even worse than rum-and-water in a close atmosphere. Then there is the whole train of evils consequent on a change of the coachman; and the misery of the discovery — which the guard is sure to make the moment you begin to doze — that he wants a brown-paper parcel, which he distinctly remembers to have deposited under the seat on which you are reposing. A great deal of bustle and groping takes place, and when you are thoroughly awakened, and severely cramped, by holding your legs up by an almost supernatural exertion, while he is looking behind them, it suddenly occurs to him that he put it in the fore-boot. Bang goes the door; the parcel is immediately found; off starts the coach again; and the guard plays the key-bugle as loud as he can play it, as if in mockery of your wretchedness.

Now, you meet with none of these afflictions in an omnibus; sameness there can never be. The passengers change as often in the course of one journey as the figures in a kaleidoscope, and though not so glittering, are far more amusing. We believe there is no instance on record, of a man's having gone to sleep in one of these vehicles. As to long stories, would any man venture to tell a long story in an omnibus? and even if he did, where would be the harm? nobody could possibly hear what he was talking about. Again; children, though occasionally, are not often to be found in an omnibus; and even when they are, if the vehicle be full, as is generally the case, somebody sits upon them, and we are unconscious of their presence. Yes, after mature reflection, and considerable experience, we are decidedly of opinion, that of all known vehicles, from the glass-coach in which we were taken to be christened, to that sombre caravan in which we must one day make our last earthly journey, there is nothing like an omnibus.

We will back the machine in which we make our daily peregrination from the top of Oxford-street to the city, against any 'buss' on the road, whether it be for the gaudiness of its exterior, the perfect simplicity of its interior, or the native coolness of its cad. This young gentleman is a singular instance of self-devotion; his somewhat intemperate zeal on behalf of his employers, is constantly getting him into trouble, and occasionally into the house of correction. He is no sooner emancipated, however, than he resumes the duties of his profession with unabated ardour. His principal distinction is his activity. His great boast is, 'that he can chuck an old gen'lm'n into the buss, shut him in, and rattle off, afore he knows where it's a-going to' — a feat which he frequently performs, to the infinite amusement of every one but the old gentleman concerned, who, somehow or other, never can see the joke of the thing.

We are not aware that it has ever been precisely ascertained, how many passengers our omnibus will contain. The impression on the cad's mind evidently is, that it is amply sufficient for the accommodation of any number of persons that can be enticed into it. 'Any room?' cries a hot pedestrian. 'Plenty o' room, sir,' replies the conductor, gradually opening the door, and not disclosing the real state of the case, until the wretched man is on the steps. 'Where?' inquires the entrapped individual, with an attempt to back out again. 'Either side, sir,' rejoins the cad, shoving him in, and slamming the door. 'All right, Bill.' Retreat is impossible; the new-comer rolls about, till he falls down somewhere, and there he stops.

As we get into the city a little before ten, four or five of our party are regular passengers. We always take them up at the same places, and they generally occupy the same seats; they are always dressed in the same manner, and invariably discuss the same topics — the increasing rapidity of cabs, and the disregard of moral obligations evinced by omnibus men. There is a little testy old man, with a powdered head, who always sits on the right-hand side of the door as you enter, with his hands folded on the top of his umbrella. He is extremely impatient, and sits there for the purpose of keeping a sharp eye on the cad, with whom he generally holds a running dialogue. He is very officious in helping people in and out, and always volunteers to give the cad a poke with his umbrella, when any one wants to alight. He usually recommends ladies to have sixpence ready, to prevent delay; and if anybody puts a window down, that he can reach, he immediately puts it up again.

'Now, what are you stopping for?' says the little man every morning, the moment there is the slightest indication of 'pulling up' at the corner of Regent-street, when some such dialogue as the following takes place between him and the cad:

'What are you stopping for?'

Here the cad whistles, and affects not to hear the question.

'I say [a poke], what are you stopping for?'

'For passengers, sir. Ba — nk. — Ty.'

'I know you're stopping for passengers; but you've no business to do so. WHY are you stopping?'

'Vy, sir, that's a difficult question. I think it is because we perfer stopping here to going on.'

'Now mind,' exclaims the little old man, with great vehemence, 'I'll pull you up to-morrow; I've often threatened to do it; now I will.'

'Thankee, sir,' replies the cad, touching his hat with a mock expression of gratitude; — 'werry much obliged to you indeed, sir.' Here the young men in the omnibus laugh very heartily, and the old gentleman gets very red in the face, and seems highly exasperated.

The stout gentleman in the white neckcloth, at the other end of the vehicle, looks very prophetic, and says that something must shortly be done with these fellows, or there's no saying where all this will end; and the shabby-genteel man with the green bag, expresses his entire concurrence in the opinion, as he has done regularly every morning for the last six months.

A second omnibus now comes up, and stops immediately behind us. Another old gentleman elevates his cane in the air, and runs with all his might towards our omnibus; we watch his progress with great interest; the door is opened to receive him, he suddenly disappears — he has been spirited away by the opposition. Hereupon the driver of the opposition taunts our people with his having 'regularly done 'em out of that old swell,' and the voice of the 'old swell' is heard, vainly protesting against this unlawful detention. We rattle off, the other omnibus rattles after us, and every time we stop to take up a passenger, they stop to take him too; sometimes we get him; sometimes they get him; but whoever don't get him, say they ought to have had him, and the cads of the respective vehicles abuse one another accordingly.

As we arrive in the vicinity of Lincoln's-inn-fields, Bedford-row, and other legal haunts, we drop a great many of our original passengers, and take up fresh ones, who meet with a very sulky reception. It is rather remarkable, that the people already in an omnibus, always look at newcomers, as if they entertained some undefined idea that they have no business to come in at all. We are quite persuaded the little old man has some notion of this kind, and that he considers their entry as a sort of negative impertinence.

Conversation is now entirely dropped; each person gazes vacantly through the window in front of him, and everybody thinks that his opposite neighbour is staring at him. If one man gets out at Shoe-lane, and another at the corner of Farringdon-street, the little old gentleman grumbles, and suggests to the latter, that if he had got out at Shoe-lane too, he would have saved them the delay of another stoppage; whereupon the young men laugh again, and the old gentleman looks very solemn, and says nothing more till he gets to the Bank, when he trots off as fast as he can, leaving us to do the same, and to wish, as we walk away, that we could impart to others any portion of the amusement we have gained for ourselves.

Morning Chronicle, *26 September 1834*

OMNIBUS LAW

1. Keep your feet off the seats.

2. Do not get into a snug corner yourself, and then open the windows to admit a nor'wester upon the neck of your neighbour.

3. Have your money ready when you desire to alight. If your time is not valuable that of others may be.

4. Do not impose on the conductor the necessity of finding you change; he is not a banker.

5. Sit with your limbs straight, and do not let your legs describe an angle of 45 degrees, thereby occupying the room of two persons.

6. Do not spit upon the straw. You are not in a hog-sty, but in an omnibus travelling in a county which boasts of its refinement.

7. Behave respectfully to females, and put not an unprotected lass to the blush because she cannot escape from your brutality.

8. If you bring a dog, let him be small and confined by a string.

9. Do not introduce large parcels; an omnibus is not a van.

10. Reserve bickerings and disputes for the open field. The sound of your own voice may be music to your own ears – not so, perhaps, to those of your companions.

11. If you will broach politics or religion, speak with moderation; all have an equal right to their opinions, and all have an equal right not to have them wantonly shocked.

12. Refrain from affectation and conceited airs. Remember you are riding a distance for sixpence which, if made in a hackney-coach, would cost you as many shillings; and that should your pride elevate you above plebeian accommodations, your purse should enable you to command aristocratic indulgences.

The Times, *30 January 1836*

AN EARLY OMNIBUS ACCIDENT

Last Saturday afternoon an omnibus with twelve inside and nine outside passengers was upset in the Tottenham-court-road, the hind axletree having broken. One gentlemen had his leg fractured, and another his shoulder dislocated, both were conveyed to Middlesex Hospital. The driver and the rest of the outside passengers were all more or less injured. The inside passengers fortunately escaped without any further injury than a few cuts from the broken glass.

Illustrated London News, *18 September 1847*

A DEMAND FOR OMNIBUS REFORM

'An Omnibus Traveller' proposes a Fixed Price for Omnibuses, instead of leaving the amount of the Fare to the capricious taste of the Conductor. This plan would certainly put an end to the numerous squabbles that take place at undetermined distances. Charing Cross is generally the focus of all these disturbances.

CHARLES'S Statue may be called the Omnibus Seat of War. Pass when you will, you are pretty sure to hear some noisy altercation, in which a female voice takes the high notes and the Conductor the very low ones, as to whether the Fare is to be 3d or 6d. This is not so bad, however, as when the Omnibus is kept waiting for ten-minutes in the middle of a high road whilst the Fare is being argued. It is terrible then to hear the fierce invectives of the three Outsides, and the loud grumbling of the Insides, all anxious to get home to their dinners. Ladies generally hold out the longest. It takes such a long time to convince a woman she can be wrong, especially in Omnibus matters; and we have seen a lady, with a beautiful ermine tippet, run half way down the Kensington Road, sooner than sacrifice three miserable coppers. She was perfectly right in the long run, (we really believe there are women who would walk round the wall of China to save a halfpenny toll,) and we admired her dauntless spirit, though we were pained, as we looked at her muddy boots, at the dirty cause in which it had been exercised.

A FIXED PRICE, made intelligible to the smallest capacity, would remedy this far-spreading evil, and stop all those numerous stoppages, and quell those frightful émeutes, which at present disturb the jog-trot equanimity of the most amiable Bus. At present the Fare is 6d. and a fancied imposition or 3d. and a row thrown in. We should like to see it else fixed at the latter sum, without the usual appendage. How strange it is, that Conductors never know how to conduct themselves!

Punch, *Jul–Dec 1849*

A horse-drawn 'knifeboard' bus, c. 1895

THE KNIFEBOARD

Perhaps the most noteworthy date during this period was 1850, when the 'knifeboard' or longitudinal back-to-back outside seat was introduced, to be retained until the coming of the 'garden seat' in the Eighties. The 'knifeboard' furnishes us with a curious sidelight on Victorian manners and morals. In those days it was not considered proper for a woman, and especially an unescorted female to travel on the top of an omnibus. Some were, however, sufficiently daring to do so, just as there were flighty young things who rode in hansoms. As protection from the gaze of the public, the bus tops were fitted with 'decency boards' which also found another use as advertising hoardings.

from London's Buses: The Story of a Hundred Years 1829–1929

OMNIBUS INFORMATION

Peter Cunningham

OMNIBUSES. The total number traversing the streets of London is about 3,000, paying duty, including mileage, averaging 9*l.* per month each, or 324,000*l.* per annum. The number of conductors and drivers is about 7,000, paying annually 1,750*l.* for their licenses. The earnings of each vehicle vary from 2*l.* to 4*l.* a day.

OMNIBUS ROUTES IN LONDON lie principally north and south, east and west, through the central parts of London, to and from the extreme suburbs. The majority commence running at 9 in the morning, and continue till 12 at night, succeeding each other during the busy parts of the day every five minutes. Most of them have two charges-threepence for part of the distance, and sixpence for the whole distance. It will be well, however, in all cases to inquire the fare to the particular spot; wherever there is a doubt the conductors will demand the full fare. The Atlas omnibuses (marked 'Atlas') run from St. John's-wood down Oxford-street, Regent-street, past Charing-cross, over Westminster Bridge, to Camberwell-gate. The Paddington omnibuses run from the top of the Edgeware-road through Oxford-street and Holborn, to the Bank, and from the Edgeware along the New-road to the Bank. The Waterloo omnibuses (marked 'Waterloo') run from the north-east extremity of the Regent's Park, down Regent-street, Strand, and over Waterloo Bridge to Camberwell-gate. The King's-cross omnibuses run from the North-Western Railway station, at Euston-square, to Kennington-gate. The Chelsea and Islington omnibuses run from Sloane-square, along Piccadilly, Regent-street, Portland-road, and the New-road, to Islington ; the Chelsea and Shoreditch from Battersea Bridge to Shoreditch, along Piccadilly, the Strand, Fleet-street, and Cheapside. The red Kensington run from London Bridge to Kensington; the Royal Blue and Pimlico from the Blackwall and Eastern Counties Railway station to Pimlico. The omnibuses inscribed 'Favorite' run between Westminster, Islington, and Hoxton. Putney and Brompton omnibuses run from Putney Bridge to the Bank and the London Bridge Railroad station. The green Bayswater run to the Bank, along Oxford-street and Holborn, and also Regent-street and the Strand. The Brixton and Clapham run from Oxford-street, along Regent-street and Parliament-street, over Westminster Bridge, to Kennington, Brixton, or Clapham. These are the principal routes.

from Hand-Book of London (1850)

WORKING ON THE BUSES

Henry Mayhew

—

OMNIBUS DRIVER

—

From a driver I had the following statement:

'I have been a driver fourteen years. I was brought up as a builder, but had friends that was using horses, and I sometimes assisted them in driving and grooming when I was out of work. I got to like that sort of work, and thought it would be better than my own business if I could get to be connected with a 'bus; and I had friends, and first got employed as a time-keeper; but I've been a driver for fourteen years. I'm now paid by the week, and not by the box. It's a fair payment, but we must live well. It's hard work is mine; for I never have any rest but a few minutes, except every other Sunday, and then only two hours; that's the time of a journey there and back. If I was to ask leave to go to church, and then go to work again, I know what answer there would be – 'You can go to church as often as you like, and we can get a man who doesn't want to go there.' The cattle I drive are equal to gentlemen's carriage-horses. One I've driven five years, and I believe she was worked five years before I drove her. It's very hard work for the horses, but I don't know that they are overworked in 'busses. The starting after stopping is the hardest work for them; it's such a terrible strain. I've felt for the poor things on a wet night, with a 'bus full of big people. I think that it's a pity that anybody uses a bearing rein. There's not many uses it now. It bears up a horse's head, and he can only go on pulling, pulling up a hill, one way. Take off his bearing rein, and he'll relieve the strain on him by bearing down his head, and flinging his weight on the collar to help him pull. If a man had to carry a weight up a hill on his back, how would he like to have his head tied back?

Perhaps you may have noticed Mr. ----'s horses pull the 'bus up Holborn Hill. They're tightly borne up; but then they are very fine animals, fat and fine: there's no such cattle, perhaps, in a London 'bus – least-ways there's none better – and they're borne up for show. Now, a jib-horse won't go in a bearing rein, and will without it. I've seen that myself; so what can be the use of it? It's just teasing the poor things for a sort of fashion. I must keep exact time at every place where a timekeeper's stationed. Not a minute's excused – there's a fine for the least delay. I can't say that it's often levied; but still we are liable to it. If I've been blocked, I must make up for the block by galloping; and if I'm seen to gallop, and anybody tells our people, I'm called over the coals. I must drive as quick with a thunder-storm pelting in my face, and the roads in a muddle, and the horses starting – I can't call it shying, I have 'em too well in hand, – at every flash, just as quick as if it was a fine hard road, and fine weather. It's not easy to drive a 'bus; but I can drive, and must drive, to an inch: yes, sir, to half an inch. I know if I can get my horses' heads through a space, I can get my splinter bar through. I drive by my pole, making it my centre. If I keep it fair in the centre, a carriage must follow, unless it's slippery weather, and then there's no calculating. I saw the first 'bus start in 1829. I heard the first 'bus called a Punch-and-Judy carriage, 'cause you could see the people inside without a frame. The shape was about the same as it is now, but bigger and heavier. A 'bus changes horses four or five times a-day, according to the distance. There's no cruelty to the horses, not a bit, it wouldn't be allowed. I fancy that 'busses now pay the proprietors well. The duty was 2d. a-mile, and now it's 1d. Some companies save twelve guineas a week by the doing away of toll-gates. The 'stablishing the three-pennies – the short 'uns – has put money in their pockets. I'm an unmarried man. A 'bus driver never has time to look out for a wife. Every horse in our stables has one day's rest in every four; but it's no rest for the driver.'

OMNIBUS CONDUCTORS

The conductor, who is vulgarly known as the 'cad', stands on a small projection at the end of the omnibus; and it is his office to admit and set down every passenger, and to receive the amount of fare, for which amount he is, of course, responsible to his employers.

From one of them, a wry intelligent man, I had the following statement: –

'I am 35 or 36, and have been a conductor for six years. I'm a conductor now, but wouldn't be long behind a 'bus if it wasn't from necessity It's hard to get anything else to do that you can keep a wife and family on, for people won't have you from off a 'bus. The worst part of my business is its uncertainty. I may be discharged any day, and not know for what. If I did, and I was accused unjustly, I might bring my action; but it's merely, 'You're not wanted.' I think I've done better as a conductor in hot weather, or fine weather, than in wet; though I've got a good journey when it's come on showery, as people was starting for or starting from the City. I had one master, who, when his 'bus came in full in the wet, used to say, 'This is prime. Them's God Almighty's customers; he sent them' I've heard him say so many a time. We get far more ladies and children, too, on a fine day; they go more a-shopping then, and of an evening they go more to public places. I pay over my money every night. It runs from 40s. to 4l. 4s., or a little more on extraordinary occasions. I have taken more money since the short 'uns were established. I never get to a public place, whether it's chapel or a playhouse, unless, indeed, I get a holiday, and that is once in two years. I've asked for a day's holiday and been refused. I was told I might take a week's holiday, if I liked, or as long as I lived. I'm quite ignorant of what's passing in the world, my time's so taken up. We only know what's going on from hearing people talk in the 'bus. I never care to read the paper now, though I used to like it. If I have two minutes to spare, I'd rather take a nap than anything else. We know no more politics than the backwoodsmen of America, because we haven't time to care about it. I've fallen asleep on my step as the 'bus was going on, and almost fallen off. I have often to put up with insolence from vulgar fellows, who think it fun to chaff a cad, as they call it. There's no help for it. Our masters won't listen to complaints: if we are not satisfied we can go. Conductors are a sober set of men. We must be sober. It takes every farthing of our wages to live well enough, and keep a wife and family.'

OMNIBUS TIMEKEEPERS

Another class employed in the omnibus trade are the timekeepers. On some routes there are five of these men, on others four. The timekeeper's duty is to start the omnibus at the exact moment appointed by the proprietors, and to report any delay or irregularity in the arrival of the vehicle. His hours are the same as those of the drivers and conductors, but as he is stationary his work is not so fatiguing. His remuneration is generally 21s. a week, but on some stations more. He must never leave the spot. A timekeeper on Kennington Common has 28s. a week. He is employed 16 hours daily, and has a box to shelter him from the weather when it is foul. He has to keep time for forty 'busses. The men who may be seen in the great thoroughfares noting every omnibus that passes, are not timekeepers; they are employed by Government, so that no omnibus may run on the line without paying the duty.

from London Labour and the London Poor *(1851)*

FOR BETTER OR FOR WORSE

The Well-conducted conductor

1. Never bawls out 'Bank—Bank—City—Bank!' because he knows that passengers are always as much on the look-out for him as he is for them, so that these loud and hideous shouts are quite unnecessary.

2. Never bangs the omnibus door after he has let a passenger in or out, but makes it a rule to shut it as quietly as possible.

3. Always takes care that there are two check strings or straps running along the roof of the omnibus, on the inside, and communicating with the arms of the driver by two large wooden or other rings which are easily slipped on and off.

4. Is careful also to have a direction conspicuously placed inside the omnibus, announcing to the passengers that if they wish to be set down on the right hand they will pull the right-hand check-string or strap, and if they wish to be set down on the left hand they will pull the left-hand check-string. By this arrangement the passenger is set down exactly where he wishes to be, and all the bawling is prevented.

5. Never stands at the omnibus door staring in upon the passengers, but sits down upon the seat provided for him outside. In this way he knows that he gains a double advantage: he is saved the fatigue of standing during a whole journey, and by looking backwards as the driver looks forwards, persons who wish to ride are more easily seen than if the driver and conductor are both looking the same way.

6. Never allows the driver to go on till the passengers are safely seated, and always directs him to pull up close either to the right or left hand of the street or road.

The Ill-conducted Conductor

1. Always bawls out 'Bank—Bank—City—Bank—Bank—Bank—City—City—Bank—Bank—Bank!' by which disgusting noise his own lungs are injured, the public peace is disturbed, and not any advantage gained.

2. Always bangs the door violently that if you are sitting next the door you are likely to be deafened for life.

3. Never provides any check-string, but compels the passengers who want to be set down to use their sticks, canes, and umbrellas, and loud shouts into the bargain, thereby creating a most intolerable nuisance.

4. Always takes up and sets down his passengers in the middle of the street; by which rudeness they are sometimes bespattered with mud and always exposed to danger.

5. Always stands at the door of the omnibus staring in upon the passengers, particularly after he has been eating his dinner of beef-steak, strong onions, and stale beer; and generally has some cad or other crony standing and talking with him. The air that would otherwise circulate through the omnibus, in the way of ventilation is obstructed and poisoned.

6. Always bawls out 'All right!' before the passengers have taken their seats, by which gross carelessness great inconvenience and even danger are often occasioned.

The Times, *January 1841*

A PENNYWORTH
OF LOCOMOTION

Charles Manby Smith

We are going to take a ride in a penny omnibus. Here we are at Holborn-hill: the omnibus, a white one, has just turned round, and we are the first to jump in and ensconce ourselves in a further corner. Now we can ride to Tottenham Court-road for a penny, or to Edgware-road, if we choose, for two-pence. We are hardly seated, when an elderly dame literally lunettes in, having a large brown-paper parcel, almost as big as a pannier, and a crushed and semi-collapsed bandbox, which she quietly arranges on the cushioned seat, as though she had engaged that whole side to herself. She is followed in an instant by an elderly and portly figure in patched boots, and well-worn dingy great coat, who takes the right-hand door corner, where he sits with clasped horny hands, nursing a corpulent umbrella, upon the handle of which he rests his unshaven chin, as with rueful face he peers over the low door. Bang! goes something on the roof; the explosion startles him from his contemplations, and causes him to poke out his head, which is instantly drawn in again, as the conductor opens the door, and keeps it open while a living tide rushes in – one, two, three, four, five, six, seven, eight, nine! 'No more room here, conductor: full here!' 'Full inside!' roars the conductor, in reply. But we don't move on yet; there is a vision of muddy high-lows, corduroy garments, and coat-tails, clambering up consecutively in the rear tinder the guidance of the conductor, and making a deafening uproar on the roof in the ceremony of arranging themselves upon what has been not inappropriately styled the 'knife-board.' 'All right' bursts involuntarily from the lips of the conductor, as the last pair of bluchers disappears above our heads. Now the ''bus' gets under way, and we begin to look around us, and find that we form one of a very mixed company indeed. Opposite us sits the old lady with the bandbox and monster bundle. By her side is a very thin journeyman baker in his oven undress, and next to him a young man carrying a blue bag, and wearing a diamond ring on his little finger, a pair of false brilliants by way of shirt studs, and a violet-coloured neck-tie. To his left is the wife of a mechanic, carrying a capless, bald-headed fat baby in her arms – baby sputtering, staring, and kicking in an ecstasy of delight, and stretching out its little puddings of fingers to reach the diamond-ringed hand that grasps the blue bag. Next to the mother of the baby is a blue-jacket, a regular tar, who, it would seem, has entered the omnibus for the sake of enjoying a 'turn-in,' and is endeavouring to compose himself to sleep. Next to him is our friend with his companion the stout umbrella, which he still hugs with undiminished affection.

Of the party sitting on our side we cannot give so good an account, by reason of a very voluminous widow, weighing, at a rough guess, some twenty stone, who has almost eclipsed our view in that direction, and whose presence oppresses us with an idea of the cheapness of land-carriage in the present day – estimating it by weight. We stop for half a minute at the top of Chancery-lane, to put down the owner of the blue bag; somebody too drops from the roof, but another climbs up, and another rushes in as we are again getting under way, and, still full, we proceed onwards. We drop three more of our company at the corner of Red Lion-street, and among them, greatly to the relief of the horses and the writer, the ponderous widow. Now we find ourselves sitting next to a shoe-maker, who is taking home a pair of new boots of his own manufacture; we can tell that much by the channels cut by countless wax-ends through the hardened skin of his little fingers. Next to him are a couple of boys, who, we suspect, have no other business to follow just now than to enjoy a penny ride for the pleasure of walking back again. We are soon in New Oxford-street, and now the elderly and portly man whom we first noticed lifts his corpulent umbrella carefully out of the omnibus, and disappears in the shop of an advertising tailor, probably in search of a new great-coat, which indeed it is high time that he had provided. Nobody gets up in place of the last few departures – for a good and sufficient reason, namely, that we are approaching the end of the pennyworth, and that all who go beyond Tottenham Court-road must pay a double fare. Now the conductor pops his head in at the window, and, to save time, collects the pence of all the penny passengers, so that there will be nothing to do beyond letting them out when we stop. At Tottenham Court-road all the passengers alight but ourselves, even the old lady emerging from behind her bandboxes, and walking off towards St. Giles's. But new customers are waiting, and in less than two minutes we are crammed again with a new cargo as various as the preceding one, and on we roll towards the Edgware-road. We set out with twelve insiders, and we stop at the end of our route with but four, and yet the conductor has taken twenty-two fares, by an accurate calculation, without actually pulling up to a stand-still once on the way.

The necessity of despatch is recognised by both parties to the contract, and passengers, paying their money before they alight, are seen to step out while the vehicle goes on at an easy pace, and others clamber in or on to the roof in the same way.

We have got to the end of the journey, and nothing better offering on our return, we ascend to the roof, and ride back on the outside to our starting-point. There is a great deal of the world to be seen in the inside of an omnibus, as those who are accustomed to ride in them very well know, but there is still more to be seen on the outside. The 'knife-board', that is, the longitudinal seat which stretches from end to end of the roof, is a very favourite position with a numerous class of the metropolitan world. It is sufficiently far above the noise of the wheels to allow of undisturbed conversation, and is a point of eminence from which everything going forward below and around can be plainly seen. We have ourselves made from this point some curious surveys of men and things which we could not possibly have made in a less elevated position, or which did not, like that, afford us an ever-moving panorama of social life and action.

The boorish incivility and savage behaviour of omnibus drivers and conductors was, not many years ago, the theme of universal irritation and complaint, and very justly so. At the present moment, the reverse is the case, a civil and obliging demeanour being the general characteristic of the profession. The key to the transformation is, doubtless, to be found in the fact, that civility pays better than its opposite.

from Curiosities of London Life *(1853)*

THE FRENCH TAKE-OVER

The London General Omnibus Company

At the beginning of 1856 it became known that a French undertaking was about to enter the already congested sphere of omnibus operation in London. The busmen posted up placards strongly denouncing the foreign intruders. The alarm subsided when it became known that the new company intended to acquire the established services at full market value, and to work with existing staff. The London proprietors, perceiving a good bargain in the offing, thereupon joined with Press in paying graceful compliments to the Omnibus *Entente Cordiale*.

The new enterprise, the Compagnie Générale des Omnibus de Londres, although formed in Paris, was really Anglo-French. Two of the three managing directors were English, as were five of the council of surveillance. The subordinate officials were all English.

The Compagnie Générale took over the initial instalment – 27 omnibuses – on January 7, 1857, and by the close of the summer of that year 600 of the 800 omnibuses that comprised the London services had been acquired. The price paid was £400,000, of which amount no less than £242,000 was represented by the 'times' or running-rights.

from One Hundred Years of the London Omnibus 1829–1929

THEY DO IT BETTER IN PARIS

Charles Dickens

Most persons who have sojourned in the capitals of England and France, and have availed themselves of the commercial comforts proper to either city, must have noted that the spacious and commodious vehicle, to which from its catholic capacities the name 'omnibus' has been applied in both countries, plays a much more important part in Paris than in London. It is not too much to say that in the former you can go from anywhere to anywhere else, at a price which is not varied by the length of your journey, whereas, in the latter, there is not only a variation of charge, but there are many points which, from certain other points, cannot be reached by omnibus at all. In Paris all classes are alike accommodated; in London the most favoured class consists of the persons who have business in the city. On this account the Bank of England, as a city focus, can be reached from almost any district you could name, inhabited by business men, and on this account likewise the privileges of the Bank of England are exceptional.

The result of the London system, or rather want of system, is a great diversity in the small assemblies that travel at different hours by the same omnibuses. At the time when city men leave their residences at the West-end or in the suburbs, the vehicles which they use are crowded, and the same phenomenon is observed when the time for returning home has arrived. These city men comprise employers as well as clerks, and thus nine and ten am and four and five pm, or thereabouts, may be termed the aristocratic hours for those omnibuses that ply to and from the Bank of England, the morning hours being considered in reference to those who seek, and the afternoon hours to those who leave that important point. During the intermediate hours, and at those very hours when the course of the omnibus is contrary to the course of business, the travellers belong for the most part to a far humbler class, and are by no means numerous. And with the omnibuses that do not ply city-wards this is almost always the case. Indeed, with the exception of persons who for some important reason are impelled towards the centre of traffic, every one who is in the slightest degree opulent and luxurious makes a point of patronising the more expensive cab. The cab will at any rate take us to any point we may choose to name, whereas the choice for the travellers by the omnibus is limited. Of course, we leave out of the account the state of traffic on Sundays and holidays, when the omnibuses that ply to and from the city are almost empty, and those that convey the passengers to Richmond, and other places of pleasant resort, are full.

Now, in Paris the travellers by omnibus are much more numerous, and comprise throughout the day a much more opulent class of persons than those who use a similar mode of locomotion in London. This fact may be ascribed, in a great measure, to a system of so-called 'correspondances,' by means of which there is scarcely a point in Paris which is not connected with every other. When the point which the traveller desires to reach lies in the direct line of the omnibus which he takes, there is, of course, no difference between the practices of the two countries. It is when the point lies apart from the track of the omnibus that the difference begins. In that case the London traveller must consider where he must get out to complete his pilgrimage to the desired spot. He may perhaps be aware of an intermediate point, whence another omnibus will proceed to it directly; or he may be convinced that a cab or a tedious journey on foot will be indispensable. At all events, a judicious choice of the course he ought to pursue demands an amount of topographical knowledge which cannot be expected in a casual visitor to the capital, or even in those confirmed Cockneys whose London movements have been confined to a beaten track.

The difficulty here indicated is met by the French system of 'correspondances'. Paris is dotted all over with omnibus stations, which for some vehicles are starting points, for others houses of call. To one of these the traveller proceeds, in the first instance, and tells the official personage he finds there whither he desires to go. If the spot does not lie in the route of the omnibus at this station, he is furnished not only with a ticket for his place, but another ticket entitling him to a seat in another omnibus, which he will enter at an intermediate station, and, thence proceeding, will complete his journey. Let us make matters intelligible to purely British traders, by imagining a similar arrangement in London. The traveller, being at the Bank of England, would proceed to Russell-square a journey which, according to the actual system, is altogether impossible. He would find a station erected (say) by the Wellington statue, and, armed with a 'correspondance,' would take an Oxford-street omnibus. The conductor would set him down at the most convenient intermediate station, which would be at the corner of the Gray's Inn-road or Southampton-street, and there he would find another omnibus, which would take him to Russell-square, or its immediate vicinity. This journey costs him no more than it would have done had the square in question lain on the route of the first vehicle. The uniform fare from any given point to any other is thirty centimes, or three-pence, for an inside place; twenty centimes, or twopence, for a seat on the roof. The first conductor alone receives money, the second receives, in its stead, the correspondance ticket.

As crowding at French theatres is prevented by a regulation which compels every one to follow those who have reached the entrance before him, so that first come is sure to be first served, however strong the will and the muscles of second come may be; so also is crowding into omnibuses prevented, though by a more elaborate arrangement. In a Parisian omnibus there are fourteen inside seats and twelve seats on the roof; and the tickets are inscribed with numbers corresponding to this capacity, and must be used in rotation. For instance, the ticket you obtain at the station is numbered nine. The omnibus that is about to start may have two vacant places, and if persons armed with tickets numbered seven and eight are not yet accommodated, their claim will be preferred to yours, and you must await the arrival of the next omnibus, when you will find yourself similarly privileged with regard to number ten. When the vehicle is empty, or comparatively empty, this ticket system is not regarded. You may enter it without visiting the station at all, and the conductor, when you pay him the fare, will furnish you with correspondance tickets, if these are required.

If we have made the French plan intelligible to our readers, they will at once perceive that in Paris the use of the omnibus is open to a larger number of persons than in London. We are compelled, in fairness, to admit that the city man, whose course is invariably from a populous suburb to the Bank, will find an advantage in the London system to which there is nothing comparable in Paris. Here we have direct routes only, from which we have no occasion to deviate, and probably in Paris there is no omnibus route at once so-long and so direct as that which lies between Paddington and the Bank of England. In Paris the travellers who use correspondances are as much considered as anybody else, and these must be set down at the most convenient stations before the vehicle which they have entered in the first instance completes its journey. Hence there is much roundabout travelling unknown in England, the omnibus sometimes proceeding southward, and then again northward, as if the place of final destination inscribed on the vehicle had been forgotten on the route. In short, the slight convenience of the few is sacrificed to the great convenience of the many, and this sacrifice the city gentleman, who belongs to the few par excellence, will probably not be disposed to admire.

At the principal omnibus stations in Paris a little book is sold in which the merits of the English and French systems are compared in a very equitable way, on data obtained in the year 1866. Its author is M. C Lavollee, an administrator of the Omnibus Company of Paris, who evidently speaks rather in an official than in a personal capacity, and its object is partly to show that the capitalist will find French omnibus shares a more profitable investment than the shares of the English company. With this object we have nothing to do. Those facts, which as presented by M. C

Lavollee, concern the general public the people who trust their persons to the vehicle, not the persons who trust their money to the enterprise alone come under our consideration.

According to M. C Lavollee who always speaks, be it remembered, with the year 1866 before his eyes, the number of lines taken by the General Omnibus Company of London, whose pre-eminence above other omnibus proprietors is incontestable, is sixty-eight. But he remarks that these lines would not be considered so many from a French point of view. When one route is the mere continuation of another, these, according to the French routes, constitute but one line; whereas, it is otherwise here. Nor does the competition of the other omnibus proprietors necessarily bring with it increased accommodation to the people of London, inasmuch as several vehicles, independent of each other, frequently take the same route, while some districts are altogether unprovided. An observation made on London Bridge on the 23rd of May 1865, gave a transit of three thousand nine hundred omnibuses between the hours of nine am and eleven pm, that is to say, about two hundred and seventy-eight per hour, and more than four per minute.

An observation made on Westminster Bridge on the 11th of the following June, and consequently in precisely the same season, gave a transit, between the corresponding hours, of five hundred and forty omnibuses, that is to say, about thirty-eight per hour. These statistics forcibly illustrate what we have said above with regard to favoured routes.

In London the omnibuses begin to run between the hours of seven and eight in the morning, and some of the latest return home after midnight. But they are only in full activity from ten am until between nine and ten pm, after which latter hour there are no omnibuses running, save those bound for the remote suburbs. These are the statements made by M. Lavollee. It is bold to question so careful an observer, but we cannot help remarking that ten o'clock in the morning seems rather a late hour for the commencement of expeditions to the city, and we know how important these are in promoting omnibus traffic.

In Paris the omnibuses begin to run before seven am, and most of the lines continue till after midnight. Sunday increases the French and diminishes the English traffic. This fact does not touch the question of accommodation, but is to be attributed to the different habits of the two countries.

The number of passengers carried by one vehicle is exactly the same in the two capitals, viz., twenty-six; but the distribution is different, inasmuch as there are twelve inside places in the London, and fourteen in the Parisian omnibus. Attempts have been made in Paris to find room for two additional outside passengers, and this would, of course, increase the total number to twenty-eight.

The London omnibus, when empty, weighs only twelve hundred and fifty kilogrammes, whereas the Parisian vehicle weighs sixteen hundred and twenty or sixteen hundred and thirty, the former figure corresponding to the newer, the latter to the older construction.

(The kilogramme, it may be observed, is equal to rather less than two pounds and a quarter avoirdupois). This apparent advantage on the English side is attributed not only to the greater number of passengers accommodated inside the French vehicle, but also to the fact that nearly two inches more space is allowed for each person. Additional causes of the weight of the Paris omnibus are to be found in the dial, which registers the entrance of each passenger; four lanterns, against which we can only set off a small inside lamp; and a casing of sheet iron, used to lessen the damage caused by collisions. To the dial which we have just mentioned, and which in French is called 'cadran', there is nothing analogous in this country. All who know anything of Paris, are familiar with it as a matter of course ; for those, not so privileged, the simple statement will suffice, that it is an apparatus worked by the mere entrance of the passengers, and that, as it records the number of travellers by mechanical means, over which the conductor has no control, it necessarily makes fraud on his part a sheer impossibility. We learn from M. Lavollee that an attempt to introduce this useful institution by the General Omnibus Company of London was effectually resisted, not only by the conductors but also by the public. The fact is curious. That the conductors dis-liked such an application of practical science to the prevention of petty fraud seems natural enough ; and if one of those useful members of society were represented on the stage of a transpontine theatre, slapping his left side, and declaring that the honour of a poor man was far superior to machinery, we have not the slightest doubt that a hearty round of applause would manifest the satisfaction of the gallery. But why the public, who are by no means the necessary allies of the conductor, should be equally sensitive on the subject, we cannot at all understand. Is it possible that the sharp tinkle, which marks the action of the machine, is found objectionable to fastidious ears?

This odd sympathy between passengers and conductors seems more difficult to explain, if we consider that in London the passengers can easily be defrauded by the conductor, whereas in Paris the conductor can cheat no one. The passenger in the French omnibus knows that however far he goes, he has only to pay thirty centimes (threepence) if he travels inside, and twenty (twopence) if he sits on the roof; but there is no such uniformity in England, where prices are roughly measured by distance. The absence of uniformity favours imposition on travellers in general and on foreigners in particular, as M. Lavollee shrewdly observes, his remark being probably grounded on his own personal experience. The interior of the London omnibus is indeed decorated with a certain tin placard, on which the tariff of prices, as regulated by distance, is stated in the blackest black and the whitest white. But how many are the persons, English or foreign, who can exactly comprehend the tariff?

The rapidity of the London omnibus exceeds that of the Parisian, the former travelling at the rate of from five to six English miles an hour (seldom six), that is to say, of from eight to nine and a half kilometres, whereas seven and a half kilometres is the extent of the French rate. To reduce this fact to its proper value, we should recollect that the English is, as we have said, lighter than the French vehicle, and take other circumstances into consideration. The slopes in London are less formidable, the streets are wider, and the passages are less numerous than in Paris. Stoppages are also less frequent. The system of 'correspondances' forces the French omnibus to stop at various stations, thus causing a slight inconvenience, which is to be taken into account when the two systems are balanced with each other.

When M. Lavollee compares the number of omnibus travellers in Paris with those in London during 1866, the advantage is unquestionably on the side of the former. Confining his observations to the London General Omnibus Company, he tells us, that whereas the company with six hundred and two vehicles carried during the year forty-four millions three hundred and fifty thousand passengers, the Paris company, with six hundred and twenty-five vehicles carried one hundred and seven millions two hundred and two thousand, that is to say, considerably more than double the number. The searcher after truth will, like M. Lavollee, balance this fact with the circumstance, that in Paris there is nothing analogous to the penny-steamboat, or to the Metropolitan and North London Railways. The steamers which connect all the important points on the left bank of the Thames from London Bridge to Chelsea may easily be over-looked by many of the sojourners in London, but their importance, derived from rapidity and extreme cheapness, is immense.

The accidents that occur in Paris, through the employment of the omnibus, are, according to M. Lavollee, more numerous than those that take place in London. To account for this difference he finds several reasons. In the first place, the streets of our capital are broader and straighter than those of Paris, and the advantage on the side of London is not counterbalanced by the crowd of vehicles which are seen daily in the city, but which diminishes at a very early hour in the evening. In the second place, M. Lavollee admits that both in skill and temper, the English drivers are far superior to the French, and have to deal with more docile horses. A third cause of accident is the number of trucks and light carts frequently driven by women, which in Paris is greater than in London, and leads to collisions by which the weaker side suffers. Fourthly and this is an advantage on the side of London, which at once strikes every Englishman at the very first walk which he takes in Paris, unless he confines himself to the Boulevards and such novelties as the Rue de Rivoli our streets are, with exceptions scarcely worth noting, uniformly provided with foot-pavements on each side of the road, whereas, in many of the streets of the French capital, there is no such thing as a distinct path for pedestrians, but horse and foot move in the same track, the latter taking care of themselves as best they may. In the opinion of M. Lavollee, this Parisian order, or rather disorder of things, leads to a general habit of carelessness, which does not exist in London. The Briton, accustomed to find his foot-pavement everywhere, never thinks of leaving it; the Gaul, forced in many cases to dispense with this luxury, does not always take advantage of it when it is offered, and hence the carriage-roads of Paris are often thronged with pedestrians, even where especial accommodation has been provided for them.

Conning over the facts thus briefly enumerated, and perhaps consulting also his own personal experience, the reader will perceive at a glance, that if the French streets were widened and uniformly provided with foot-pavements, the French drivers were better trained, and the traffic in light carts were diminished, the comparison between London and Paris would show an unqualified advantage on the side of the latter, and, moreover, that the allowances made in favour of England were but trifling after all.

Why, then, should we not adopt the Parisian mode without hesitation?

This question is not to be answered without grave deliberation. The great efficiency of the Parisian scheme, and the perfection of its system of correspondances, are the results of a monopoly; all the omnibuses in the French capital belonging to one company, with whom it is unlawful to compete. Now, to every thinking Englishman the very word monopoly is suggestive of fallacy, and whenever a particular case arises where protection in any form seems to have an advantage over free competition, he will doubt whether a partial benefit is to be sought by the sacrifice of a grand principle. Who can say that, properly developed, the London system of free competition may not ultimately attain in the small matter of the omnibus, the same degree of perfection that in Paris is enforced by monopoly.

All Year Round 30, 12 June 1869

WE GIRLS IN THOSE OMNIBUSES

Anonymous

'Charing Cross, Fleet Street, Westminster, fourpence aa the way!' So sings that never-sitting bird, the conductor of the 'Favourite' omnibus. Here we stand, three scared country ladies, outside that unangelic spot, the 'Angel' Islington. Won by the blandishments of the 'Favourite,' we carefully adjust our skirts, hitherto so innocent of London mud, and daintily step into the middle of the road, wondering why the omnibus does not drive quite close up to the pavement for us. First sister – in, with a mighty effort; second sister, with a gasp at the height of the step, follows. 'Now, then, ma'rm – right!' and off we go, the last sister's last foot in a state of suspense between London mud and a London omnibus. Fear soon decides the question; clutching wildly at a greasy hand from the interior, and aided by a propelling force from without in the shape of a conducting arm, No 3 is in, only, however, to augment the awful consternation her sisters are experiencing, arising from the unsolved riddle – 'Where are we to sit?'. No 1 is dignified. No 2 is plaintive, No 3 is nervous. 'He said there was room,' murmurs No 2, in accents vague. 'Here's room for one,' says a stout, rosy-faced woman, indicating, with her thumb, an imaginary space between herself and a cadaverous-looking shadow of a man, whose legs are rendered invisible by the mud-fringed drapery of his facetious neighbour.

At last all are seated, No 3 having been startled into an unnaturally small compass by a remark from the owner of the greasy hand at the door, who says: 'If there ain't room, anyhow, there's my knee at your service, miss.'

Our journey is a long one; really, we shall get our money-worth. One by one the passengers are 'put down,' and others 'taken in;' but by this time, having all the right and dignity of precedence, we have so far regained our composure as to admire the internal economy and decorations of the 'Favourite.' First of all, there is that mysterious brass bar down the centre, reminding us of a lightning-conductor. What is its purport? We soon discover, to our cost. Plaintive No 2 is suffering severely from compression, and though the half of the side to which she does not belong is only occupied by two small children, and something that looks like the thin moiety of an ordinarily sized woman, yet she cannot encroach upon their rights, for that brass bar – oh, it must have a heart of iron! – is their firm friend; it 'stands up' for them, towers far above her small agonies, and insists upon her keeping her proper place, limited and previously occupied though that place may be; for she is seated between a portly lady and a more portly gentleman; and well it is for her in this respect she cannot compete with her neighbours, for, otherwise, what would become of her? And this brings to mind another omnibus enigma. Why, we pathetically ask, why is it that the three stout people invariably found in an omnibus invariably sit in the same compartment, and as invariably turn upon each other those bitter looks of mingled suffocation and hatred? Must like always seek like?

Alack-a-day! The muddy drops yclept rain by the Londoners are falling fast; our omnibus becomes popular and populous; and we soon find we suffer as severely from the shower as if we were outside. In vain we embrace our crinolines, our pet new expanders – in vain endeavour to delude ourselves and others into the belief that we have no legs; each passer-by leaves a token of remembrance in the shape of adhesive London mud on our magenta petticoats, and their unhappy-looking umbrellas revenge themselves for the wetting they have just received, by shedding dirty, spiteful tears on our boots. Our boots! Now, if we have a weakness, it is for neat boots, and we never allow them to be trifled with in any way whatever.

We are full (twelve inside); wherefore, then, does that resolute-looking woman in black stand on the step, as if with a determination to ignore the existence of somebody, and find room? We should not like to contradict that woman; we should not like to say we are in this omnibus, if she chooses to assert that we are not. She is not pretty. At some 'long time ago' her mouth evidently took up too much room, and she, of too orderly and economical a turn of mind to stand this, had tried to pucker it up into a smaller compass. The struggle seems to have been severe, for its traces still remain in the shape of long seams radiating from the centre of suffering, reminding us the entrance of a pudding-bag when the pudding is yet inside. There she is, standing on the step, peering at us with her avaricious eyes, while over her shoulder our untiring bird sings again: 'Will that young gentleman in the corner get outside to oblige a lady?' Almost personal this; but 'that young gentleman' looks straight before him, under pretence of believing that the conductor is speaking to some one else. 'Will any gentleman get outside to oblige a lady?' We don't know what he can mean, it is so so unlikely in this pouring rain. Perhaps he is asking that funny question to make us laugh. Ought we to laugh? May we laugh? We look around to see what every one else is doing; all are grave. Are they humouring this joke? But no; that man in the brown alpaca coat is speaking, and half-a-dozen voices chorus: 'This gentleman will ride outside.'

Conductor, blandly – 'Will you be pleased to come out, sir?'

Alpaca coat, firmly – 'No I won't. I only said I should get out at Charing Cross, and that then she could have my place.'

So on we drive, our friend just standing inside, grasping the door with an iron grasp. The end of her shawl is in poor No 3's left eye; her elbow is in No 3's mouth, who is thereby precluded from making any objection, even could she have found courage to do so. No 1 is not behaving at all well, her mouth being most untidily open; No 2 is afraid that this strange journey has given No 1 a fit, never having seen her with such an aspect before. Her gaze is riveted on certain many-coloured poles gleaming through the glass ventilators. She ventures to make a timid enquiry of her left-hand neighbour, not being sure that it is quite safe; he looks disdainfully at her, and shouts: 'Thems the legs of the gents as rides outside.'

Stoppage, 'Charing Cross.' He of the alpaca coat gets out, and the woman in black fiercely pounces on his seat. No more adventures until Westminster, where we get out, and No 1 presents the conductor with a shilling, which he puts into his mouth. Does silver assist the conductive digestion? Gravel is said to agree with hens. Perhaps, though, he has a pouch within his cheek. Has nature, as a small compensation for many disadvantages, provided him with such a ready-made purse?

Now, we honestly confess, indeed we have never endeavoured to conceal the fact, that we are only country people; and now that we are once more at home, this mighty London, this great metropolis, seems to us a great wonder, a mightier mystery than before; and within us arises a restless, ceaseless longing – a wild wish to know somewhat more of the natural history of conductors. Do conductors ever sit down? Can conductors sit down? Did they grow up standing, and so find their places just fitted to them? Did their mothers all know they were going to be conductors, and regulate their conduct accordingly? For surely peculiar circumstances and treatment alone could produce the eccentricities we call conductors.

Have conductors any homes? Had they ever time to marry? Do old mothers sit by their firesides? Do they kiss baby-faces before they go to their short sleep? We almost think so, for we have seen them deal very lovingly with little children; and wherefore else is it that one stops a dozen times in half-an-hour to answer an old woman's querulous inquiry as to 'Ha we come to Piccadilly Cirkis yet?' Whence comes their stern patience? Why is their authority so unquestioned? But stop! We remember – yes indeed, we do remember a woman once raising her voice against the prevailing vice of saying 'Right,' and moving on whilst the passenger is yet on the step, instead of the seat, and calling the conductor 'a naughty boy' for so doing; insisting, moreover, on the vehicle's stopping until she and her dog were comfortably inside; but then she was French, and he evidently yielded in contemptuous pity for her continental ignorance.

Fellow country-women, have you ever been in an omnibus at night? We were once, and No 1 immediately found her company unpleasant. Bounded on one side by the brass rod, on her other sat a man who had taken seven or eight drops too much, though he was old enough to have known better. The worst of it was he was not at all ashamed of it. Now what were we to do? True, there was our escort; but he was three seats off, asleep, as we thought; but, as he afterwards assured us, merely 'shutting his eyes to keep them warm.' Everyone says 'patience is a virtue;' but was it our duty to suffer indignities? We had almost decided not, when our tribulations were brought to a sudden end by the determination of the old sinner to perform the remainder of his journey on foot.

Well, if we stand talking here any longer, we shall be told to 'move on with our great lumbering box-of-all-sorts,' as quoth a cabman to an omnibus-driver, and we would much rather go before it comes to that; so let us end. Our visit to London is among the things that were. When next we go there, we shall doubtless find many changes in our old enemies, for we hear rumours of their having interior spiral staircases to enable ladies to 'ride' outside, and of first- and second-class seats. But, be they ever so magnificent, no future vehicles shall make us forget those omnibuses of 1860.

Chambers's Journal of Popular Literature Science and Arts *No 420,*
Saturday 18 January 1862

BENT CONDUCTORS

James Greenwood

I don't know how many omnibuses, each requiring a conductor, are constantly running through the streets of London, but their number must be very considerable, judging from the fact that the takings of the London General Omnibus Company alone range from nine to ten thousand pounds weekly. Now it is well known to the company that their conductors rob them. A gentleman of my acquaintance once submitted to the secretary of the company an ingenious invention for registering the number of passengers an omnibus carried on each journey, but the secretary was unable to entertain it. 'It is of no use to us, sir,' said he. 'The machine we want is one that will make our men honest, and that I am afraid is one we are not likely to meet with. They will rob us, and we can't help ourselves.' And knowing this, the company pay the conductor four shillings a day, the said day, as a rule, consisting of seventeen hours – from eight one morning till one the next. The driver, in consideration it may be assumed of his being removed from the temptation of handling the company's money, is paid six shillings a day, but his opinion of the advantage the conductor still has over him may be gathered from the fact that he expects the latter to pay for any reasonable quantity of malt or spirituous liquor he may consume in the course of a long scorching hot or freezing cold day, not to mention a cigar or two and the invariable parting glass when the cruelly long day's work is at an end.

It would likewise appear that by virtue of this arrangement between the omnibus conductor and his employers, the interference of the law, even in cases of detected fraud, is dispensed with. It is understood that the London General Omnibus Company support quite a large staff of men and women watchers, who spend their time in riding about in omnibuses, and noting the number of passengers carried on a particular journey, with the view of comparing the returns with the conductor's receipts. It must, therefore, happen that the detections of fraud are numerous but does the reader recollect ever reading in the police reports of a conductor being prosecuted for robbery?

To be sure the Company may claim the right of conducting their business in the way they think best as regards the interests of the shareholders, but if that 'best way' involves the countenancing of theft on the part of their servants, which can mean nothing else than the encouragement of thieves, it becomes a grave question whether the interests of its shareholders should be allowed to stand before the interests of society at large. It may be that to prosecute a dishonest conductor is only to add to the pecuniary loss he has already inflicted on the Company, but the question that much more nearly concerns the public is, what becomes of him when suddenly and in disgrace they turn him from their doors? No one will employ him. In a few weeks his ill-gotten savings are exhausted, and he, the man who for months or years, perhaps, has been accustomed to treat himself generously, finds himself without a sixpence, and, what is worse, with a mark against his character so black and broad that his chances of obtaining employment in the same capacity are altogether too remote for calculation. The respectable barber who declined to shave a coal-heaver on the ground that he was too vulgar a subject to come under the delicate operations of the shaver's razor, and who was reminded by the grimy one that he had just before shaved a baker, justified his conduct on the plea that his professional dignity compelled him to draw a line somewhere, and that he drew it at bakers. Just so the London General Omnibus Company. They draw the line at thieves rash and foolish. So long as a servant of theirs is content to prey on their property with enough of discretion as to render exposure unnecessary, he may continue their servant; but they make it a rule never again to employ a man who has been so careless as to be found out.

As has been shown, it is difficult to imagine a more satisfactory existence than that of an omnibus conductor to a man lost to all sense of honesty; on the other hand it is just as difficult to imagine a man so completely 'floored' as the same cad disgraced, and out of employ. It is easy to see on what small inducements such a man may be won over to the criminal ranks. He has no moral scruples to overcome. His larcenous hand has been in the pocket of his master almost every hour of the day for months, perhaps years past. He is not penitent, and if he were and made an avowal to that effect, he would be answered by the incredulous jeers and sneers of all who knew him. The best that he desires is to meet with as easy a method of obtaining pounds as when he cheerfully drudged for eighteen hours for a wage of four-shillings. This being the summit of his ambition, presently he stumbles on what appears even an easier way of making money than the old way, and he unscrupulously appears not in a new character, but in that he has had long experience in, but without the mask.

I should wish it to be distinctly understood, that I do not include all omnibus conductors in this sweeping condemnation. That there are honest ones amongst them I make no doubt; at the same time I have no hesitation in repeating that in the majority of cases it is expected of them that they will behave dishonestly, and they have no inclination to discredit the expectation. I believe too, that it is much more difficult for a man to be honest as a servant of the company than if he were in the employ of a 'small master.' It is next to impossible for a man of integrity to join and work harmoniously in a gang of rogues. The odds against his doing so may be calculated exactly by the number that comprise the gang. It is not only on principle that they object to him. Unless he 'does as they do,' he becomes a witness against them every time he pays his money in. And he does as they do. It is so much easier to do so than, in the condition of a man labouring hard for comparatively less pay than a common road-scraper earns, to stand up single handed to champion the cause of honesty in favour of a company who are undisguisedly in favour of a snug and comfortable compromise – and has no wish to be 'bothered.'

It is a great scandal that such a system should be permitted to exist; and a body of employers mean enough to connive at such bargain-making, can expect but small sympathy from the public if the dishonesty it tacitly encourages picks it to the bones. What are the terms of the contract between employer and employed? In plain language these: 'We are perfectly aware that you apply to us well knowing our system of doing business, and with the deliberate intention of robbing us all you safely can; and in self-defence, therefore, we will pay you as what you may, if you please, regard as wages, two-pence three farthings an hour, or four shillings per day of seventeen hours. We know that the probabilities are, that you will add to that four shillings daily to the extent of another five or six. It is according to our calculation that you will do so. Our directors have arrived at the conclusion, that as omnibus conductors, of the ordinary type, you cannot be expected to rob us of a less sum than that, and we are not disposed to grumble so long as you remain so moderate; but do not, as you value your situation with all its accompanying privileges, go beyond that. As a man who only robs us of say, five shillings a day, we regard you as a fit and proper person to wait on our lady and gentleman passengers; to attend to their convenience and comfort, in short, as a worthy representative of the LGOC. But beware how you outstrip the bounds of moderation as we unmistakably define them for you! Should you do so, we will kick you out at a moment's notice, and on no consideration will we ever again employ you.'

Taking this view of the case, the omnibus conductor, although entitled to a foremost place in the ranks of thieves non-professional, can scarcely be said to be the least excusable amongst the fraternity.

from The Seven Curses of London *(1869)*

Busy traffic on Ludgate Hill, including horse-drawn buses, in an 1872 illustration by Gustave Doré

TRAFFIC TROUBLE

Thomas Hardy

To the City. Omnibus horses, Ludgate Hill. The greasy state of the streets caused constant slipping. The poor creatures struggled and struggled but could not start the omnibus. A man next to me said: 'It must take all heart and hope out of them! I shall get out.' He did; but the whole remaining selfish twenty-five of us sat on. The horses despairingly got us up the hill at last. I ought to have taken off my hat to him and said: 'Sir, though I was not stirred by your humane impulse I will profit by your example'; and have followed him. I should like to know that man; but we shall never meet again.'

Diary – 8 January 1889

BALLADE OF AN OMNIBUS

Amy Levy

Some men to carriages aspire;
On some the costly hansoms wait;
Some seek a fly, on job or hire;
Some mount the trotting steed, elate.
I envy not the rich and great,
A wandering minstrel, poor and free,
I am contented with my fate --
An omnibus suffices me.

In winter days of rain and mire
I find within a corner strait;
The 'busmen know me and my lyre
From Brompton to the Bull-and-Gate.
When summer comes, I mount in state
The topmost summit, whence I see
Crœsus look up, compassionate --
An omnibus suffices me.

I mark, untroubled by desire,
Lucullus' phaeton and its freight.
The scene whereof I cannot tire,
The human tale of love and hate,
The city pageant, early and late
Unfolds itself, rolls by, to be
A pleasure deep and delicate.
An omnibus suffices me.

Princess, your splendour you require,
I, my simplicity; agree
Neither to rate lower nor higher.
An omnibus suffices me.

'To see my love suffices me.' from Ballades in Blue China (1889)

IN PARTIBUS

Rudyard Kipling

The 'buses run to Battersea,
The 'buses run to Bow
The 'buses run to Westbourne Grove
And Nottinghill also;
But I am sick of London town
From Shepherd's Bush to Bow.

I see the smut upon my cuff
And feel him on my nose;
I cannot leave my window wide
When gentle zephyr blows,
Because he brings disgusting things
And drops 'em on my 'clo'es'.

The sky, a greasy soup-toureen,
Shuts down atop my brow.
Yes, I have sighed for London town
And I have got it now:
And half of it is fog and filth,
And half is fog and row.

And when I take my nightly prowl
'Tis passing good to meet
The pious Briton lugging home
His wife and daughter sweet,
Through four packed miles of seething vice
Thrust out upon the street.

Earth holds no horror like to this
In any land displayed,
From Suez unto Sandy Hook,
From Calais to Port Said;
And 'twas to hide their heathendom
The beastly fog was made.

I cannot tell when dawn is near,
Or when the day is done,
Because I always see the gas
And never see the sun,
And now, methinks, I do not care
A cuss for either one.

But stay, there was an orange, or
An aged egg its yolk;
It might have been a Pears' balloon
Or Barnum's latest joke:
I took it for the sun and wept
To watch it through the smoke.

It's Oh to see the morn ablaze
Above the mango-tope,
When homeward through the dewy cane
The little jackals lope,
And half Bengal heaves into view,
New-washed—with sunlight soap.

It's Oh for one deep whisky peg
When Christmas winds are blowing,
When all the men you ever knew,
And all you've ceased from knowing,
Are 'entered for the Tournament,
And everything that's going.'

But I consort with long-haired things
In velvet collar-rolls,
Who talk about the Aims of Art,
And 'theories' and 'goals,'
And moo and coo with women-folk
About their blessed souls.

But that they call 'psychology'
Is lack of liver pill,
And all that blights their tender souls
Is eating till they're ill,
And their chief way of winning goals
Consists of sitting still.

It's Oh to meet an Army man,
Set up, and trimmed and taut,
Who does not spout hashed libraries
Or think the next man's thought
And walks as though he owned himself,
And hogs his bristles short.

Hear now, a voice across the seas
To kin beyond my ken,
If ye have ever filled an hour
With stories from my pen,
For pity's sake send some one here
To bring me news of men!

The 'buses run to Islington,
To Highgate and Soho,
To Hammersmith and Kew therewith
And Camberwell also,
But I can only murmur "'Bus'
From Shepherd's Bush to Bow.

first published in The Civil and Military Gazette, *23 December 1889*

POOTLING WITH MR POOTER

The archetypal Victorian commuter

George and Weedon Grossmith

June 7.—A dreadful annoyance. Met Mr Franching, who lives at Peckham, and who is a great swell in his way. I ventured to ask him to come home to meat-tea, and take pot-luck. I did not think he would accept such a humble invitation; but he did, saying, in a most friendly way, he would rather 'peck' with us than by himself. I said: 'We had better get into this blue 'bus.' He replied: 'No blue-bussing for me. I have had enough of the blues lately. I lost a cool 'thou' over the Copper Scare. Step in here.'

from The Diary of a Nobody *(1892)*

THE ROMANCE OF A LONDON OMNIBUS

Fred T Jane

ANGEL, Stoke Newington, 'Igate — Hangel, Hangel,' roared a 'bus conductor in a voice that would have made the fortune of a Trafalgar Square Orator.

'Do you go to the Angel?' inquired an old lady of the type these busmen know all too well.

'Yes 'um — Angel. Any more for the Angel, Hangel, Angel!'

'Conductor,' said the same old party, 'are you quite sure you go to the Angel?'

'Well, mum,' came the answer, 'it's writ all over the 'bus, and I've been callin' it for the last 'arf hour, so I believe we do; but I'll arsk a policeman if you like.'

The trodden worm had turned; but how very gently.

And yet they class the conductor under the head of unskilled labour — a man who must be born, not made — he must be dead to all sensitiveness and feeling. Study his back on a muddy day, and you will see it covered with innumerable dark spots; each of these represents a dig from the umbrella point of a female rider who has wanted to alight!

The Angel incident, recorded above, first drew my attention to what may be termed the hidden side of bus traffic. All of us are familiar with the bus itself, and most of us know how to distinguish the particular vehicle we want to travel in, but our knowledge ends, here; we only know that it comes from somewhere and goes on to somewhere. On the fare board inside are names of places it passes on its journey, but to most people they are names only. Queen of England, Windsor Castle, World's End, Weavers' Arms, Sands End, Crooked Billet, and a host of other unknown spots confront us on the fare boards of different conveyances, and we fall to wondering in a dim sort of way whether Windsor Castle is the Windsor, or merely a 'pub' of that name, and if Sands End is where hen-pecked Johnnie Sands enacted the historical scene with Mrs. S., until by and by the places get enshrined in our memories with a good substantial halo of romance around them. To systematically visit all these localities would be almost impossible; the buses of the London General Omnibus Company alone pass along no less than sixty-seven different routes. Besides this company, which by the way owns 1,037 buses, 10,000 horses, and Car Company with 310 buses, 3,248 horses, and 1,523 men to manage them; Tilling's, Andrew's

'Star' Buses, the 'John Bull', Bus Proprietors' Association, Railway Buses, and legions of 'pirate' buses and private enterprises.

In addition to these come numerous trams (which are but buses running on rails), halfpenny buses, and one-horse trams. Most people have noticed the huge umbrella that marks the Metropolitan Railway's vehicles, the more modest star of the District Railway, or the flag of the Road Cars, and the broom sported some short while since by the strikers from the LGOC – unfortunately suggestive of a similar emblem hoisted by the Dutch admiral Van Tromp, and equally short-lived. The 'London General' have no distinguishing mark save the inscription of the Company's name, which is of great benefit to 'pirates,' who imitate it near enough to deceive all save the most observant. 'London General Post Office' is the usual beginning, and so they capture the country cousin who has been directed to get a 'London General'; and the sequel thereof usually consists of double fares, or else just after paying to go to some distant destination he finds that the bus 'don't go no further this 'ere jerney.'

The law has taken to interfering in this last case, but the difficulty has been got over before now by a wheel that goes wrong – after the fares have been collected. This necessitates stoppage, the passengers tired of waiting get into another bus, and then the programme is re-enacted. In the case of the double-fare buses, grumblers are referred to the fare board, where they note that what looks like 'Piccadilly to Oxford Circus, 1d.', is really a big black '1' with a gray '2' painted over it. Some pirate conductors go so far as to wear a strap and bag in imitation of the bell punch and ticket-roll of the Companies' buses.

All buses not belonging to the well known companies are known as 'pirates' but it is only fair to state that many of them make merely the regulation charge. *A propos* of pirates, I once overheard a dear old lady remark to a friend as she gazed at a 'Road Car ' with a somewhat ancient flag, 'Now you mustn't get into that bus, it's a 'pirate'; *don't you see the back flag*' and forthwith they got into a 'London General Post Office, etc.,' that was following astern.

The pirate conductor is usually, as his name would imply, a scowling and bearded bully, and old ladies never prod him in the back; in return for which he'll book them to all parts of London, and both ways at once.

A conductor's life cannot be a happy one; his notion of heaven is probably a place where no women are. This un-gallant idea is fostered by the way in which three women living next door to each other will each stop the conveyance at her own door, utterly regardless of the unfortunate horses, which would probably last eight years instead of five if men were the only passengers. Men are of course better able to jump in and out of a moving bus; but, apart from all this, it is a melancholy fact that they are the sex who show the most consideration, despite the fact that the great majority of members of the RSPCA are women.

A very misogynistic conductor recently gave me some of his experiences with women passengers. They ranged from the excitable female, who having forgotten her purse (as usual) wants to ride on the credit system, down to the lady, who finding she has got into a bus going in the wrong direction threatens to call the police unless it turns round and drives her way. He dwelt sorrowfully on one carrying an umbrella and sunshade, whose first act on boarding is to hurl them violently to the other end of the bus, leaving him to settle with damaged passengers; and he said grievous things of another who had stopped the bus and sent him to ask the price of some dress material displayed in a shop window! He had many more tales, but I forbear.

Certain parts of London are centres from which bus and tram traffic radiates, and the '*Helefant an' Cawsle*' in South London is perhaps the principal of these, six roads, each with its service of bus or tram, meeting there. The 'Elephant' itself is an ordinary enough public-house, pleasantly situated in a square well strewn with cabbage stumps, and surrounded with fish stalls; and not very far off is the now historical Old Kent Road. Next in importance come the 'Angel,' Islington; Charing Cross; Piccadilly Circus; and other spots too well known to need either illustration or description.

Hammersmith Broadway; the 'Weavers' Arms; 'King's Cross; the 'Salisbury'; these, and many others, have their meed of buses. The 'Salisbury' is a great starting place for Road Cars, and likely enough inspired the

> '*Is ab ille, heres ago,*
> *Fortibus es in aro*'

that we have most of us puzzled over in our school days. Places like the 'Queen of England' and the 'Crooked Billet' represent the Ultima Thule of bus traffic, and adjacent to them are sheds and stables belonging as a rule to the ubiquitous LGOC. Beyond these points trams connect with the outlying suburbs.

The 'Crooked Billet' in Upper Clapton is a strange sort of place altogether, a passenger between it and the 'Weavers' Arms' being so rare that the outward bound one asking for a ticket for 'all the way' is never booked beyond the latter place.

There is a good deal of rivalry between the different companies, factories and stables being jealously guarded, and races between their buses are common scenes. Sometimes these terminate disastrously for all concerned, and woe betide the crawling 'growler' that does not get out of the way. Steering these huge vehicles, the 'ironclads of the streets,' is always difficult, but the 'rule' simplifies it —

> 'The rule of the road — make way for the bigger,
> But as for the small, why, we don't care a jigger.'

Occasionally, when a bus starts on a new route, a rival appears and tries to drive it off by competition. Two blue ones have for some time been running between King's Cross and Camberwell, each ever trying to get ahead of the other; and as along every portion of the route at least three other lines of omnibuses are running, somebody must be losing money, for to start and keep a bus going costs a good deal more than most people are aware of, and the profits are apt to become a deficit on most roads unless the price of horses' keep is low.

Another sort of bus race is that of the passenger who, getting to the corner just after the thing has started, tears down the street amidst the cheering of small boys, and the encouraging "Urry up, guv'ner,' of the conductor. Passengers are always very persevering in their efforts to save time by attempting to catch the conveyance ahead of the one they could easily reach; and I remember seeing a man rush some hundred yards up Holborn after a bus. Near the Tottenham Court Road he caught it. 'Marble Arch,' he gasped, as he stumbled into the conductor's arms. 'No, Piccadilly Circus; yours is the one you've been running away from,' came the answer wrapped in a sardonic smile. The last tram or bus is always a scene of excitement; there is a mad rush of passengers to fill the empty seats — commonly enough there is room for them all twice over; but this is a detail that never enters into their calculations.

On the variety of form and shape in buses much might be said, but since the majority of people care nothing whatever about the conveyance so long as it takes them where they want to go to, it is best left unwritten; yet, at the risk of being prolix, I would remark on the great advantage of the modern 'garden-seat' bus over the old 'knife-board' it is superseding, though the latter are regretted by those who daily use the same bus, and look on a certain seat beside the driver as their own especial place. Somebody or other has remarked that the garden-seat, and its consequent isolation of the driver, has evolved a new type of Jehu, surly-tempered and un-Weller-like. If this be true, the LCC will doubtless endeavour to remedy matters at some future date. The knife-board bus has decided disadvantages; everybody kicks everybody else when getting on or off the roof; four seats beside the driver can only be reached after a perilous climb; and when a big man getting down from one gives the final jump into a crowded street, accidents are apt to occur.

The origin of the term 'knife-board' is lost in obscurity; some asserting that it is due to the shape of the board whereon the Jehu rests his legs, while others are of opinion that it is a corruption of 'knave-bored' – referring to him who sits beside the driver and listens to his yarns.

There is plenty of room for other improvements in omnibuses besides the arrangement of seats; something to obviate the jolting one experiences in them would be decidedly welcome, and pneumatic tires loom in the near future.

With them will probably come the electric bus that was mooted in 1890, and has already been tried in London. Benzine has also been used as a motive power in Germany. Vienna has the smoking bus, divided into two compartments with a door between the wheels; and since these are controlled by the directors of the London General, it is strange that we have not yet had them introduced here.

We got the idea of 'buses from the French; and it will be seen that the vehicle started in London by one Shillibeer does not differ much from that in use to-day. The LGOC was founded some forty years since, and its early buses were practically the same as those now employed, save in the form of steps by which the roofs are reached. Progress cannot be said to have been very rapid, and any radical change when it comes will probably entail the doing away with altogether of the bus as we know it.

Already the pavements in the City cannot properly hold the pedestrians, and it is not unreasonable to suppose that by and bye vehicular traffic will have to be relegated to underground and overhead.

About the level of the first-floor windows footways could be erected, alongside which electric trams would run; lifts every here and there leading to higher stations, between which a service of air ships or dirigible balloons would fly.

The day may also come when the ever-moving pavement, which one will just step on to be moved along automatically at speeds up to ten miles an hour, will be something more than the dream of a German engineer. The configuration of our streets is against its practical use now; but there is no reason why it should not work in subterranean passages, ventilated and worked by tidal force.

To come back from dreams of the future to the realities of the present; this article would be incomplete without some reference to bus fares, both as regards ordinary curiosity thereupon and for the benefit of those who like to know where they can get the most for their money.

The longest penny fare is from Hammersmith to Sloane Street. Other distances Liverpool Street to Tottenham Court Road, Chancery Lane to Victoria, Tottenham Court Road to Chapel Street, and Charing Cross to Liverpool Street. Against these may be placed Queen's Road to Notting Hill Gate, which is little over 500 yards; or Gray's Inn Road, corner of Holborn, to the bottom of Chancery Lane, which is hardly half-a-mile. The longest route covered by the LGOC is from Fulham to Old Ford; the shortest from Highbury Barn to Highbury Place. The Road Car routes vary from thirteen to seven miles in length.

* Since the above was written the Companies have reduced the distances of some of these fares.

According to police regulations, every omnibus must once a year undergo a thorough overhaul and re-fitting; and as this takes about a month, the London General has usually about eighty buses 'in hospital.' At the factory in Islington, buses may be seen in all stages, from the broken-down veteran to the last thing out of the painting shop, spick and span in all the glory of its brilliant colours. A row of newly-painted buses makes a fine bit of colour composition; the colours though bright are not too crude, and make a decidedly harmonious whole. Here, too, may be seen buses in course of construction; in one case a mere skeleton yet unpanelled, in another, complete save for the paint and cushions.

I made a partially successful attempt to discover why bus wheels are painted yellow – 'because they always have been, and so it's our colour,' – one of the employees gave as the reason.

The English Illustrated Magazine V.11, 1894

SOME DEFINITIONS

Bus. A contraction of *omnibus (q.v.)*. The word is used by airmen and motorists in a humorous, almost affectionate, way for their conveyances.

Busman's holiday. There is a story that in old horse-bus days a driver spent his holiday travelling to and fro on a bus driven by one of his pals. From this has arisen the phrase, which means occupying one's spare and free time in carrying on with one's usual work, in other words, a holiday in name only.

> Brewer's Phrase and Fable (*first published 1898, although these entries are likely to have made their first appearance in a later edition*)

The Man on the Clapham Omnibus. This is a familiar expression commonly used by journalists and other writers to denote an archetypal member of the public, who is by inference an intelligent and sensible person. However, it is perhaps less well known as a legal expression used by English courts where it is necessary to infer whether someone has acted in the manner that a reasonable person would be expected to, and so their conduct is measured against that universal representative of propriety, the Man on the Clapham Omnibus. It has been in use in English law since Victorian times, and may have been coined by the famous constitutional writer Walter Bagehot.

The use of this expression within English law was reviewed by the Supreme Court in 2014, where Lord Reed said:

> 1. The Clapham omnibus has many passengers. The most venerable is the reasonable man, who was born during the reign of Victoria but remains in vigorous health. Amongst the other passengers are the right-thinking member of society, familiar from the law of defamation, the officious bystander, the reasonable parent, the reasonable landlord, and the fair-minded and informed observer, all of whom have had season tickets for many years.
>
> 2. The horse-drawn bus between Knightsbridge and Clapham, which Lord Bowen is thought to have had in mind, was real enough. But its most famous passenger, and the others I have mentioned, are legal fictions. They

belong to an intellectual tradition of defining a legal standard by reference to a hypothetical person, which stretches back to the creation by Roman jurists of the figure of the bonus paterfamilias...

3. It follows from the nature of the reasonable man, as a means of describing a standard applied by the court, that it would be misconceived for a party to seek to lead evidence from actual passengers on the Clapham omnibus as to how they would have acted in a given situation or what they would have foreseen, in order to establish how the reasonable man would have acted or what he would have foreseen. Even if the party offered to prove that his witnesses were reasonable men, the evidence would be beside the point. The behaviour of the reasonable man is not established by the evidence of witnesses, but by the application of a legal standard by the court. The court may require to be informed by evidence of circumstances which bear on its application of the standard of the reasonable man in any particular case; but it is then for the court to determine the outcome, in those circumstances, of applying that impersonal standard.

4. In recent times, some additional passengers from the European Union have boarded the Clapham omnibus. This appeal is concerned with one of them: the reasonably well-informed and normally diligent tenderer.

Healthcare at Home Limited v. The Common Services Agency [2014] UKSC 49 at [1]–[4]

2 THE BELLE EPOQUE BUS

In 1800 the population of London had only marginally exceeded that of Paris. By 1900 it was two and half times its French rival's and London was by far and away the largest city in the world. At the time of Queen Victoria's death in January 1901, just a few weeks into the new century, some 3,700 horse buses were ferrying Londoners to their various destinations. But the arrival that April of the first electric trams was a harbinger of the technological revolutions that would transform the capital's transport network in the run up to World War I. That same year, the American businessman Charles Tyson Yerkes acquired the District Line Railway and announced extensive expansion plans that would ultimately produce the Bakerloo, Northern and Piccadilly Lines. The petrol-powered internal combustion engine would, in any case, call time on horse-drawn buses, trams and hansom cabs. By 1913, the latter would dwindle to a mere 400 in the capital down from a high Victorian peak of 7,000, while the London General Omnibus Company's fleet of bespoke B-type motorbuses reached 2,500.

TOO HOT FOR OMNIBUS HORSES

Ruth Slate

It has been hot again; 88 degrees in the shade. On Monday it was 90. Grandpa back last night and said it was dreadful up in the City; the Omnibuses had to keep stopping to get fresh horses, as the others would suddenly be taken so ill, that they could get no further. Most of them wore large straw hats and presented an amusing sight.

Diary — 21 July 1900

THE OMNIBUS HORSE

W J Gordon

THE omnibuses are the most characteristic feature of London; and they increase, while the cabs decrease. What London would be like without them a recent strike gave us the opportunity of knowing, and there can be no doubt that from an aesthetic point of view its streets would be considerably improved.

But the omnibus is for use, not for beauty; it exists for the convenience of the many. It is a money-making machine, and it looks it, with its crowd of passengers, who pay up amongst them some forty-four shillings a day for its hire, as they sit between screens of patchy advertisements, which add a shilling a day to its takings, and spoil every attempt at improving its form and decoration.

We shudder, however, at the thought of depriving a poor man of his omnibus, and for a writer on horses to even hint at such a thing is peculiarly ungrateful, inasmuch as the London General Omnibus Company are the greatest users of living horse power in London. They have, in round numbers, ten thousand horses, working a thousand omnibuses, travelling twenty million miles in a year, and carrying one hundred and ten million passengers. In other words, every omnibus travels not sixty miles an hour, but sixty miles a day, and every horse travels twelve miles a day. And as an omnibus earns a little over eightpence-halfpenny a mile, and the average fare paid by each passenger is a little under three-halfpence, it follows that each omnibus picks up six passengers every mile.

In practice, a fifth of the omnibuses are daily at rest or under repair, and allowing for these, each vehicle carries thirty-nine passengers during a journey, so that, with its accommodation for twenty-six, three passengers enter and leave for every two of its seats. The average number in an omnibus at any one time is given as fourteen, and averaging these passengers at ten stone apiece, and throwing in the driver and conductor, we get a ton of live weight, to which we can add the ton and a half which the omnibus weighs, making up two-and-a-half tons for the pair to draw, and thus we arrive at the easily-remembered formula that the London omnibus horse draws a ton and a quarter twelve miles a day. He draws this at the rate of five miles an hour; he is bought when he is five years old; he works five years; he costs 35*l.* to buy and half-a-sovereign a week to feed;

he is sold for a 5*l.* note; and lastly, and by no means less importantly, 'he is not a horse, but a mare.'

Most of these mares are English, some of them are Irish, only a few of them are foreign — that is, according to the dealer, if he can be trusted in his verbal guarantee of nationality. And although the omnibus is of French extraction, and the London company has a French offshoot, it is curious that there is so little avowedly foreign about either the omnibus or its horseflesh.

Let us be off to some typical yard to see how these horses live and how they are cared for; and let the yard be one of the newest, say, that at Chelverton Road. Here are the 375 horses working the 'white bus' line from Putney to Liverpool Street. The white 'buses are well known for their trimness. Their colour precludes their being carelessly looked after, but they are no better kept than the others. Like the rest, they are cleaned and overhauled every morning, their locks looked to, their tires examined, their wheels tapped, just as if they were railway carriages, the minor repairs being done on the spot, the more serious being executed at Highbury.

Each of these omnibuses has its driver, its conductor, and its stud of ten or eleven horses, the eleven being required when the vehicle does its four full trips and a short one in a day. The full trip averages three hours and a half, and the day's work thus employs eight horses, giving each pair in turn a day's rest, but the extra short trip means an extra horse and a different system of relief, which we can deal with later on.

The horses are of all colours, bay, roan, brown, chestnut, grey, and that most promising of all colours, flea-bitten grey, which is seldom worn by a bad horse. All over the country, at the fairs and the provincial stables, buyers are at work for the company, picking out the peculiar class of horse which will best bear the constant stopping and starting of the London omnibus traffic. When an omnibus is full it weighs three and a quarter tons, a considerable weight for a pair to start. Think of it, ye exigent women, who rather than walk a yard will stop an omnibus twice in a minute; the sudden stopping and starting, so often unnecessary, taking more out of a horse than an hour's steady tramp on the level, and being the chief cause of the London horse's poor expectation of life.

When the horses are bought they are sent to the depot at Paddington or to that at Spitalfields, where they are sorted out for the different roads. Five years on the London streets takes as much out of a horse as ten years elsewhere; and a horse that will suit one road will not suit another, owing to the different kinds of paving. There is one road worked over by one of the 'Favourite' lines on which there is no asphalt; there are others which have every variety of material the worst being asphalt when slightly wet, the best being wood when lightly sprinkled with gravel. But it is not so much the paving as the change from one sort to another which is so puzzling to the horses, the sudden break from granite to asphalt, or macadam to wood, requiring an instant change in the step, to which not every horse is equal, though by some the knack is caught in a week or so.

The new horse is sent off to the yard from which the road he has been chosen for is worked. This is the headquarters from which the omnibus begins its travels in the morning, and to which it returns at night after its four or five journeys to and fro. The 'Putneys,' for example, start eastwards to Liverpool Street, and their last journey is a westerly one; the Walham Green 'Favourites' work northwards to Islington and back; the Victoria 'Favourites' work southwards from Holloway and back; the 'Royal Blues' from Victoria, northwards and back; and so with all the rest, always out and home, though on some lines the horses are not changed at the yard, but at some corner close by. The London General owns newly half the omnibuses in London, and is the largest concern of the kind in the world. Next to it in London comes the Road Car Company, which carries 37,000,000 passengers a year, and has about 300 cars and 3,000 horses. The company has been running about ten years, and is favourably known as the introducer of the garden seat and the pioneer of the penny fares and the roll tickets. It is worked on much the same system as the London General, but being a younger company has fewer survivals.

At Farm Lane, Fulham, the Road Car Company has the finest omnibus yard in Britain. At half-past seven in the morning when the first car comes out, and indeed at any time, it is one of the sights of London. In the central court are over sixty cars which have been washed and examined during the night, the cleaning of each seven being one man's night's work. Around the quadrangle are the stables, on two storeys, and in them are 700 horses. Four of the floors have each about fourteen studs of eleven in a long double line standing in peat, the gas jets down the middle alight in the fading darkness flickering on the double set of harness for each stud, which gleams black and shiny on the posts that make the long lines look longer, while the growing daylight streams in from the high windows on the inner wall and from the ventilators overhead.

There is a strong Caledonian element in the 'Road Car,' and even the horses are most of them Scotch. Like those of the 'General' they cost about 35l. each, begin work when about five years old, last about five years, and fetch about thirty shillings each as carcases for the cat's-meat man. When they first come into the stable they are put to light work with an experienced companion, and it is on an average eight weeks before they get into full working order. The studs are all elevens, the car doing five full trips a day. The eleven, with the one horse working round as a relief, means one horse resting every day, and Sunday being a short day with a trip the less, affords a chance of a rest for three horses every seventh day.

The day's work of an omnibus horse is, in fact, severe but short, and he spends at least five-sixths of his time in the stable, making friends with his neighbours, or trying to get the better of them, for there are many points of resemblance other than pathological between equine and human nature. And surely a little touchiness can be forgiven after a worrying trip through noisy London in rain or snow or fog, varied at all sorts of irregular intervals with sudden stops and starts on greasy asphalt; the start, as we said before, being for a full load a pull of between three and four tons.

Besides the 'General' and the 'Road Cars,' there are the Omnibus Carriage Company, the Railway omnibuses, including the Metropolitan, now lighted by oil gas or electricity; the omnibuses owned by the Tramway Companies, the Camden Town, and Star, and other associations, and the private owners, ranging down to that fortunately rare 'unfairest of the fare,' the man with one vehicle, the so-called pirate or 'flat-catcher,' who cruises as he likes and charges what he pleases; an irregular man who makes up for the erasures in his fare-table by an exuberance of expletives – at least, as a rule, though there are in London some of the honestest and mildest-mannered pirates imaginable, with the very neatest and completest of turn-outs.

Every omnibus or road car allowed to ply in London has to be approved of and licensed by the Scotland Yard authorities. About five per cent, are refused a licence every year, and thus weeded out by the police, for being too old or unsafe to pass muster – some of them condemned in the daylight at the annual examination, some of them discovered and doomed in the night time at the monthly inspection. The annual police return gives the present number of licensed omnibuses at 2,210. These 2,210 vehicles we can assume to require 22,000 horses and 11,000 men to look after them and their burden. The horses, at something under 35*l.* each, would represent three quarters of a million of money, and the stables and buildings they occupy are worth at least another quarter of a million, for those of the London General and the Road Car are valued at 200,000*l.* The million is thus made up by the bus horse and his home, and his food costs over 10,000*l.* a week; the 2,200 odd vehicles average 150*l.* apiece to build, which means a third of a million for the lot; and if we add to this a sixth of a million for the value of the harness and the stores generally, after making all allowance for depreciation on every point, we shall make up another half million, and, adding our figures together, be well within the limit in estimating that it takes fifteen hundred thousand pounds to work the omnibus trade of London.

from The Horse World of London *(1893)*

A HORSE-LESS DREAM

R D Blumenfeld

Yerkes, the projector of the new Charing Cross, Euston, and Hampstead electric Underground, for which he has a charter, said to me that in spite of the opposition which he meets at every turn he proposes to go through with it. He has secured the backing of some large American financiers to the extent of £30,000,000, and he predicted to me that a generation hence London will be completely transformed; that people will think nothing of living twenty or more miles from town, owing to electrified trains. He also thinks that the horse omnibus is doomed. Twenty years hence, he says, there will be no horse omnibuses in London. Although he is a very shrewd man, I think he is a good deal of a dreamer.

R D B's Diary, 6 October 1900

THE ROUTE TO REVOLUTION

Lenin's fondness for the London Omnibus

N K Krupskaya

Ilyich studied living London. He liked taking long rides through the town on top of the bus. He liked the busy traffic of that vast commercial city, the quiet squares with their elegant houses wreathed in greenery, where only smart broughams drew up. There were other places too — mean little streets tenanted by London's work people, with clothes lines stretched across the road and anaemic children playing on the doorsteps. To these places we used to go on foot. Observing these startling contrasts between wealth and poverty, Ilyich would mutter in English through clenched teeth: 'Two nations!'

But even from the top of the bus one could observe many characteristic scenes. Ill-clad lumpen-proletarians with pasty faces hung around the pubs, and often one would see among them a drunken woman with a bruised eye wearing a trailing velvet dress from which a sleeve had been ripped off. Once, from the top of a bus, we saw a huge 'bobby' in his typical helmet and chin strap hustling before him with an iron hand a puny little urchin, who had evidently been caught stealing, while a crowd followed behind them whooping and whistling. Some of the people on the bus jumped up and began hooting at the little thief too. 'Well, well!' Vladimir Ilyich would mutter sadly. Once or twice we took a ride on top of the bus to some working-class district on pay-day evening. An endless row of stalls, each lit up by a flare, stretched along the pavement of a wide road; the pavements were packed with a noisy crowd of working men and women, who were buying all kinds of things and satisfying their hunger right there on the spot. Vladimir Ilyich always fell drawn to the working-class crowd. Wherever there was a crowd he was sure to be there — whether it was an outing in the country, where the tired workers, glad to escape from the city, lay about for hours on the grass, or a public house, or a reading room. There are many reading rooms in London — just a single room opening straight on to the street, where there is not even a seat, but just a reading desk with newspaper files. The reader takes a file and when he is finished with it, hangs it back in its place. Ilyich, in years to come, wanted to have such reading rooms organized everywhere in our own country. He visited eating houses and churches. In English churches the service is usually followed by a short lecture and a debate. Ilyich was particularly fond of those debates, because ordinary workers took part in them. He scanned the newspapers for notices of working-class meetings in some out-of-the-way district, where there were only rank-and-file workers from the bench — as we say now — without any pomp and leaders. These meetings were usually devoted to the discussion of some question or project, such as a garden-city scheme. Ilyich would listen attentively, and afterwards say joyfully: 'They are just bursting with socialism! If a speaker starts talking rot a worker gets up right away and takes the bull by the horns, shows up the very essence of capitalism.' It was the rank and-file British worker who had preserved his class instinct in face of everything, that Ilyich always relied upon. Visitors to Britain usually saw only the labour aristocracy, corrupted by the bourgeoisie and itself bourgeoisified. Naturally Ilyich studied that upper stratum, too, and the concrete forms which this bourgeois influence took, without for a moment forgetting the significance of that fact. But he also tried to discover the motive forces of the future revolution in England.

from Reminiscences of Lenin: Life in London 1902–1903

(Nadezhda Krupskaya was a prominent Bolshevik revolutionary, and was also married to Lenin. In her account of their life together in exile she describes how they would take the bus to Parliament Hill in North London in order to benefit from walking in the fresh air, and also to visit the grave of Karl Marx in Highgate cemetery. Lenin was not the first to realise that the top deck of a bus was an ideal vantage point for studying both London and Londoners, but the research that he undertook in this way was perhaps more consequential than that of any other passenger before or since.)

THE LESSER-SPOTTED LONDON 'BUS

Henry Charles Moore

It is a quarter past seven, and the driver of the first 'bus to leave one of the London General Omnibus Company's many extensive yards is already up, standing with his legs astride the brake pedal, and wrapping his rug around his body. A stout, grey-whiskered, red-faced old man, with his rug already strapped around him, is climbing laboriously to the box seat of the second bus. He is a conservative fellow, and wears a tall hat, in spite of the fact that such headgear is going out of fashion among 'busmen. Drivers, ranging in age from twenty-one to seventy, and conductors, mostly under forty, hurtling into the yard, greeting and chaffing each other in vigorous language. The only man who appears at all depressed is an 'odd' driver who has been three days without a job; but soon his spirits revive, for a bustling little woman enter the yard and informs the foreman that her husband is 'that bad with rheumatism he can't raise a hand, let alone drive a pair of young horses like he had third journey yesterday.' The 'odd' driver takes out the sick man's 'bus, and the 'odd' conductors regard his luck as a good omen.

By half-past eight 'buses of almost every colour, except black, are arriving in rapid succession from all quarters of the Metropolis, and, setting down the last of their passengers at the Bank, rumble onwards to join the queue toward Broad Street Station or to add to the busy scene in London Bridge Station yard. An hour later the London General's Kilburn express 'six pence any distance' is rattling Citywards along Maida Vale; and at Oxford Circus 'buses are passing north, south, east and west. Here too, are the large motor omnibuses — yearly increasing in number — of the London General Omnibus Company, the Road Car Company, the Atlas and Waterloo Association, and Tilling Limited, as well as others which only came into existence with the introduction of the modern horse-less 'bus. Before mounting to the top of one of these motor omnibuses we notice, crossing the Circus, a 'Royal Blue' — a name which has been familiar to Londoners for more than half a century — and during our ride down Regent Street towards Piccadilly we meet Balls Brothers' 'Brixtons' and the very old-fashioned blue 'Favourites' of the London General Omnibus Company.

Near by, crossing Trafalgar Square we see the yellow 'buses (dubbed by 'busmen 'mustard pots') of the Camden Town Association, the oldest omnibus body in London. To this and other associations belong the majority of the leading proprietors, including several very old-established firms and such comparatively youthful limited liability companies as the Star Omnibus Company and the Associated Omnibus Company. Proceeding to Victoria, we find 'bus after 'bus starting from the railway station yard, including the well-lighted red 'Kilburns' of the Victoria Station Association.

Now it is early in the afternoon – a slack time for 'busmen. Here comes a Road Car with every seat vacant, but the silk-hatted driver is keeping a sharp look out and soon picks up three ladies for Westbourne Grove. Not far away an empty London General is standing at a 'point'. Here is a 'pirate'. Two ladies enter this 'bus believing it to belong to the London General Omnibus Company. It is painted and lettered to give the public that impression, but the company's name is not on the panels, and the horses, instead of being well-fed animals are lean 'cabbers'.

Later on, an almost empty 'bus, which belongs to one of the great companies is coming along Fleet Street from Ludgate Circus. The driver glances up at the Law Court clock, and calculates that by driving somewhat slowly he will arrive at the earliest closing theatre just as the people are coming up. But the Strand policemen's duty clashes with his, and they hurry him on, with the result that, instead of leaving Charing Cross with a full complement of passengers, he has only five.

***

Quarrels among the passengers were of everyday occurrence, and the cause of the discord was, almost invariably, the windows. There were usually five windows on each side of the omnibus, which could be opened or closed according to the passenger's fancy. An arrangement better calculated to breed discord could scarcely have been made. The quarrels concerning them were usually somewhat ludicrous—from the fact that the ten windows rattled fearfully, compelling the disputants to yell at each other to make themselves heard. One day a Frenchman and an Italian chanced to be sitting side by side in an omnibus. The Italian pulled up a window just behind them. The Frenchman promptly, and indignantly, lowered it. The Italian excitedly pulled it up again, and this ding-dong performance was continued for some little time, greatly to the amusement of the other passengers. At last, the Frenchman grew desperate, and shattered the glass with his elbow, exclaiming, 'Now, Monsieur, you can have ze window up if you likes!'

both extracts from 'Tram 'Bus and Cab London'
published in Living London *periodical (1905)*

THE JUST-OUTSIDE-LONDON BUS

Ford Madox Ford

London manifests itself slowly with high-banked and gravelled footpaths, with those same blackened tree trunks, in a certain coarseness of the grass, in houses of call that you feel uninclined to call at. Dogcarts and governess cars begin to look a little out of place, indefinably, you don't know why. And suddenly you meet a 'bus.

I don't know whether it is to me alone that a 'bus running between hedgerows seems forlorn and incongruous. They 'link up' all sorts of outlying villages — Mitcham with Tooting, all sorts of hamlets with Kingston-on-Thames, Islington with I don't quite know where. There is a network of what are called 'bus-routes' all over England, but these are mostly carrier's carts.

Some have tarpaulin hoods and go at a walk, others look like the station omnibuses of country hotels. Their existence is largely unsuspected, yet it is possible to go from Lewes to York by changing from link to link in market towns, or from Canterbury to Sydenham.

But the just-outside-London 'bus carries no parcels. It is, as a rule, bright green, and has a brilliant orange knifeboard atop. It goes at a good pace, and it is the sign that you have reached the sphere of influence of the very outer suburbs. I at least have never entered London by road without meeting or passing one of them.

They are due to the enterprise of large job masters near the great tram and London omnibus termini; they are the signs of London's reaching out its arms still further; they are really the pioneers. In older days they started from Whitehall, from the Bank, from the Borough, and were called Short Stages. As real London spreads they cease to pay; they travel farther afield, and their place is taken by our municipal services or by those of the larger trusts.

from The Soul of London *(1905)*

WHY ARE LONDON BUSES RED?

Matt Brown

As a symbol of our city, the red double-decker is up there with Big Ben and Tower Bridge. But did you ever wonder why the colour was chosen? You have to go back to 1907, when most buses were still horse-drawn, to witness the crimson dawn.

Before that time, buses came in all manner of shades, with rival companies operating different routes. In 1907, the London General Omnibus Company rouged-up its entire fleet in an effort to stand out from the competition. The LGOC soon became the largest bus company, and its livery came to dominate the streets. When London Transport formed in 1933, it extended the convention to most (though not all) London buses, a decision whose effects remain with us today.

A quick glance through Transport for London's colour standards guide reveals that buses under its purview should be coloured in Pantone 485 C. This popular hue is also used on the tube roundel and Central line, as well as by Royal Mail, Kit Kat, McDonald's and the Russian flag.

Actually, the surfaces of London buses are mostly not red. This becomes clear when seen from above. Bus roofs are largely white. This is to reflect sunlight and thereby reduce heating in summer. Their underbellies aren't red, either. Now if you subtract the area taken up by the windows and adverts — the latter can encanker the whole backside of a bus. At a guess that the typical vehicle is probably only 30-40 per cent red.

Finally, we have to acknowledge there are those buses that get the all-over, wrap-around advertising. At any given time then, a small percentage of London's buses don't feature any red at all. Could this symbol of our city be in danger of disappearing? The London red bus might actually be a red herring.

from an article originally published on the Londonist website, 2016

Joe Clough poses in front of an early LGOC motorbus on route 11 in 1908

JOE CLOUGH

The first black bus driver

Ian Thomas

Joe Clough was born in Jamaica in 1887 and orphaned at an early age. As a boy, he was employed by a Scottish doctor, Dr R C White, to look after his polo ponies. In 1905 while they were returning from a dance at the governor's house in Kingston, they had a conversation that was to change Clough's life. Dr White asked him, 'How would you like to go to England?' 'Well,' replied Clough, 'I'd like that very much'. He was 18 years old.

In winter 1906 Clough came over to Britain as White's servant and companion. He would have needed the brand new warm underwear he was wearing when he landed in Bristol. The first things Clough noticed were the trees. On remarking, 'Dr White, why are there so many dead trees about?' he was told that it was winter. Clough commented later, 'We don't have trees like that in Jamaica, I'd never seen anything like it before.' He was never to see his old home again.

When Clough arrived in London, he drove Dr White around town in his coach and horses. However, the doctor was keen to try out the new motorcars, which were becoming popular; so Clough learnt to drive and became the doctor's chauffeur.

Clough remembered later that, after he had left the doctor's employ, the Whites would entertain him in the drawing room, treating him as an equal in spite of the attitudes of the day. 'The doctor was a lovely man. After I left him, I could go to see him, go up to the front door, knock, saying 'Is the doctor in?' He treated us just the same as you and me talking together, no nose in the air.'

In 1910, Clough applied to work at London General Omnibus Company (LGOC). He became a spare driver. He passed his bus driving test and started driving a No 11 B-type bus between Liverpool Street and Wormwood Scrubs. Joe Clough was the first Black London bus driver.

This was also the year that he began taking his wife-to-be on weekly visits to the music hall. The daughter of a local publican, Margaret worked as a domestic servant. She and Joe married in 1911, and enjoyed a happy married life together. Margaret was always prepared to support her husband in the face of racism. Clough wanted to rise above it, however, and met people's stares and comments by raising his hat and wishing the person a good day.

When World War I started, Clough wanted to join up to help defend his adopted country. He enlisted in the Army Service Corps based at Kempston barracks in 1915. He drove a field ambulance for four years in Ypres on the Western Front, the area that saw some of the bloodiest battles.

After the war in 1919 Joe, his wife and two daughters moved to Bedford. He was almost the only Black inhabitant there until after the Second World War. He first worked for the National Omnibus Company, before buying his own taxi in 1949.

Joe died in 1976 at the age of 91. In the last decade of his life he had become a local celebrity thanks to a book, *The Un-melting Pot* by John Brown, published in 1970, which featured a chapter about Joe and Margaret Clough. Many local people remember him with great affection.

originally published on the Black History Month website in 2015

3 THE BUS GOES TO WAR

World War I began on 5 August 1914. As we know only too well, the sheer scale of the slaughter of this conflict dwarfed anything seen before. It was war advanced with a lethal combination of technical innovation (new-fangled motorised tanks, aeroplanes, machines guns and mustard gas), and military incompetence. Thanks to German Zeppelin bombing raids, London's streets joined the battlefields as war zones, for perhaps the first time since the English Civil War. A fleet of London's B-type buses on the other hand were dispatched to Flanders and France to serve as troop transporters. Lacking enough able-bodied men to keep those left on the capital's bomb-pocked roads running, women stepped into the breech. And a small victory in the ongoing battle for sexual equality, one waged so courageously by the suffragettes before the war, was duly won.

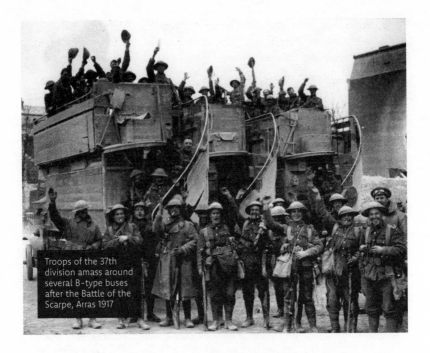

Troops of the 37th division amass around several B-type buses after the Battle of the Scarpe, Arras 1917

THE BUS DURING WORLD WAR I

Sam Mullins

The first motor buses had first been tried in the capital from 1898, but they proved under-powered and unreliable. A period of rapid technical development followed as these primitive motor vehicles worked alongside the well-established fleets of horse buses. In 1910, the London General Omnibus Company or 'General' introduced the B-type bus, which soon proved itself as the world's first reliable motor bus. The design was simple, essentially a double-deck horse bus body powered by a 30 hp petrol engine driving the rear wheels. It carried 16 inside and 18 passengers on the open upper deck, weighed 3.5 tons and was restricted to 12mph. The B-type was mass-produced, with up to 30 buses a week leaving the works at Walthamstow, and more than 2,900 being built between 1910 and 1914.

The General built the B-type in the former Vanguard (London Motor Omnibus Company) works at Walthamstow. In the competitive world of bus services, a motor vehicle which could be relied upon to work long days on the demanding stop/start London services, brought a revolution. Within a year, the General had replaced all its horse-drawn services and by August

1914, within four years, the new motors had brought about the end of the horse bus across London; stables were emptied and drivers retrained, garages created and the new trade of motor mechanic arose.

The motor buses of 1910 were, mostly, red. The Vanguard company had pioneered two key features of the London bus; from 1906 the company had introduced the first five route numbers to replace vehicles being a different colour for each route. Vanguard's other significant innovation was the introduction in 1905 of a distinctive red livery for all its fleet, to stand out from the competition and be highly visible on the street. Both of these key characteristics of the London bus were inherited and developed by the General when it acquired Vanguard, its fleet and Walthamstow works in 1908.

By the hot dusty summer of 1914, London was served by a fleet of over 3,200 motor buses and by a number of bus companies of which the General was by far the largest. The General had in turn been absorbed in the Underground Group or Combine, the Underground Electric Railway Company of London, owners of the new tube railway system and a network of tram lines.

The cheering crowds that thronged Whitehall, Trafalgar Square and the Strand to welcome the outbreak of war with Germany in August 1914 expected the conflict to be short and victorious. The bus drivers whose buses were stuck in the sea of revellers and from which there was a grandstand view from the top deck, had little idea that both they and their buses might be on the Western Front within a matter of weeks. Certainly, the duration and profound effect of the war on London was not anticipated, nor could those drivers guess the loss and destruction they would witness and write home about to loved ones and work colleagues.

The War was on the Capital's doorstep and the city became the centre of the war effort; headquarters, a place for transit to the Front or on the way home on leave or wounded, to the many hospitals created in and around London and the centre of the munitions industry.

At the outbreak of war, the War Office requisitioned a third of the London bus fleet, around 1,200 buses, as troop transports. Many were accompanied by their crews who volunteered for active service in the Royal Corps of Transport (RCT). A reminder of London was brought to the war zone by convoys of buses carrying soldiers up to the front lines and bringing out the tired and wounded.

The first batch of blue-liveried Metropolitan Electric Traction company buses rushed to Flanders to rescue soldiers and civilians from the invading German army at the siege of Antwerp in October 1914. The buses were deployed in such haste that they still carried adverts for West End theatres, including, to the Tommies' ironic delight, a musical revue entitled 'Never A Dull Moment'.

During the euphoric early days of the War in London, buses brought volunteers to recruiting stations, transported them the railway stations for journeys to mobilisation and to training depots or for embarkation to France. Soon they were bringing casualties from the mainline stations and dispersing them to hospitals around the capital.

Once in France some London buses were relieved of their passenger saloons and converted into lorries. Others had their side windows boarded up and were painted khaki. For large movements of troops behind the front line, the buses were used in convoys of 70 or more, usually at night to avoid observation and artillery bombardment, manned by pairs of volunteer drivers who lived with their vehicles and often worked through the safety of the night. During the day, the convoys were parked up in village streets for protection from artillery. The drivers had to be able to make repairs on the road and avoid slipping into ditches from the cobbled pave. They were skilled men and were paid received 4-6 shillings a day, more than the one shilling a day of the infantrymen they carried. They were known as great sources of news and gossip and to be able to supply contraband whisky, German regalia, eggs, a chicken or other delights for the hard-pressed Tommy;

> 'One of the transport men, who were noted for their tall stories... Our transport men were marvels: They knew everything that was happening on the Western Front. The Old Soldier, when he was with the Battalion, used to say they has a private telephone line to the Commander-in-Chief's bedroom... When the rations came up to the village, the Old Soldier exchanged two nosecaps for about a pint or rum...with one of the transport men'.

For the men at the Front, the bus was a poignant reminder of the pre-war life they had left behind:

> '... it was the first time the Riflemen had not had to march. The buses arrived at ten o'clock in the evening of 5 July. There were twenty of them to transport the Battalion, and they had seen better days since they trundled around the peacetime streets of London, shiny red and cheerfully noisy. They were still noisy, and here and there, where the drab khaki of their wartime paint was chipped, a glint of red still hinted at the days when they had plied along Oxford Street,

*travelling north of Kilburn, or honked through Piccadilly
and south to Kensington. The windows were boarded up
but, miraculously, on some the conductor's bell was still
functioning, and, as the boys clambered aboard, one
wag inevitably positioned himself on the platform and
rang the bell.*

*'Do you stop at the Savoy Hotel?' It was the old, old joke
that Joe Hoyles couldn't resist asking.*

*'No sir!' The 'conductor' was equally familiar with the old
chestnut. 'can't afford it. Did you say a twopenny one, sir?
Comes cheaper if you take a return.'*

The Chaplain to the Rifle Brigade also found the buses reminded him
of home:

*'You may paint a motor bus dark green, and you may
remove the advertisements and cover the windows with dark
green boards, but you cannot conceal the identity of the old
familiar friends who have done their duty in Piccadilly. When
we saw them all drawn up in some side road waiting for
their 'fares' there was nothing to be said except, 'How did
they bring them all across the Channel?'*

With so many men away on war service, the transport system in London
was obliged by the gaps in its own ranks to consider engaging women in
the workforce for the first time. The emancipation of women had been a
major political issue in the years before the War. As the services consumed
more and more men, they could only be replaced by women. Many
employed women had previously been hidden away as domestic servants,
enthusiastically took up roles in transport as cleaners, guards, platform
staff, lift attendants, mechanics and 'conductorettes'. In general, they
valued the comparative freedom of regular hours, better pay and a job out
of the home.

The Metropolitan Railway began to recruit and train women in 1915.
They were dressed in a blue uniform with red flashes on the collar and a
pair of sensible shoes, with a modest heel. Their roles were porter, ticket
inspector and later guards. The General began to train women at Millman
Street, Chelsea in March 1916. The interest in these jobs was considerable,
the LGOC alone receiving 20,000 applications of whom around 3,500
were employed over the next three years. The women had to pass IQ and
medical tests and prove they did not have a criminal record. An album of

photographs of the training centre was produced to mark the graduation of the 2,000th woman later that year. It is a remarkable record of their training. Discipline was strict though, as the staff register confirms.

The appearance of women in such visible roles on buses and station platforms was indeed a cultural revolution for London. When one notes that women only routinely entered the transport workforce in the 1950s, and the first female bus driver (1974) and train driver (1972) had to wait for a further generation to pass, the impact on the class conscious and gender stereotypes of Edwardian London must have been profound.

Postcards from this period suggest men remained unreconstructed in their views of women. They depict women in highly elegant versions of the uniforms and exhibit a sexist disparagement of these female pioneers. Private Christopher Massie, of the Medical Corps (RAMC) was much taken with this new world when on leave:

> 'Those wonderful girls working the trams and buses and railway stations delivering papers, milk and bread. To Tommy, 'on leave', London is a dazzling revue of enchanting feminine uniforms. These girls are nice to us chaps who have come back for a breather. They have a special inflection in their voices all for us. A special greeting, a quiet sympathy, for all the world as if we were invalids who require special treatment. And so we do.'

The busmen who remained at work in London were also at risk. On the night of 8 September 1915, bus B304 on route 8 was hit during a bombing attack by a Zeppelin airship. Driver Tarrant and Conductor Rogers were killed. Their funeral on 20 October was a huge civic event. The cortege passed through Dalston; two B-type buses bedecked with floral tributes, carried their coffins, followed by a long line of their colleagues in white summer duster uniform coats with black armbands. A set of commemorative postcards was issued. The bus on which they died was repaired and put back into service.

Post-war London still suffered from the war; men continued to be scarred, to die from wounds or from the terrible influenza epidemic of 1918–19. Public transport struggled to return to normal with makeshift khaki-coloured lorry buses drafted into emergency service. Women lost their transport jobs as men returned from the forces. The Underground Combine issued the women dismissed in 1919 with certificates of appreciation and held a large tea party over which the chairman, Lord Ashfield, presided. Nonetheless, 8.4 million women gained the vote in

1918, having proved themselves in transport, in munitions and many other aspects of life and work in the previous four years.

Surprisingly, around 40 buses were returned by the Army and resumed public service. The B-type bus had proved to be remarkably resilient, despite irregular maintenance and hard use. Memorials to fallen comrades were placed in many bus garages, on railway stations and in every parish church.

The contribution of the busmen to the war effort attracted the attention of King George V. In February 1920, a group of 25 veteran busmen from Middle Row Garage were invited with a B-type bus to Buckingham Palace. Recorded by Pathé News, the bus drove around the yard, the busmen on the top deck doffing their caps and the King his top hat. George remarked that this was the first time he had stepped on a London bus. So taken was he with their war service, that a transport contingent was invited to join the newly conceived Remembrance Sunday parade in November 1920.

B43 was one of the buses which had returned from service across the Channel. It was repaired, given a new body and became a mobile war memorial. With a radiator cap based on cartoonist Bruce Bairnsfather's 'Ole Bill' character, a shell mounted on the dashboard and battle honours including Ypres, Amiens and the Somme above its side windows, 'Ole Bill' became a feature of the Remembrance Sunday parade and was used by the Auxiliary Omnibus Association to raise funds for wounded soldiers and donated to the Imperial War Museum in 1970. It is currently displayed at London Transport Museum.

In November 1920 at the dedication of the new Cenotaph memorial in Whitehall, marching behind the three armed services, uniformed busmen followed by 'Ole Bill' placed their wreath on the newly dedicated Cenotaph. The contingent of transport workers has remained a feature of the Remembrance Sunday commemoration ever since.

King George V salutes the crew of a B-type bus 'Ole Bill' at Buckingham Palace, 1920

BLOWN TO BITS

W N P Barbellion

My first experience of a Zeppelin raid. Bombs dropped only a quarter of a mile away and shrapnel from the guns fell on our roof. We got very pannicky and went into a neighbour's house, where we cowered down in our dressing-gowns in absolute darkness while bombs exploded and the dogs barked.

I was scared out of my life and had a fit of uncontrollable trembling. Later we rang up ---- and ----, and thank Heavens both are safe. A great fire is burning in London, judging by the red glare. At midnight sat and drank sherry and smoked a cigar with Mr ---- — my braces depending from my trousers like a tail and shewing in spite of dressing-gown. Then went home and had some neat brandy to steady my heart. H---- arrived soon after midnight. A motor-omnibus in Whitechapel was blown to bits. Great scenes in the city.

from Journal of a Disappointed Man — *8 September 1915*

OMNIBUS CONDUCTORETTES

Michael MacDonagh

It occurred to me to go for a long walk through the main thoroughfares, starting from Whitehall, to see in what respects the daily life of London has been altered by two years of war, so far, at least, as change is to be observed in the streets.

The Strand, into which I turn from Whitehall, is still the busiest and most animated street in London, but its aspect is changed – its traffic and pedestrianism being so very different from what they were in the days of peace. The omnibus service is restricted; the use of private motor-cars is discouraged; horse-drawn vehicles are far more numerous. Among the walkers on the pavements khaki is predominant. Soldiers are everywhere. The military hustle and bustle to be seen in Whitehall is purposeful, being concentrated on War service and administration. In the Strand there is military relaxation, and some indiscipline. Obviously the men are from the training camps, spending a day off in London. They have not the seriousness which mark most soldiers back from the trenches on furlough. They have the idle vacancy of sheep wandering on the hill-side.

The drabness of civilians is very noticeable! What shabbiness in dress! A remarkable change in the point of view regarding clothes has set in. The cause is to be found on the walls and hoardings. Recruiting posters have been replaced by economy posters. 'Spend Less; Save More.' 'Buy only War Savings Certificates.' Accordingly it is the mode to assume a studied air of personal untidiness... The fashion among men of all classes is to wear hat, coat and trousers long – as long as possible, in time. The only short wear is the feminine skirt.

Women are to be seen at work everywhere. 'Men must fight and women must work – and weep.' You see them at the wheel of motor-cars and motor-drays. You see them handling the reins of horse-drawn vehicles. They are ticket-collectors at Underground and tube stations. At hotels and offices the lift-boy has become a lift-girl. The hall-porter at some of the big hotels is an Amazon in blue or mauve coat, gold-braided peaked cap and high top-boots – a gorgeous figure that fascinates me. But my favourite is the young 'conductorette' on trams and buses, in her smart jacket, short skirts to the knees and leather leggings.

from In London During the Great War: The Diary of a Journalist – *7 August 1916*

89 newly qualified women conductors – one week's output from the LGOC training school – pose in their new uniforms with a B-type bus, c.1917

THE LURE OF THE OMNIBUS

Hurry-Along Girls and World War I

Emmanuelle Dirix

In March 1916 newspapers up and down the country covered the latest story from the capital: the introduction of female bus conductors by the London General Omnibus Company (LGOC).* Regardless of the fact that women had already taken on several other traditionally male roles to aid the war effort, the news that the company was sending out the 'first 80 women conductors, with 250 more in training, a number that was added to each day' (*Aberdeen Press and Journal* – Friday 17 March 1916) was considered worthy of extensive coverage.

The reason for this interest can be put down to several factors, all revealed in these articles and indeed the extensive subsequent newspaper coverage of conductresses that lasted for the duration of the war. By closely analysing and contextualizing these contemporary writings a clear

---

* The LGOC was not the first company to employ female conductors. Tillings had employed the first 'clippie' in November 1915 but the LGOC was the first company to employ women on this scale.

picture starts to emerge of why these Hurry-Along girls* elicited so much interest and discussion.

The initial wave of articles in March 1916 all centred on two things: training and pay. Conductresses, as most newspapers informed their readers, were trained for 14 days at the Chelsea training facility in subjects such as route orientation, customer service, fares, ticket dispensing and most importantly what was referred to in the bus trade as acquiring 'sea-legs' – being able to keep one's balance while traipsing up and down the stairs and collecting fares and whilst the bus was in motion. During their training women received food and an allowance but once in active service they received wages of £2 per week, exactly the same amount as their male counterparts. This unprecedented pay equality, while applauded by certain newspapers, became the topic of some serious debate and indeed accounts in part for the countrywide interest in the London conductresses. Many questioned the fairness of this equal pay system citing that women were clearly not suited to this type of physically demanding work: 'the standing up and long hours seem particularly unsuited to women' (*The Graphic* 17 February 1917) and that 'willing as they may be (they) are not capable of doing the same amount of work as a man for mere physical reasons alone'. (*The Tatler* – Wednesday 4 September 1918).

This attitude, while certainly problematic to some contemporary eyes, was very much in line with assumptions and gender stereotypes about women that had been societally ingrained since the previous century. A few months prior to the outbreak of war the *London Times Weekly* set out the widely accepted view of the difference between the sexes and why women were incapable of contributing to the economy in any meaningful manner:

> '*Men cannot imagine a woman, dressed as women have seen fit to dress for the last few years, being competent to take any serious or worthy part in the work of the world. He cannot believe in a woman being capable of efficient, vigorous or independent action when hampered by the skirt of the period. A man knows that if for a year he were to submit himself to the restraints which a woman puts upon herself he would be mentally, morally and physically degenerate*' (London Times Weekly, 17 April 1914)

Indeed the idea that women were physically and mentally weak and belonged in the domestic sphere was oft repeated in the coverage of the conductresses; thus when special seats were added to buses so female

---

* Their nickname was derived from the phrase conductors would call out to passengers boarding buses

bus conductors could sit down on longer routes, newspapers once again picked up the story and reignited the debate of female physical inferiority. But it was not merely the press who peddled these feminine stereotypes. The Vehicle Workers Union went further and tried to block women from working in public transport, citing the work as 'Unsuitable to women from a moral and physical point of view' thus affirming this idea of female mental and physical inferiority. Interestingly at this same union meeting a representative from the London General Omnibus Company actively denied this assertion and quoted figures that showed only '3.86 per cent of women (had) resigned because they found the work too hard versus 2.13 men', clearly a negligible difference. He also stated that no disproportionate sick leave had been taken by female conductors (*Reading Observer* – Saturday 25 November 1916) thus showing that, physically women were fast proving themselves as capable as men.

If it wasn't her supposed physical weakness that was being debated it was her fragile and impressionable mental state that was a cause for worry. Certain commentators 'feared women would harden of disposition and would have a coarsening of manners' (*Liverpool Daily Post* – 20 March 1916) or simply put become more 'masculine' in their demeanour. The arguments that women mixing freely in society, women in employment or women obtaining the vote would turn them into masculine creatures who were ugly, refused to do housework and gave up on marriage had been used since the late 19th century to dissuade support for, and undermine the women's suffrage movement. This worry for women's spiritual well-being grew in part out of the increased female engagement with, and visibility in, wider society that the War had enacted. Prior to the conflict middle-class women were very much trapped in the domestic sphere and much female employment was either invisible (domestic work) or subservient by nature (sales assistants and waitresses). The city was very much the domain of men, and if women wished to enter it they were bound by the strict societal rules of the chaperoning system, which meant that for many, large parts of the city were off limits. But while the War put a stop to chaperoning out of simple practicality and necessity, employing women in roles of authority on omnibuses that travelled the length and breath of the city, was for many one uneasy step too far. As one article put it 'Fleet street was un-known ground to them til today' (*Aberdeen Press and Journal* – 15 March 1916).

For many of the women who signed up for the training programme, it was exactly these new opportunities and freedoms that attracted them to the role. Interestingly every single article that discussed the popularity of conductress work failed to see this point, and this inability of commentators to conceive why these roles would be attractive to women shows just how deeply engrained ideas around the sexes were, and just how little men understood women and their frustrations with their position in life. Instead of realising this type of role afforded them a host of previously unknown freedoms that they so craved, and that took them away from the monotony of their existence, newspapers instead speculated that women signing up in droves was simply down to the £2 weekly wage. Only just over a week after their introduction the *Daily Gazette for Middlesborough* reported that '300 "young women" are working as conductresses or are in training, but that soon 1,000 will be required if not 2,000 in due course' (23 March 1916). Unsurprisingly it blamed the favourable wages and went on to speculate about the detrimental impact that this would no doubt have on the domestic labour workforce; the entire article reads more like a covert warning of the evils that will befall society when women are given employment options rather than a genuine appraisal of the situation.*

There is no doubt that women were leaving domestic posts in favour of bus conducting or indeed one of the many other new employment opportunities offered by the War, however to merely put this down to the wages misses the point entirely.

In an article titled 'Lure of the Omnibus' the *Daily Mirror* stated that 38 per cent of the new recruits had been domestic servants, that the rest had been typists, shop assistants, waitresses or had worked for the postal service, but most importantly it noted that 10 per cent had formerly stayed at home and had not previously had any formal employment (28 April 1916). While some of this last group no doubt took on a conductress role to 'do their bit', for many the lure of excitement, responsibility and freedom no doubt played a deciding role. The happiness this new role afforded those women who had signed up is well conveyed in an unfortunately titled article in the *Globe*, 'Joys of Bus Conducting', which discussed the death of Violette Newman, a bus conductress who had been killed falling off her bus in Whitehall. At the inquest her mother testified that Violette 'had been happy as a bird and never wanted to return to typing' (15 February 1916).

While criticism and doubts regarding their capabilities continued to be published, soon after their introduction a steady stream of articles also appeared praising these women as 'they were after all, releasing fit men for service' (*Daily Gazette for Middlesborough*, 5 March 1918). Others lauded them for their efficiency and several were convinced that their presence

---

* Scaremongering stories regarding all the imagined ills that will befall society were women to be given the vote, equal rights etc. had become a staple in many news outlets for a good two decades. Cautionary tales used fear to maintain the status quo.

encouraged better manners on public transport* which meant that 'she is winning good opinions and good wishes' (*The Illustrated War News* April 5, 1916).

These more favourable articles were often accompanied by a photograph of a conductress in her newly designed uniform. This navy blue Norfolk jacket with white piping and a *General* badge, a plain skirt 3 inches below the knee, leather and cloth gaiters, and the felt hat in the 'colonial style' turned up at one side, drew more attention and had more column inches dedicated to its discussion than all the aforementioned issues combined. The more conservative commentators remarked on the 'uncommonly short skirt' which had been designed to allow the women to rush up and down the stairs with relative ease, yet this logical design decision did not detract from their outrage. Other, predominantly male, writers, worried condescendingly that women would not take to the austerity and functionality of the uniform, citing the stereotype that women's main preoccupation in life was appearance and that without their frills and individuality they could not be happy. Others used a focus on the uniform to detract from the vital service these women were providing: 'nobody yet saw two women omnibus conductors who wore their becoming shiny hats at the same angle or for that matter the straps of their money bags and ticket punches in the same manner' (*Daily Mirror*, 9 May 1916) This type of reporting which borrowed tone and terminology from fashion reporting trivialised their employment by positioning it as just another opportunity for accessorising.

Illustrations of conductresses featured in certain publications and on popular postcards of the time also often misrepresented the uniform; in several instances the skirt was depicted as either far shorter or far more figure hugging than it was in reality, and in certain images the 'uniform' looked more like the latest Paul Poiret Parisian *Haute Couture* frock than the functional outfit that it was in reality. This glamorisation of the conductress hints at her fetishisation in popular culture and undoubtedly her uniform, combined with her position of authority, titillated many a man unaccustomed to this novel sight. These 'sexy' representations did her no favours in terms of being taken seriously as a vital war worker and instead merely reduced her to a pleasant spectacle there for the enjoyment of men, which in turn of course also reduced the perceived threat she posed in trespassing on the male domain.

The majority of female writers however took a very different stance on the uniform and were quick to point that 'women have taken to uniform like ducks to water' (*Daily Record*, 13 June 1917). It was not just

---

* In 1913 New York omnibus company T Edison made the decision to employ women as it was though they would be more polite than male conductors

the comfort of the uniform (minus the spats – there are multiple accounts to be found of how much women hated the spats), or the fact they were classless as opposed to civilian dress, that made the uniform popular; its most appealing aspect resided with the authority and visibility this official uniform afforded women for the first time in their lives and the manner in which it commanded respect from civilians. Because it was a symbol of their contribution to society, their authority, and the fact they had secured important, serious and well-respected employment, the uniform was a symbol of pride.

A contributor to the letters page of the *Daily Mirror*, only identified as 'a woman war worker', asked whether uniforms would survive the war. She discussed how the simplicity and functionality of the uniform suited women far better than the extravagant fashions of the day, and she predicted women would continue to wear well-designed suits that afford her comfort and mobility (*Daily Mirror*, 26 January 1917) Arguably her predictions foresaw the simpler more comfortable cuts that would come to dominate the postwar female wardrobe.

By 1918 press reporting on the conductresses was almost wholly positive and supportive, perhaps because the initial shock had worn off, and more importantly because the conflict which many had predicted would last only a few months was in its fourth year, and anyone making a direct or indirect contribution to war work was unilaterally praised and supported. Nothing makes this change in attitude clearer than the reporting on the 1918 strike by conductresses over pay. While basic pay had been set at the same rate for male and female conductors, men were also awarded a wartime bonus denied to the women workers. To highlight the injustice of this system the women went on strike, and were surprisingly backed by reporters, who argued that these women had proved their worth and delivered an invaluable contribution both to the war effort and to London life, and hence should be awarded the same bonus. This time no arguments of physical or mental inferiority were used to justify the discrepancy in pay,* showing just how far public attitudes to conductresses and, to an extent women in general, had shifted.

This support and gratitude did not prevent conductresses from the London General Omnibus Company – like so many other women who had undertaken vital war work– from being dismissed at the end of the war. In total more than 3,500 women had served the role. There was little newspaper coverage about this demobilisation process at the time, except for a small piece in the *Daily Herald* entitled 'Bus Girls Make Merry,'

---

* However *Tatler*, a magazine for women often written by women, dragged up the same old stereotypes of women being incapable of the same work as men, regardless of the fact women had been doing exactly that for two years

describing how 500 Hurry-Along girls gathered at the People's Palace in Mile End for a demob beano: 'The most interesting feature of the evening was the presentation of an artistic souvenir certificate to the girls who had rendered service in the war' (*The Daily Herald*, October 22, 1919). Thus men received medals, but women an artistic certificate!

The conductress, who had taken over so many column inches and elicited so much debate about a woman's nature and ability, disappeared almost entirely from the London landscape, until she was once again called upon during World War II when the Hurry-Along girls came back as clippies.

4 THE MODERNE METROPOLIS

Perhaps there can be no greater emblem of interwar London casting out the old than the dumping in the Thames in 1929 of hundreds of horse-bus badges deemed irredeemably obsolete. But by then the congestion by motorised vehicles in the capital had already forced the introduction of 'one-way', or 'roundabout', traffic systems in the Haymarket and Piccadilly. What had added to London's traffic problems in the early 1920s though was a large increase in 'pirate' bus operators. In 1922, a canny cabby called Mr A G Partridge, noticing the shortage of buses caused by war-time requisitions and exploiting a legal loophole, had begun running his own bus up against those run by the London General Omnibus Company on route 11. Within two years it is estimated that there were as many as 200 independent buses with 74 different owners, chasing after the firm's business. They were run along have-a-go to gung-ho lines, with buses, staffed by cheap, easy-come, easy-go off-the-books labour, switching routes at the drop of a hat if potential passengers were spotted waiting elsewhere. The situation became so chaotic that the first Labour government passed The London Traffic Act 1924, forcing operators to deposit details of schedules with the Metropolitan Police and restricting the number of buses allowed on key routes. By the end of the 1920s most of the pirates had either gone bust or been swallowed up by the General and its allies.

A VERY MODERN DEATH

Virginia Woolf

It's not catastrophes, murders, deaths, diseases, that age and kill us; it's the way people look and laugh, and run up the steps of omnibuses.

from Jacob's Room *(1922)*

FIXED OMNIBUS STOPS. TODAY'S LONDON TRAFFIC EXPERIMENT.

From today all omnibuses running between Cricklewood and Victoria, and Hammersmith and Piccadilly will stop only at points indicated by conspicuous notice boards.

The following thoroughfares are affected:

Cricklewood Road, part of the Edgware Road, Kilburn High Road, Maida Vale, Park Lane and Grovesnor Place.

Hammersmith Road, Kensington Road, Kensington High Street, Knightsbridge, Hyde Park Corner and Piccadilly. This is an experiment which has been arranged by the Advisory Committee on London Traffic to regulate the number of stops made by omnibuses.

The stopping posts are of two types, 'Compulsory' and 'By Request', and are fixed roughly 300 yards apart, so that in no event will the public have to walk a distance of more than 150 yards to a point.

The Times, *18 February 1920*

ELIZABETH'S BUS RIDE

Virginia Woolf

And Elizabeth waited in Victoria Street for an omnibus. It was so nice to be out of doors. She thought perhaps she need not go home just yet. It was so nice to be out in the air. So she would get on to an omnibus. And already, even as she stood there, in her very well cut clothes, it was beginning... People were beginning to compare her to poplar trees, early dawn, hyacinths, fawns, running water, and garden lilies; and it made her life a burden to her, for she so much preferred being left alone to do what she liked in the country, but they would compare her to lilies, and she had to go to parties, and London was so dreary compared with being alone in the country with her father and the dogs.

Buses swooped, settled, were off – garish caravans, glistening with red and yellow varnish. But which should she get on to? She had no preferences. Of course, she would not push her way. She inclined to be passive. It was expression she needed, but her eyes were fine, Chinese, oriental, and, as her mother said, with such nice shoulders and holding herself so straight, she was always charming to look at; and lately, in the evening especially, when she was interested, for she never seemed excited, she looked almost beautiful, very stately, very serene. What could she be thinking? Every man fell in love with her, and she was really awfully bored. For it was beginning. Her mother could see that – the compliments were beginning. That she did not care more about it – for instance for her clothes – sometimes worried Clarissa, but perhaps it was as well with all those puppies and guinea pigs about having distemper, and it gave her a charm. And now there was this odd friendship with Miss Kilman. Well, thought Clarissa about three o'clock in the morning, reading Baron Marbot for she could not sleep, it proves she has a heart.

Suddenly Elizabeth stepped forward and most competently boarded the omnibus, in front of everybody. She took a seat on top. The impetuous creature – a pirate – started forward, sprang away; she had to hold the rail to steady herself, for a pirate it was, reckless, unscrupulous, bearing down ruthlessly, circumventing dangerously, boldly snatching a passenger, or ignoring a passenger, squeezing eel-like and arrogant in between, and then rushing insolently all sails spread up Whitehall. And did Elizabeth give one thought to poor Miss Kilman who loved her without jealousy, to whom she had been a fawn in the open, a moon in a glade? She was delighted to be free. The fresh air was so delicious. It had been so stuffy in the Army and Navy Stores. And now it was like riding, to be rushing up Whitehall; and to each movement of the omnibus the beautiful body in the fawn-coloured coat responded freely like a rider, like the figure-head of a ship, for the breeze slightly disarrayed her; the heat gave her cheeks the pallor of white painted wood; and her fine eyes, having no eyes to meet, gazed ahead, blank, bright, with the staring incredible innocence of sculpture.

It was always talking about her own sufferings that made Miss Kilman so difficult. And was she right? If it was being on committees and giving up hours and hours every day (she hardly ever saw him in London) that helped the poor, her father did that, goodness knows, — if that was what Miss Kilman meant about being a Christian; but it was so difficult to say. Oh, she would like to go a little further. Another penny was it to the Strand? Here was another penny then. She would go up the Strand.

She liked people who were ill. And every profession is open to the women of your generation, said Miss Kilman. So she might be a doctor. She might be a farmer. Animals are often ill. She might own a thousand acres and have people under her. She would go and see them in their cottages. This was Somerset House. One might be a very good farmer — and that, strangely enough though Miss Kilman had her share in it, was almost entirely due to Somerset House. It looked so splendid, so serious, that great grey building. And she liked the feeling of people working. She liked those churches, like shapes of grey paper, breasting the stream of the Strand. It was quite different here from Westminster, she thought, getting off at Chancery Lane. It was so serious; it was so busy. In short, she would like to have a profession. She would become a doctor, a farmer, possibly go into Parliament, if she found it necessary, all because of the Strand.

The feet of those people busy about their activities, hands putting stone to stone, minds eternally occupied not with trivial chatterings (comparing women to poplars — which was rather exciting, of course, but very silly), but with thoughts of ships, of business, of law, of administration, and with it all so stately (she was in the Temple), gay (there was the river), pious (there was the Church), made her quite determined, whatever her mother might say, to become either a farmer or a doctor. But she was, of course, rather lazy.

And it was much better to say nothing about it. It seemed so silly. It was the sort of thing that did sometimes happen, when one was alone — buildings without architects' names, crowds of people coming back from the city having more power than single clergymen in Kensington, than any of the books Miss Kilman had lent her, to stimulate what lay slumbrous, clumsy, and shy on the mind's sandy floor to break surface, as a child suddenly stretches its arms; it was just that, perhaps, a sigh, a stretch of the arms, an impulse, a revelation, which has its effects for ever, and then down again it went to the sandy floor. She must go home. She must dress for dinner. But what was the time? – where was a clock?

She looked up Fleet Street. She walked just a little way towards St Paul's, shyly, like some one penetrating on tiptoe, exploring a strange house by night with a candle, on edge lest the owner should suddenly fling wide his bedroom door and ask her business, nor did she dare wander off into queer alleys, tempting by-streets, any more than in a strange house open doors which might be bedroom doors, or sitting-room doors, or lead straight to the larder. For no Dalloways came down the Strand daily; she was a pioneer, a stray, venturing, trusting.

In many ways, her mother felt, she was extremely immature, like a child still, attached to dolls, to old slippers; a perfect baby; and that was charming. But then, of course, there was in the Dalloway family the tradition of public service. Abbesses, principals, head mistresses, dignitaries, in the republic of women – without being brilliant, any of them, they were that. She penetrated a little further in the direction of St. Paul's. She liked the geniality, sisterhood, motherhood, brotherhood of this uproar. It seemed to her good. The noise was tremendous; and suddenly there were trumpets (the unemployed) blaring, rattling about in the uproar; military music; as if people were marching; yet had they been dying – had some woman breathed her last and whoever was watching, opening the window of the room where she had just brought off that act of supreme dignity, looked down on Fleet Street, that uproar, that military music would have come triumphing up to him, consolatory, indifferent.

It was not conscious. There was no recognition in it of one fortune, or fate, and for that very reason even to those dazed with watching for the last shivers of consciousness on the faces of the dying, consoling. Forgetfulness in people might wound, their ingratitude corrode, but this voice, pouring endlessly, year in year out, would take whatever it might be; this vow; this van; this life; this procession, would wrap them all about and carry them on, as in the rough stream of a glacier the ice holds a splinter of bone, a blue petal, some oak trees, and rolls them on.

But it was later than she thought. Her mother would not like her to be wandering off alone like this. She turned back down the Strand.

A puff of wind (in spite of the heat, there was quite a wind) blew a thin black veil over the sun and over the Strand. The faces faded; the omnibuses suddenly lost their glow. For although the clouds were of mountainous white so that one could fancy hacking hard chips off with a hatchet, with broad golden slopes, lawns of celestial pleasure gardens, on their flanks, and had all the appearance of settled habitations assembled for the conference of gods above the world, there was a perpetual movement among them. Signs were interchanged, when, as if to fulfil some scheme arranged already, now a summit dwindled, now a whole block of pyramidal size which had kept its station inalterably advanced into the midst or gravely led the procession to fresh anchorage. Fixed though they seemed at their posts, at rest in perfect unanimity, nothing could be fresher, freer, more sensitive superficially than the snow-white or gold-kindled surface; to change, to go, to dismantle the solemn assemblage was immediately possible; and in spite of the grave fixity, the accumulated robustness and solidity, now they struck light to the earth, now darkness.

Calmly and competently, Elizabeth Dalloway mounted the Westminster omnibus.

from Mrs Dalloway *(1925)*

RULES & REGULATIONS
FOR OPERATING EMPLOYEES

The London General Omnibus Company, Limited

Entering Public Houses

Drivers and Conductors are strictly forbidden to enter a Public House when the bus is in service. They must not enter shops and make purchase.

Taking Meals

Drivers and Conductors shall not take meals or any refreshment when the bus is on a journey, nor at a terminus if their duties are thereby interfered with or the omnibus delayed.

Bell Signals

Drivers and Conductors must observe the following code of bell signals.

One Ring. To stop.
Two Rings. To Start.
Rapid Succession of Rings. Emergency Stop.

In no circumstances are buses to be started on signals such as whistling, stamping of feet or the hitting of the side of the bus.
Private signalling from one employee to another is strictly forbidden.

Luggage

Drivers and Conductors are strictly forbidden to accept any fee or gratuity for carrying luggage or parcels of any description unless a charge is authorised under the Fare Table. No large boxes, baskets, parcels or other articles likely to injurious or to cause inconvenience to other passengers shall be carried on any bus, and any passenger leaving property on the platform is to be informed respectfully that such can be carried only at the passenger's risk.

Unnecessary Noise Early Morning and Last Buses

Drivers and Conductors on the early morning buses or late buses shall conduct their traffic as quietly as possible, so as to avoid inconvenience and annoyance to residents.

SPECIAL RULES AND REGULATIONS FOR DRIVERS

Wearing of Clogs
The wearing of clogs by Drivers is not permitted.

Hands to be Kept on Steering Wheel
Drivers shall not take both hands off the steering wheel or look back into the bus when the bus is in motion.

Descending Hills
Drivers are strictly forbidden to descend hills with their speed in neutral, or with their clutch disengaged.

Excessive Speed
Drivers are strictly warned of the dangers due to excessive speed, and to the legal penalties to which they subject themselves by breaches of the law in this connection.

Passing Churches, &c.
When buses are being driven past Churches, &c., on Sundays, or Hospitals at night, they are to be driven slowly and quietly, so as to minimise any noise.

SPECIAL RULES AND REGULATIONS FOR CONDUCTORS

Counterfeit Coin, &c.
Conductors will be held responsible for any counterfeit, foreign, obsolete or mutilated coins taken by them, and when taking coins to give change, they must mention the name of the coin to the passenger, before putting it into their cash bag, thus minimising the possibility of disputes.

Passengers Travelling Excess
Conductors shall exercise all possible vigilance in order to detect any passengers travelling beyond the distance for which payment has been made.
The name and address of any such passenger who may refuse to pay the excess fare due is to be obtained and reported to Chief Office, with the names and addresses of witnesses.

Improper Language or Conduct by Passengers

Conductors shall be regardless of the comfort of passengers on all occasions, and must not permit any improper language or conduct on the part of any passenger, or allow any passenger to smoke in a bus, or enter a bus with a lighted pipe, cigar or cigarette.

Passengers Under Influence of Drink

Passengers under the influence of drinks shall not be permitted to ride on any bus. Should such persons refuse to leave when requested, Conductors must remove them in the presence of a Police Constable, who will assist the Conductor should resistance be offered. Care must be taken to use no more force than is necessary for the purpose.

Knowledge of Routes, &c.

Conductors shall acquaint themselves with the routes worked by the Company in order to be able to reply to enquiries from passengers, and are to do their utmost to familiarise themselves with the various places of interest on or near the route upon which they are working,

Persons or Animals liable to be Objectionable not to be carried

No person whose clothing is in a condition liable to cause damage to other passengers, or to whom other reasonably objections may be taken, shall be allowed to travel on any bus, and no property or animal likely to be injurious or offensive to the passengers may be carried on the bus. Small dogs or other animals may be carried by passengers travelling outside, provided such animals are small enough to be carried on the laps of their owners, and are not allowed to annoy other passengers.

first published 1927

PICTURING THE LONDON BUS

Richard Dennis

In the 20th century, the red double-decker became a symbol of London, as emblematic of the metropolis as Big Ben or Tower Bridge, so it is unsurprising that buses feature prominently in cityscapes by painters like L S Lowry or, earlier in the century, C R W Nevinson. A typical example is Ludovic-Rodo Pissarro's *Hyde Park Corner*, in which we can count no fewer than 15 double-deck, open-top London General buses passing in front of Apsley House and Decimus Burton's Ionic Screen which spans the entrance to Park Lane. There are more buses than all the other motor vehicles added together in this scene! To many Londoners, even the route numbers displayed on the front of buses could signify the location of a photograph, film or painting. The No 9 has run through Hyde Park Corner since 1908, the No 19 has been running through Piccadilly Circus (where it was depicted by Charles Ginner in 1912) since 1906.

But until the beginning of the 20th century, London buses were not necessarily red, nor did they carry route numbers. Horse buses were painted different colours according to their ownership and the route they followed – the red 'Paddington', the yellow 'Camden Town'; they often carried distinctive names – 'Favorite', 'Atlas', 'Perseverance'; and their destinations were either painted on, or displayed on boards affixed to, their sides, which must have made it very difficult to tell where a bus was headed until it was already passing by! Paintings of buses were less about the city in which they operated and more about the characteristics of the buses themselves, their crews and passengers. Buses were emblematic of modernity: they were the latest fashion, they embodied up-to-date technology, and they could, especially by the late 19th century, be 'democratic' in their use by both sexes and (apart from the poorest) a range of social classes.

Consider the representation of Shillibeer's omnibus when it was introduced in 1829*. This is really a high-class advertisement. It oozes messages about class and elegance: three horses, a very smartly dressed driver, and a not only smart, but attentive, conductor ushering well-dressed passengers onto the vehicle through the rear door. The other passengers, glimpsed through the windows of the bus, are equally well attired in fine bonnets and top hats, and the setting is pastoral, probably outside Regent's Park, which lay on the route from Paddington to the City.

* See lithograph on page 18

This is almost a large private and personal means of transport, definitely for the middle classes.

Surprisingly, given the London bus's subsequent reputation for stolid slowness, moving in convoy through congested city streets, many early paintings emphasised the exhilaration of travelling at speed on open suburban roads. James Pollard's paintings of buses in northeast London were an extension of his interest in painting stagecoaches and racehorses at speed. But now we have a distinction between female passengers, confined to the lower deck, and male passengers who can enjoy the excitement and camaraderie of riding on the upper deck, either engaging in banter up front with the driver or seated on the 'knifeboard', the seat which ran lengthways along the roof. The passengers may be on their way to catch a train (the *Upper Clapton Omnibus* (1852) advertises its connection with the 'Birmingham Railway' at Euston Square), or to work or to go shopping in the West End (and Pollard's *Favorite Omnibus at Islington Green* (1852) also advertises that it serves the Houses of Parliament).

Seventy years after Pollard, as the double-deck (though still open-top) motor bus assumed its dominance of public transport on London's streets, Claude Flight produced his linocut entitled simply *Speed* (1922), depicting a succession of fast-moving buses almost stampeding down the street like a herd of buffalo, the foremost moving so quickly that we can

'The Sunshine Roof' Cyril Power, c. 1934; a 4-block linocut depicting the speed and movement of a Green Line coach travelling between London and Hertford, and driven by the artist's son

only catch the letters 'SPEE' on its advertising board, the buildings lining the streets rippling as if we cannot keep them in focus as we keep our eyes on the buses, and anxious pedestrians hurriedly crossing the road between buses under the supervision of a London bobby. Flight's colleague, Cyril Power, offered the impression of speed from inside the bus. *The Sunshine Roof* (1934) seats us at the back of a single-deck Greenline country bus, behind the other passengers, as we lean into a bend, almost as if we were on a motor bike.

Speed implies the oppression (at least for pedestrians and other road users) as much as the excitement of the all-conquering motor bus. In Charles Ginner's *Piccadilly Circus* (1912), a less speedy, but equally oppressive, pair of motor buses blot out the sky and, in company with one of the first motorised taxis, hem in the pedestrians, who are in turn hurrying past a flower-seller. The more prominent of the two buses is a London General B-type, which Ginner is careful to identify as B1218, based at B5 Garage (Battersea). The class had been introduced in 1910 but Ginner's bus is an even more recently constructed one. The painting makes a perfect accompaniment to E M Forster's almost contemporaneous passage in *Howards End*, where Forster has Margaret Schlegel sensing the 'architecture of hurry':

> '... month by month the roads smelt more strongly of petrol, and were more difficult to cross, and human beings heard each other speak with greater difficulty, breathed less of the air, and saw less of the sky ... she noted for the first time the architecture of hurry, and heard the language of hurry on the mouths of its inhabitants – clipped words, formless sentences, potted expressions of approval or disgust.' (E M Forster, Howards End (1910), chapter XIII)

A lot of Victorian genre art features studies of characters observed boarding, alighting, or sitting on omnibuses, along with the drivers and conductors. Early horse-buses were entered from a door in the rear of the bus, with the conductor perched outside on a rear step from which a ladder gave access to the open upper deck. The inside deck comprised facing benches running the length of the bus, along which artists imagined a range of ages, classes and genders. In *Omnibus Life in London* (1859), William Maw Egley portrayed the scene end-on – looking out from the innermost end of an already overcrowded lower deck as more passengers are attempting to board. To paint his picture, Egley constructed a mock-up out of old boxes and planks in his back garden, and then posed sitters including his own wife to make up a 'typical' set of passengers: 'every class of society, from an old country woman, perhaps a family servant, with her piles of baggage, to the city clerk with his cane'. A generation later, and a similar viewpoint, but understandably less crowded, Alfred Morgan fantasised *An Omnibus Ride to Piccadilly Circus — Mr Gladstone Travelling with Ordinary Passengers* (1885). It is hard to conceive of a senior politician travelling by public bus today on any but carefully stage-managed occasions, and the scene also contrasts sharply with the (possibly apocryphal) observation of a more recent prime minister that 'a man who, beyond the age of 26, finds himself on a bus can count himself as a failure'.

George William Joy (1895) imagined he was sitting on one bench of a bus, facing an orderly, if tightly squeezed, row of passengers on the opposite bench, again painting his own family into the picture: 'In the farthest corner sits a poor anxious mother of children, her foot propped on an untidy bundle; beside her, full of kindly thoughts about her, sits a fashionable young woman; next to her the City man, absorbed in his paper; whilst a little milliner, bandbox in hand, presses past the blue-eyed, wholesome looking nurse in the doorway.' From the view through the windows, the bus seems to be passing Hyde Park or Kensington Gardens and, indeed, the painting is entitled *The Bayswater Omnibus*. The painting also features advertisements for 'black lead', used as polish for indoor metalwork, and Pear's Soap. It is paralleled in literature by George Gissing's *In the Year of Jubilee* (1894) in which Nancy Lord travels from Camberwell to Westminster Bridge by horse-tram, trying to avoid the 'persistent glances' of her tiresome companion

> *By reading the rows of advertisements above his head. Somebody's 'Blue'; somebody's 'soap'; somebody's 'High-class jams'; and behold, inserted between the Soap and the Jam — 'God so loved the world, that He gave His only-begotten Son ...* (George Gissing, In the Year of Jubilee (1894), Part I, Chapter 7)

A less well-known image, featuring exclusively female, working-class passengers, is Maria Brooks' painting, *Down Piccadilly: Returning From Covent Garden Market One June Morning* (1882). This is among the more ambitious of Brooks' paintings — she mostly produced rather sentimental portraits of young women, children and pets. It was exhibited at the Royal Academy, before emigrating along with its maker, first to Canada and then the USA, where it attracted the interest of art critics in Ottawa, Toronto and New York. One critic drew attention to the 'fine colouring of the brilliant blooms on sale in the baskets of the flower girls' contrasted with 'the sombre garments in which the poor women are clad'. In Toronto, it was 'the most popular picture in the Exhibition'. Praise was also offered for the depiction of 'the blind woman and her neighbour on the left with the

Down Piccadilly: Returning From Covent Garden Market One June Morning, Maria Brooks (1882)

flower in her mouth'. The subject was 'as English as the advertisements on the roof of the bus'.

While women might travel on the lower deck, it was much harder – both physically and culturally – for them to climb the rear ladder to ride on the 'knifeboard'. Things began to change in the 1880s with the introduction of spiral staircases and 'garden seats' (seats facing forwards with a central gangway). Drivers were known for their laconic wit (a bit like taxi drivers later on) and could be both the object and the instigator of flirtation. Writing in 1892 in the magazine, *Good Words*, the Rev. A R Buckland observed that 'The old-fashioned bus-driver ... is often a man with whom it is worth talking. He can enliven the monotony of a long drive by anecdotes not always, perhaps, veracious, but passing for truth in his own circle.'

But the most powerful – and enigmatic – image of the 'new woman' must be Sidney Starr's *The City Atlas* (1888–9), an over-the-shoulder rear view of a young woman seated alone on the front seat of an 'Atlas' omnibus as it made its way between Baker Street and St John's Wood. Starr's painting corresponds in date almost exactly with Amy Levy's novel, *The Romance of a Shop* (1888), in which we encounter Gertrude, one of four sisters who run a photographer's shop on Baker Street, 'mounting boldly to the top of an Atlas omnibus' and later 'careering up the street on the summit of a tall, green omnibus, her hair blowing gaily in the breeze'.

The figure of the bus conductor, usually standing on the rear platform, was also a popular one. Thomas Musgrave Joy pictured a good-natured conductor ushering a young woman carrying a dog into an already crowded Charing Cross to Bank omnibus (c.1861). Other images portrayed the conductor as a London 'character', as in Elijah Albert Cox's *Bus Conductor*, used as the artwork for a poster produced by Underground Electric Railways Ltd, which by this time (1920) had absorbed the London General Omnibus Company. There were also depictions of female conductors, hired to keep the transport system operating during both world wars: George Studdy depicted a jaunty *London Bus Conductress* (1916), while Eric Kennington, an official war artist in both wars, made serious and dignified portraits of a bus driver (Albert Coe) and a conductor (Mary Morgan), who had each displayed acts of bravery during air raids in 1940.

Until World War I there were no bus stops, merely customary stopping places where intending passengers would congregate to hail passing buses. But the dissemination of the iconic London bus stop through the 1920s and 1930s offered new opportunities to artists. The bus stop could be depicted as a cipher for social isolation on the streets of the big city, as in Elwin Hawthorne's elegiac painting of *Bow Road* (1931) — no traffic, just a few lone individuals on the street, one of whom is waiting patiently for the bus. At the opposite extreme, bus queues could be metaphors for competitive urban life — a survival of the fittest as passengers fought to board already full buses. William Roberts (1895–1980) produced artwork for a poster popularising the new bus stops in 1925, drawing on his early enthusiasm for Cubism and Vorticism, and emphasising the scarlet redness of the latest motor buses contrasting with the greyness of their passengers; but he returned to the subject after World War II, with paintings including *Bus-stop* (1957) and culminating in the anarchic chaos of *Rush Hour* (1971). Buses not only signify London as a place; they also embody the state of metropolitan society — fashions, gender relations, social etiquette.

'Seeing it through: bus conductress' poster (1944) by Eric Kennington; a portrait of Mrs M J Morgan who as one of the first clippies in 1940 saved two young children by shielding them with her own body during an air raid

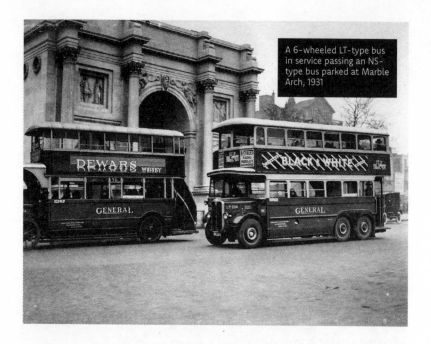

A 6-wheeled LT-type bus in service passing an NS-type bus parked at Marble Arch, 1931

MORE WHEELS ON THE BUS

Arnold Bennett

Took one of the new 6-wheel buses, just to try it, to the Ritz, and walked up to Bond Street to the Queen's Hall to look at programmes.

Journals – 5 November 1928

Arnold Bennett's eye for detail is impressive. The distinctive 6-wheel AEC LT-Type bus is normally described as being introduced in 1929, so he must have travelled on one of the very first to enter service. And these were magnificent buses, and one of the first on which diesel engines were fitted. In the words of one commentator: 'For the first time, perhaps, this was a really good-looking bus. They had style. They had presence. They were the monarchs of the road. They were, as Flanders and Swann put it so memorably, the big six-wheeler, diesel-engined, 97 horse-power omnibus.' (Ian Smith, countrybus.org)

LOST IN THE THAMES

Matt Brown

A peculiar ceremony took place on the Thames in the opening days of 1929. A solitary policeman stood in salute as 60,000 pieces of metal were poured into the river.

That lone sergeant was paying respect to a vanished age. His jettisoned cargo was a huge stockpile of badges, once belonging to London's horse-drawn bus and cab drivers.

Fifteen years earlier, the last horse bus had rattled across Waterloo Bridge. They'd been a familiar part of the capital for almost a century. The internal combustion engine finally and quickly put them out of service.

As part of their duties, drivers and conductors were required to wear a numbered badge, much as police officers still do. That system was shaken up when the horses were retired. More than 60,000 metal badges were collected and put into storage.

The hoard was rediscovered in the late 1920s in the safekeeping of Scotland Yard. The constabulary had no use for the relics. The sacks were taken to scrap merchants but nobody was interested. A few badges were sent to museums, but what to do with the rest? After 'grave deliberation', it was decided to bury the badges at sea.

Or, rather, in the Thames Estuary. And so it was that an unnamed police sergeant accompanied the expired insignia to the Black Deep channel at the mouth of the Thames. As the man saluted, 'unconsciously deputising for millions of horse lovers', the badges sank to the river bed.

originally published on the Londonist website in 2018

A SERVICEABLE ROUTE

C F Gregg

'First of all, sir, particulars of this bus-route. X87. Is it a busy route, for instance?

'X87 eh? No, sir. It is not a busy route. Far from it. It doesn't pay, sir. It doesn't pay. It is what we all an easy route. Every conductor on this route is within a year or two of his pension. Elderly fellows glad of the rest. Few passengers, sir. Ruinous route, I call it.'

'Then why operate it, sir?'

'Why?' the manager shouted his eyes protruding with the intensity of his feelings. 'Why? Because we have to. If we only ran the routes which paid, half the buses would be taken off London streets. But we supply service, sir. And service is not always remunerative. Yet these slack routes have one good aspect. It enables us to give some of our older employees an easier task.'

Higgins had been an interested auditor of this peroration. For the first time in his life he realised that the London Transport Corporation had a soul – that this vast organisation was human enough to give its old servants easier jobs. Then he wondered whether the fact that it was an easy route had any bearings on its use by the murdered man. Did he travel on the top deck to avoid contact with other passengers? He must make a note of that.

from Murder on the Bus *(1930)*

5 FURTHER EXCURSIONS IN THE INTER-WAR YEARS

Promoted by the railways and the Underground, speculative builders, the Ministry of Transport's road building schemes and the London County Council – who in 1920 allocated £5 million pounds for the creation of Beaconstree, a new purpose-built garden-city-style council housing estate beyond Barking – London was to become a much more sprawling entity in the 1920s and 30s. A staggering 700,000 new houses were built around London between the wars. What was sold was the dream of a home in the countryside, or at least in a greener outer suburb, within commuting distance of the city.

THE WAY TO LONDON'S COUNTRY

LGOC country area posters, 1912–1932

David Bownes

By the mid-1920s, red London buses were a familiar sight on the leafy lanes and rural byways of Surrey, Middlesex, Hertfordshire, Essex, Buckinghamshire and Kent. They carried all types of passengers, from day-trippers to commuters, on frequent services starting in the heart of the city or from local Underground stations. But it had not always been so. Just 20 years earlier regular bus services to the countryside would have seemed unimaginable. And, besides, the destinations now served would have been regarded as far outside the remit of the famous London General Omnibus Company (LGOC), only to be reached by adventurous Londoners on a rare Bank Holiday excursion. All this changed due to the entrepreneurialism of the LGOC and technological developments that made longer distance motorbus journeys possible. Poster publicity was to play a vital part in promoting these new routes and redefining the boundaries of 'London's Country'.

For the profit-hungry LGOC, the countryside around London was an especially attractive way of increasing traffic. Unlike railways, bus operators were not constrained by massive infrastructure costs or pre-existing working arrangements that had effectively carved up the south-east between powerful railway interests. Expansion did, however, require the introduction of reliable motorbuses to work the country routes. As London Underground's staff magazine commented in 1926, 'a breakdown in the London streets with garages comparatively near at hand was bad enough, but a breakdown on a rural highway, far removed from garages was a contingency not lightly to contemplate'. The introduction of the dependable B-Type bus from 1910 gave the LGOC the advantage it was looking for.

Almost immediately the company revived earlier, failed, Sunday and Bank Holiday services from the heart of the city to the countryside. The first was from Elephant and Castle to Epping Forest, with new routes opening to Hampton Court, Petersham and Edgware. Initially, shortages of buses prevented daily operation, but as the fleet expanded in 1912 so too did the frequency of services on offer. In the same year, the LGOC became part of the Underground Group, or 'Combine', under the direct control

Poster artwork for 'Take the Motor-Bus for Picknicking', Christopher Richard Winne Nevinson, 1921

of Albert Stanley (later Lord Ashfield) and Frank Pick. The number of routes was greatly expanded, so that by 1913 it was possible to travel direct from Victoria to Cockfosters, Elephant & Castle to Chingford, and Oxford Circus to Sidcup. Previously remote villages, like Lambourne End (Essex) and Stoke Poges (Hertfordshire) could now be reached without the inconvenience of having to change trains or take a complex journey of tram, tube and local bus (presuming such options were available). New services also linked Underground termini with the countryside farther afield, the first being Route 62 between Hounslow Barracks and Windsor Castle.

To be successful, however, the new services had to resonate with potential passengers, and this needed dynamic publicity. Writing in 1925, the artist and teacher Percy Bradshaw reflected that before the Underground took charge of bus publicity the average Londoner was 'apparently unconscious of the beauties of his surroundings. He would go to Hampstead Heath or Epping Forest on a Bank Holiday, but it never occurred to him to go regularly, or to explore the beauty spots within his reach'. Merger with the Underground brought the LGOC into the orbit of Pick's groundbreaking, and already famous, publicity machine. Services were promoted by leaflets and press advertisements, as before, but it was the extensive use of aspirational poster publicity which was to transform the fortunes of the Combine's country bus routes.

From 1913 until 1916, about a fifth of all 'Underground' pictorial posters directly promoted country bus services. Many more carried unspecified messages advertising 'blackberry time' or 'woodland retreats' that were equally applicable to tram, tube and bus routes. At first, Pick entrusted the commissions to his most established artists, like Charles Sharland whose flat colour representations of remote fields, sylvan lakes and charming country towns would have appealed to the day-tripper. Typically, the de-peopled bus posters of the pre-World War I era offered a vision of an unspoilt England, with minimal promotional copy to get in the way of romanticised views of Hatfield, Chigwell, Staines and Epsom. More unusual was a set of posters commissioned from the popular illustrator Tony Sarg, who chose to represent country bus destinations with figures from the towns' historical past. Presumably baffling for many Londoners, these included Edward the Elder for Kingston, Pope Adrian IV for St Albans and a caveman for Chislehurst.

The need to sell country bus routes also offered an opportunity to a new group of poster artists whose work was to transform the hoardings. Chief among them was the American Edward McKnight Kauffer, and his English contemporaries Gregory Brown and Walter Spradbery. All three received their first commissions from the Underground for designs showing destinations reached by bus. Kauffer, in particular, brought a modern aesthetic to publicity, apparent in his representation of the North Downs, Reigate, Watford, Oxhey Woods (all 1915) and Godstone (1916). Similarly, Brown's 1916 series for locations in Hertfordshire, Essex and Surrey introduced Londoners to his vivid, unreal, colourisation of rural scenes, which was to set the standard for post-war British poster art. Collectively, these young artists presented the countryside in a far from conventional manner, adding modernity and style to the already enticing offer of a day away from the hustle and bustle of the city.

Remarkably, the Underground continued to issue posters promoting trips to the country well into World War I. At least 18 were printed in 1916 alone, including the Country Services series designed by Nancy Smith — one of Britain's first professional female poster artists. A year earlier, the 'Brothers Warbis' had somehow got away with designing a poster under the slogan 'Why bother about the Germans invading the country? Invade it yourself by Underground and motor-'bus'! However, growing fuel shortages and the requisition of many London buses for military use gradually bought an end to wartime pleasure trips and associated advertising.

Country bus services were only slowly restored after the war, as the LGOC initially suffered from a shortage of serviceable vehicles. But by 1920 it was more or less business as usual, resulting in a renewed poster campaign. As *The Sphere* noted in May 1922, most of the new posters were issued 'at the opening of the 'bus riding season', suggesting that day-trippers constituted the primary market at that time. However, the Underground was keen to expand the range of routes on offer, and to develop local traffic to and from outlying tube stations. The LGOC was able to do this by working in cooperation with regional operators, such as the East Surrey Traction Company, and by investing in new, improved, vehicles. By the late 1920s, the LGOC operated more than 80 routes in the country areas, promoted by an extensive publicity campaign which included posters, daily press ads, booklets, maps and even films.

At tube stations and bus stops, and inside the vehicles themselves, a dazzling array of poster styles was deployed to ensure that the services were well patronised. As before the war, most posters featured quiet rural scenes, often married with an appropriate poetic verse (but seldom with details about times and fares). 'London's Country', as the posters proclaimed, was now 700 square miles in size, offering a range of refreshing diversions for the jaded city dweller. Unlike a lot of contemporary railway publicity, the posters were not produced in association with local authorities, resulting in a broad range of destinations and views. The most numerous were for days out in Epping Forest, St Albans and Windsor. Yet posters could also be found promoting the virtues of Harewood Downs, Green Street Green, Chaldon and other places off the beaten track.

In total, over 50 of Pick's best artists designed posters for the country bus routes in the years leading to 1932, producing a depth of quality unsurpassed anywhere in Europe at the time. Indeed, where else would you find internationally renowned fine artists like CRW Nevinson (who produced two sets of posters in 1921 and 1924), turning their skills to selling bus trips? The most prolific designers remained the poster specialists Gregory Brown, Walter Spradbery and Edward McKnight Kauffer, but many talented young women were also commissioned to depict the country routes at a time when few were able to break into the male-dominated realm of commercial art. These included Dora Batty, Dorothy Paton, Irene Fawkes, Gladys Barraclough, Vera Willoughby and Dorothy Dix.

Assessing the effectiveness of poster campaigns is notoriously difficult, as many other factors can affect passenger behaviour. It's clear, though, that ridership increased throughout the 1920s on routes that had not previously existed suggesting, at the very least, that the Underground was successful in reaching new audiences. We know, too, that the posters were well received by the press and public alike. Requests for Underground posters rose exponentially during the 20s, to the point where the company advertised surplus copies for sale. Country posters were by far the most popular, with newspapers as diverse as *The Bystander* and the *Yorkshire Evening Post* advising readers to buy the 'vivid imaginative works' of Gregory Brown, Gladys Barraclough and Fred Taylor for home decoration.

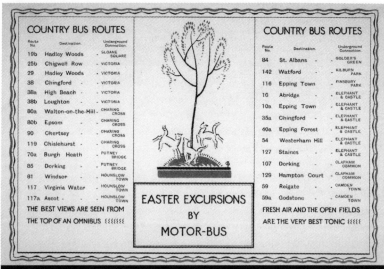

'Easter Excursions by Motor-Bus', poster for the Underground Group, by Gladys Barraclough, 1923

Even the high-end furniture retailer, Heals, used cut-down bus posters by Kauffer as room set dressing for their Tottenham Court Road store.

The posters of Gregory Brown were especially admired by the press. The *Daily Herald* regarded Brown as Britain's leading 'Tubist' (1921), a tongue in cheek reference to his modern style that was adopted by other papers. 'By his coloured confections representing scenes in the London Countryside', the article continued, 'he catches the eye in an atmosphere that makes you long to look upon their loveliness'. In fact, the press was full of praise for Pick's poster campaign, often 'reviewing' the latest offering in gushing detail. Here, for example, is an extract from the *Pall Mall Gazette* (29 March 1922): 'unless you are a hopeless Philistine you must admit that they [the posters] are a thing of beauty. The latest addition, and the work of Fred Taylor RI, is a delicate thing in water colour and charcoal depicting a caravan starting out from a spring-touched background of tender green and is as good as a country holiday'.

As an indication of how well-known the Underground's distinctive, modernist posters had become, the *Manchester Guardian* published a jokey 'Plaint to the poster artist' by M E Durham, 8 June 1927:

> *Oh, I want to see the country*
> *Like when I was a boy*
> *When the sky was blue and the clouds was white*
> *And the green fields was a joy*
> *I want to see the country*
> *But the posters seem to show*
> *The country ain't no more the place*
> *Like what I used to know*
> *For the sky is pink and the fields are mauve*
> *And the cottages all turned yellow*
> *And the sheep all green or tangerine*
> *Enough to stun a fellow*
> *Oh, I want to see the country*
> *And I wouldn't mind where I went ter*
> *So long as I knoo the trees weren't blue*
> *And the cows all turned magenta !*

Pick was so tickled by this that he had a copy typed out by his secretary and preserved in his personal papers, which are now at London Transport Museum.

Another measure of success is the extent to which the publicity campaign assisted the rapid suburbanisation of parts of Middlesex, Hertfordshire and Surrey during the 1920s. In an age before mass car ownership, country buses were essential for providing feeder services for would-be commuters travelling to outlaying stations, especially on the recently extended tube lines. In addition to promoting the bus routes, posters and other forms of publicity subtly supported changing residential patterns by stressing the closeness of an idealised countryside to London. The historian of suburban development, Alan Jackson, argued that day trips by bus 'inculcate[ed] many youngsters with the attractions of living at the edge of the country. Couples cuddling in the back-upstairs seat of the Sunday bus, legs cosy beneath the weatherproof cover, would survey the semi-rural landscape and dream of settling down'. Of course, suburban development bought its own problems as the new housing estates pushed the unspoilt countryside even further afield. But here, too, the poster artist was on hand with depictions of green fields easily reached from the new settlements by 'General' motor bus.

This behavioural shift towards viewing the Home Counties as both a potential leisure destination and residential district for Londoners, was furthered by the creation of Green Line Coaches Limited in July 1930. A subsidiary of the LGOC, Green Line operated express coach services between central London and destinations as far as Baldock to the north, Crawley to the south, High Wycombe to the west and Tilbury to the east. The distinctive single-decker green coaches were extensively promoted by press and poster publicity, including a remarkable set of 4 posters by Anthony Blunt (1932) that could be displayed separately or together to form a single panorama. The resulting services greatly expanded the LGOC's area of operation and led to the acquisition of smaller independent coach companies.

The growth of the LGOC's country bus and coach routes from 1912 was truly remarkable, and laid the foundations for the structure of London Transport in 1933, which retained an enormous country area operation until 1969. The network was created to raise revenue, but it was sold to the public by an imaginative, and innovative, publicity campaign utilising the greatest poster designers of the age. Its success helped to transform the administrative and emotional boundaries of Greater London and, in the words of the Underground's staff magazine (1926) 'restored a countryside to London'.

A DAY IN THE LIFE

H V Morton

Tom says that if he had stayed in the army he would now be a regimental sergeant-major, which, as every one knows, is a good job. But that's over. When the War ended civilian life shone before Tom in unnatural beauty, and he came back to nothing. But he could drive a motor-lorry.

To-day you will find him at the wheel of a London omnibus, his driver's cap worn at an angle which used to be known as 'gor-blimey'.

Outwardly he is still the same Tom, though older. Inwardly he is different. He has a charming wife in Battersea, and two boys with fair hair, faces like Michael Angelo's saints, and the biceps of young boxers.

When things go wrong, when he has had words with the 'missus' – as every loving husband must now and then – when old ladies wave umbrellas at him and stop him as he is trying to make up for lost time, when the traffic cop is unjust, Tom wears his cap on the back of his head and drives with a savage expression, thinking of carefree bachelor days in Gallipoli. If he could have his time over again! No blinking buses for him. No moaning women. No selfish children. But freedom glorious freedom.

But when Tom gets home from the late turn at 1 am and finds something warm waiting for him in the gas stove, and a note from Tom junior to say he has won a swimming cap at school, well, it seems worth while; and he knows that he would drive a bus through hell if necessary. In other words Tom has been domesticated.

Tom is one of the ten thousand drivers in the LPTB fleet. This fleet carries two thousand million passengers a year, or half the total passenger traffic of the London district. In this London differs from Paris, Berlin, or New York.

The bulk of the passenger traffic in Paris and New York goes underground; in Berlin, trams carry more than either omnibuses or underground. London, therefore, has the largest bus-travelling public in the world. Tom and his nine thousand and nine hundred and ninety-nine companions are admired by the public whom they serve. The provincial visitor wonders how on earth they manage to steer their big red craft so neatly through the traffic. The motorist admires them, sympathising with them as he tries to contemplate a day of stopping, starting and gear-changing.

I think you will agree that the bus-drivers of London richly deserve our admiration. They are among the most notable characters in modern London. They have inherited nothing from their predecessors, the horse omnibus-drivers, who sat aloft, a flower in their buttonholes, pointing out the sights of London with a whipstock and enlivening the day with brilliant repartee. There is nothing like that in Tom's life. He and his colleagues are sworn to silence. They are not permitted to speak to the public.

For half a century the horse bus had everything its own way. The London bus-driver became a famous character. Then, in September 1904, his doom was struck when a few motor-omnibuses were licensed. In five years the motor-buses drove twenty-five thousand horses and two thousand and two hundred horse-drawn omnibuses from the streets.

The job of the motor-bus driving is therefore a creation of only the last twenty-nine years, but in that time it has developed a type: a keen, quick, reliable type, resourceful, polite, and always on the look out for the other fellow's mistakes. It would seem that the London bus-driver developed a sense of the fourth dimension. Watch him as he steers his bus through a wheel-to-wheel traffic block in the Strand.

'I get £4 6s. 6d. a week,' says Tom. 'It's a six-day week and an eight-hour day. There is also an accident bonus. I had a cracked window last week. It wasn't my fault. You see it was like this.

'I'm this box of matches. This pipe is a motor-van loaded with planks of wood. Now I'm coming down the Tottenham Court Road. I'm not going fast, because I am a minute and a half ahead of time. Now the van's in front of me. As it comes to New Oxford Street he pulls over to the left. I sound my horn. He must be deaf! I pull over to the kerb and – bang! He hits me. But what could I do? I get down and see there's nothing but a cracked window... I give him a piece of my mind...

'On the whole, bus-driving's not bad, if you're cut out for it. If not, you don't last long! It's trying work, because there's only one thought in your mind – to run to time. All kinds of things hold you up, but you've got to run to time. The worst trial in the life of a London bus-driver is the person, generally an old lady, who stops the bus between points. If the public knew what this meant to us fellows I'm sure they wouldn't do it. They'd walk the few yards to the bus stop. Sometimes on a suburban route in the early morning, it's chronic. Gates opening and fellows rushing out waving sticks and umbrellas. It's stop, stop, stop, all the time!

'No, we don't stick to the same bus. We may get two or three different ones in a day. The new big buses are lovely to drive. You can swing 'em round and about as easy as anything. And the drivers' seats are comfortable.'

The driver and the conductor of an omnibus, although they seldom talk to each other on duty, work in close partnership. The conductor, who gets slightly less money than the driver, is actually in charge of the omnibus, and could, in certain eventualities, give orders which the driver would be forced to obey.

This is as it was in the days of the old mail-coaches. The driver was always under the orders of the guard, who could place him under arrest for drunkenness or order him to go faster – a cause of frequent quarrels and brawls on the King's Highway! A token of the mail-coach guard's superior position, and of the trust placed in him, was a Government clock in a brass case, which he wore in a pouch slung over his shoulder.

'But me and my mate are good pals,' says Tom. 'You've got no idea what a difference is makes when driver and conductor work together. He has always got his eye on the time. He knows if I am a minute late at any place, and he helps me by getting his fares quick, stopping quick and getting off again quick. A new conductor, or one that is learning a new route, will always make you late on a journey. But me and Jack work our buses smooth...

Mind you, I'm not saying he hasn't got his funny ways, but I understand him and he understands me. Well, I must be off. I'm on the late turn this week. So long...'

And Tom goes out to take his red monster through London from 4 pm until 1 am.

In the cold, small hours, when you and I are in bed, he will go home to the little basement flat in the Battersea side-road, and tiptoeing into the kitchen, discover what 'mum' has left for him in the gas stove.

From the walls of his little home, groups of soldiers riding donkeys near the Pyramids or walking together under large eastern gateways gaze down upon their old comrade as he lifts the lid from a plate of Irish stew.

from Our Fellow Men *(1936)*

THE HAND OF MOSCOW

The 1937 Central London Omnibus Strike

Communist Party of Great Britain

A lot of rubbish has been talked about the busmen striking because they wanted to spoil the Coronation, or because Moscow agents were at work among them. A glance at the conditions under which men work shows that it is the London Transport Board, with Lord Ashfield at its head, that creates discontent.

In 1932 the old London General Omnibus Co. succeeded in getting the Transport and General Workers' Union to agree to speeding-up. Since the Board took over the LCC and municipal trams, LGOC and other buses, a managerial policy of continuous speed-up has been operating. The old B-type bus carried 34 passengers and travelled at 12 miles per hour. Now we have 60-seater speeded up to 30 mph in spite of Belisha beacons, pedestrian crossings, traffic lights, and an increased stream of private car traffic. All this means a great strain on driver and conductor who are harassed by squads of inspectors to see that they are running to time.

The strain on men's health is greatly increased by irregular hours of work. On early turn week a man will get up at 4 or 5 am often having to walk to the garage. New week he will be on late turn, going to bed not much before the time he previously got up. On 'middle' shift, again a completely different set of hours. On 'spreadover', he may be up to 10 or 12 hours between starting work and finishing the day. Then remember busmen have no week-ends, work on all public holidays, and two years out of three get their annual holidays in the winter months, and you will see 'the hand of Moscow' is not necessary for discontent to be rife.

Speed, strain and irregular hours are actually shortening the lives of busmen. Remember that before the Board take on a man, he has to pass a stiff doctor's examination, and pass it as A1. Then look at these figures:—

During the five years ending 1935, the number of busmen who left the service was 3,785. Of these only 343 had reached the retiring age of 65 years, 877 had died, 1,006 were discharged through ill-health, average age being 46. Of the remainder, most left of their own decision, very often because they knew their health was going.

This means that for every two busmen who remain at work and reach 65, there are five who die on the job and six are sacked through ill-health!

There are some of the reasons why the men demanded that their working day be reduced to 7 hours, and democratically instructed their Trade Union representatives to approach the Board for a new agreement involving a reduction of 1 hour per day.

extract from The London Bus Strike, what next?: our reply to Mr Bevin *(1937)*

FELLOW TRAVELLERS

Tracing the parallel journeys of the
Green Line and the green belt

John Grindrod

Red buses are the lifeblood of London, red cells clustered in the heart of towns and dispersed around the arteries of the suburban landscape. The most exotic red bus destinations seemed to me the historic pubs with their extraordinary names. The Plough. The Pawleyne Arms. The Swan and Sugar Loaf. Places where the urban world was refracted through a haze of hops, fancy engraved glazing and the lozenge-shaped hollows of beer mugs.

But, growing up on the outskirts of Croydon in the 1970s and 80s, these red giants were not the only buses I saw. There would be occasional glimpses of elusive interlopers too. A flash of green, sneaking off down less obvious routes. The Green Line. A Pied Piper jauntily coaxing us out of our routines to different places, further out of time than even those aged London pubs. The Green Line showed destinations far from the urban mass, spun out from the centre. Hampton Court. Heathrow. Windsor. Gravesend. Buses roaming long and slow through the country and town, like pilgrims on a weary trek, holding out for the promise of distant stations.

These Green Line services had been created to take advantage of the interwar A-roads which led out into London's countryside. These new transport systems — Metroland stations on the sprawling Underground network and trunk roads leading out of the city — led to a boom in house building. Developers seized the opportunity, and soon these road and rail lines were surrounded by 'ribbon development' — that familiar sprawl of interwar tudorbethan semis. It was in reaction to this mock tudor expansion that the green belt was formed, to stop the growth of the city's land-hungry suburbs.

The Green Line coach service was founded in 1930, at a time when belief in grand government planning and coordinated centralised activity was in ascendance. 1933 would see a rationalization of London's transport system, with the Underground network and buses coming under the control of the London Passenger Transport Board. The Act was pushed through parliament by the Labour politician Herbert Morrison. A conscientious objector during World War I, he had been sent away from Stockwell to

Letchworth Garden City during the struggle, where he worked on the land. It was here he embraced the principles of the garden city movement, whose settlements were designed to combine the best of the town with the best of the country. You can see in Morrison's work on the 1933 London Passenger Transport Act and the 1938 Green Belt Act the enduring influence of these ideas. Like a generation of visionary politicians, planners and campaigners he sought to preserve the distinctive character of country and town, and to limit the creeping tendrils of suburbia. And he would work to link those two zones through an effective transport network, enabling people to benefit from both.

Another key figure in both Green Line and green belt was fellow Garden City enthusiast Frank Pick, that great moderniser and head of the London Regional Passenger Board. Shy, exacting and moralistic, he was a tricky boss but a brilliant problem-solver. Pick's ideas on urban design would influence the shape of London itself. The monumental, dislocated city could be made to feel more cohesive through the practical sleekness of his combined transport network. Where new tube and bus stations were built he hoped to encourage an explosion of similarly utopian house design. He was to be defeated by the tudorbethan semi's triumph on the outskirts of the city. Pick was also a green belt enthusiast, and so the Green Line bus network appealed to his elegant sense of connecting the countryside to the city. His position as both green belt defender and enabler of out-of-town development is familiar to anyone following the rhetoric of modern politicians, people happy to occupy simultaneously varied attitudes on the same subject, and who ask only that we do not interrogate their stance too closely. There is something of the Empire in Pick's vision for London Transport, and the Green Line was its colonizing force, bringing urban sophistication to rural backwaters, modern consumerism to the outskirts of the southeast.

Regardless of the dubious motives of their creators, Green Line buses would become the sentinels of London's green belt. They would link central locations such as Oxford Circus, Charing Cross or Golders Green with those far green belt destinations of Watford, Maidenhead, Welwyn Garden City and Guildford. After World War II satellite towns were planned and built beyond the green belt, and Green Line buses would help connect them to the centre too, from Harlow, Crawley or Stevenage. Without the notion of protected countryside, and the aspirations of that interwar period that valued rambling, health and efficiency and the Country Code, the attraction of Green Line buses for the urban population and the planners who created it would have been vastly reduced.

They both represent a steadfastly metropolitan view of the countryside. It is not a place to be seen on its own terms. The green belt exists only because its proximity to the city, and in the early days all Green Line routes connected through the centre of London. For city dwellers they were envisaged to be about escape: for country folk it was giving them access to the riches of city life; for Londoners it was a chance to gulp lungfuls of unpolluted air on Box Hill or the Thames Estuary. Frank Pick imagined that 44 per cent of Green Line custom was for shopping, 40 per cent for business, and 16 per cent to reach the attractions of the West End. The reality – that passengers were using the buses for short intra-country journeys rather than epic treks into town – was conveniently ignored.

As the Green Line and green belt reached the 1960s, changes began to affect both grand plans, just as the realities of postwar life and modernisation were altering the aspirations of London's population. Controls on development created a scramble for arcadia, rich city executives rushing to gain a foothold in the countryside before all opportunities for village infill and picturesque farmhouse conversions were exhausted. For the Green Line, the rise of a new class of rich car-owning commuters in the green belt meant that a primary purpose of the network was undermined. Car ownership created a hell for the Green Line, whose slow, country-bound buses became frequently snarled up in city centre jams, their timetables left in tatters, and the passengers who had once relied on them increasingly turning to more reliable trains or more expensive private cars. Meanwhile in town centres terrified town planners sought to channel pedestrians onto walkways, subways and decks away from the fumes and danger of traffic.

Their stories begin to diverge in the 1970s and 80s, when it became slowly apparent that the Green Line and green belt lay on different sides of a divide. Firstly there was a rebellion against big planning by local campaigners (be it for motorways, out-of-town shopping centres or town centre redevelopment). The green belt felt enshrined in a backward-looking national consciousness, despite being part of the same progressive town planning revolution as the high-rise towers and shopping precincts. Next came the selling off of public assets, such as the Green Line bus service, in the 80s. London's population hit a postwar low in 1983, with 2 million fewer people than in 1939. Meanwhile the countryside population had boomed, with stockbroker belt villages and towns housing many of the richest people in the region, masking the rural poverty of many who relied on the land, local economies and public services like the Green Line. For the rich this rural property boom was seen as one of the great dividends of planning. The green belt meant that a drawbridge could be pulled up behind the fortunate. Public transport had no place in this world of golf clubs and gated communities. The green belt was for the rich, the Green Line for the poor.

Today the affluent are returning to the city centre, in glossy towers built on the footprint of demolished council estates. London's population has once more reached those giddy 1939 highs. And buses, utilising the best in new technology, are part of a sustainable solution for our transport needs. Which is rather too late for the privatised Green Line network, now reduced from 44 routes in 1936 to five in 2018. No more the glimpsed sprites ducking round corners, making Tolkienesque epic journeys from the Great Wen to the shires, to the tamed countryside of Metroland, Frank Pick and Enid Blyton, of rambling, kissing gates and Shell Guides. The Green Line has been undone as thoroughly as our other Welfare State era advances.

But the ghosts persist. In 2017 musician Gilroy Mere produced an album called *The Green Line*, cataloguing a journey from his childhood, from town to the end of the line. It's a fantastical, whimsical and slightly absurd project, beautifully and warmly realised. It's in such works that a meaningful Green Line still exists, in the collective memory of generations old enough to recall its dismantling. In it Gilroy Mere has captured something of the elusive Pied Piper feeling I always had whenever I glimpsed one of those buses. The fading memory of a municipal fairyland, whose time on the begonia-planted floral clock is up. If you listen carefully you can still hear those engines turning over, those rivets rattling the prefabricated panels along those country roads, the swear words of daytrippers whose cars are caught in their wake. Like many of the things we have jettisoned in our rush for privatisation and profits, the need for the Green Line has not gone away, and perhaps as the pressure now mounts on the green belt instead, its time is coming once more.

A CARRIAGE FIT FOR
A FUTURE QUEEN

Marion Crawford

Presently I began to take the children out... One day we passed Hyde Park Corner people were streaming out of the Underground station and Lilibet said wistfully, 'Oh dear, what fun it must be to ride in those trains.' I thought, why not? It seemed such a simple request. I asked the Duke about it in the evening... Anyone would have thought we were going on an expedition to the stately pleasure domes of Kubla Khan rather than a ride in an Underground train. The little girls bought the tickets with their own purses. This was part of the fun...

The next grand occasion was to be a ride on a bus. On top of a bus. Lilibet insisted. It seemed to her such a wonderful idea that when you were on top of a bus you would be able to see right into other people's gardens. Sad to tell, these pleasant jaunts came to a sudden end. The Irish Republican Army started about this time to put bombs in letter-boxes, and to commit other public nuisances to draw attention to their demand for Home Rule for Ireland. It was not quite certain in what even less desirable directions their efforts might not lead them if it were known that the two Princesses were often afoot in London, unprotected.

from The Little Princesses *(1950)*

6 BUSES IN THE BLITZ

The recent centenary commemorations of World War I have perhaps overshadowed remembrance of the even greater challenges that public transport faced during World War II; when bombing and rocket attacks, mass evacuation, blackout restrictions and labour, fuel and materials shortages all presented formidable obstacles to the provision of a regular and adequate bus service. London Transport had only been in existence for six years when the outbreak of war in September 1939 presented them with the greatest logistical challenge that this city's transport infrastructure has ever faced, and led to the single most fundamental change in bus services ever undertaken. At the same time the men and women who crewed the wartime buses — and also their passengers — faced unprecedented dangers on the bomb-damaged and darkened streets of London.

East End children smile from the windows of a London Transport bus at the start of World War II – the bus will take them to a mainline railway station, from where they will be evacuated to the country

LONDON BUSES
IN WARTIME

Oliver Green

The situation in London at the start of World War II in September 1939 was as different as it could possibly be from August 1914. Twenty-five years earlier, when war with Germany was first declared, Britain was confident of an early military victory. There had been no civilian preparation for conflict or any defence measures taken in London or other parts of the country. When London buses were taken off the streets to provide motor transport for troops on the Western Front, this was considered a temporary inconvenience that would help win the war before Christmas.

There was no such simplistic optimism in the 1930s, amid widespread fears that the next conflict would be a 'bomber war' with devastating consequences for the civilian population. If war did break out again, it was clear that public transport services, including the buses, would play a vital role in keeping the capital moving and functioning.

London Transport, a new public corporation created in 1933, was now responsible for integrating and developing the capital's bus, tram and Underground railway services. An ambitious New Works Programme was soon under way to extend and improve the Underground, replace London's huge tram network with more flexible electric trolleybuses and create a larger fleet of buses and coaches with diesel rather than petrol engines. As early as 1937, when the international situation began to deteriorate in continental Europe, London Transport followed government instructions to start developing an Air Raid Precautions (ARP) strategy.

By September 1938, when the Munich Crisis arose, detailed defence plans had been prepared which would allow London's road and rail systems to remain operational under aerial attack, with the safety of passengers and staff secured as far as possible. A year later, on Friday 1 September, ARP arrangements came into effect two days before the official declaration of war.

The first major task for London Transport was to assist in the mass evacuation of London's children, hospital patients and expectant mothers to the safety of the country. This ambitious scheme was personally coordinated by Frank Pick, the LPTB's chief executive. Within a couple of days, London Transport had successfully evacuated nearly 600,000

People in gas masks wait at a bus stop in Esher during a mock poison gas attack, 1941

A bus is up-ended in one of the first raids of the London Blitz, Harrington Square, Mornington Crescent, 9 September 1940. The passengers and crew had taken refuge in a public shelter but 11 residents were killed

A Manchester Leyland Titan, one of 475 provincial buses lent to London Transport during World War II, has its blinds changed ready to start work in the capital in 1940

vulnerable Londoners. Many were transferred on to main line trains, but in other cases buses and coaches were used for the whole journey and many drivers had no sleep for 36 hours. All Green Line coach services were withdrawn at the start of the war and some 400 were converted into ambulances in just 48 hours to evacuate London's hospital patients. It was a remarkable operation.

Blackout regulations were imposed from 1 September 1939, giving London a ghostly, eerie look after dark. Buses, like all other road vehicles, had to be fitted with headlamp cowls, which reduced the beam to narrow slits. With street lighting also restricted, bus driving at night became quite hazardous – but it was equally dangerous for passengers finding their way to a stop in the pitch black, or crossing the road to get home after getting off the bus. Foggy conditions, still common in the winter months, made it worse. Bus conductors found it hard to distinguish between copper and silver coins when accepting a fare in a darkened bus and inevitably there were soon reports of attempted fiddles by passengers.

London Transport's petrol and oil supplies were cut by 25 per cent as a wartime economy measure. Bus services were heavily restricted or withdrawn altogether to save fuel and limit blackout working, but fortunately there was a considerable reduction in passenger demand because of the effect of war on business, and the evacuation of many offices from London. Travelling was pretty tiresome for everyone in the first year of the war, but there had not yet been any of the feared air attacks. The worst was yet to come and the impact was hard to predict.

London Transport staff had been receiving regular ARP training in rescue, firefighting and first aid, but in May 1940 the Board also formed its own Home Guard unit, which eventually had nearly 30,000 members. As growing numbers of male staff were called up for service in the Forces, female staff were recruited to replace them, on a much wider scale than in World War I. By 1942 women accounted for 83 per cent of bus conductors and 57 per cent of garage engineering general hands. Women enthusiastically took on virtually every job previously reserved for men, including labouring and heavy engineering work. The main exception was driving, whether on buses, trams or tubes, which remained a strictly male preserve. Bizarrely, women were not allowed behind the wheel of London buses until 1974, though in wartime they were permitted to shunt buses in depots and deliver empty vehicles between garages.

The long expected air raids finally began in the summer of 1940. The first bombs to damage London Transport equipment fell on New Malden on 16 August and immediately demonstrated the vulnerability of the trolleybus system to aerial attack by bringing down a section of the overhead wires. Heavy bombing started on 7 September with a daylight raid on the Docks and East End. London was then bombed every night until 2 November, after which the Blitz continued intermittently until May 1941.

Incidents involving London buses recorded by press photographers and newsreel cameramen gave an instant sense of place whilst avoiding wartime censorship. The high explosives which fell on Harrington Square, Mornington Crescent in one of the first night raids on 9 September 1940 blew a double-decker into a vertical position against a row of terraced houses. The bus had been left empty on the street when it was hit but 11 people were killed in their homes, which later had to be demolished. No location was given for the picture when it appeared as front page news in Britain and America, but the bus gave it drama and a London setting which highlighted the start of the Blitz.

On the night of 14 October a bomb pierced the road surface in Balham High Street and flooded the tunnels of the tube station below with water and sewage. 64 shelterers and four station staff died below ground where they thought they were safe, making this one of the worst Blitz incidents. On the surface, a bus returning to its garage with no passengers had fallen headlong into the huge crater, but fortunately both the driver and conductor were thrown clear and unhurt. No pictures of the flooded tube platforms were released but images of the red London bus with its rear end poking out of a huge bomb crater soon appeared in colour in the American magazine *Life*. It took two months to remove the bus, repair the road, reinstate the tram tracks and reopen the Northern tube line below.

In 57 raids the Luftwaffe dropped some 13,500 tons of high explosive and incendiary bombs on London, killing more than 15,000 civilians. For every person killed, another 35 were made homeless.

The damage and disruption to London's transport system was severe but it was never fatally compromised. A service of some kind could nearly always be maintained, though this was more difficult with the trams and the Underground when trackwork and tunnels were hit. Buses could always be diverted, and this was sometimes even possible with trolleybuses where temporary wiring could be erected in back streets. Frequent wartime diversions were responsible for the introduction of the first portable bus stops, with circular flags on short poles, soon referred to by staff as 'dolly stops'. When substitute services were required to replace badly hit railway, tram or trolleybus services this could only be achieved with buses.

Vehicles damaged in air raids often ran with windows missing or boarded up, and from September 1940 London Transport improvised by gluing fishnet on the side windows to protect them from splintering. This was an effective solution, but the drawback was that passengers could no longer see out of the windows. They would peel back the netting at the corners, prompting the appearance of admonitory notices, featuring cartoonist David Langdon's annoying little character Billy Brown of London Town, commenting 'I trust you'll pardon my correction, that stuff is there for your protection'. Later on in the war small diamond shaped holes were cut in the fishnet, making it slightly easier to see out, but Billy Brown's rhyming couplets of advice were often met with scrawled retorts by irritated passengers. A panel poster on bus stops offering advice on how to hail a bus in the blackout featured Billy intoning 'Face the driver, Raise your hand, You'll find that he will understand'. One reported response was 'He'll understand all right, the cuss, but will he stop the blinkin' bus?'

By October 1940 so many buses were out of action through air raid damage that London Transport had to appeal to regional bus operators for assistance. The response was very good and by the end of the year 469 provincial buses belonging to 51 different operators had arrived in London on loan. They added a range of liveries to the drab wartime capital alongside the familiar London Transport red: green from Exeter, blue and grey from Leeds and a striking blue-and-white from Hull. The last of the provincials went home in June 1941, and when subsequent German bombing was directed against new regional targets, London Transport was able to offer 334 of its own buses to help other UK cities.

In an attempt to conserve fuel, 160 buses were converted to run on producer gas generated by burning anthracite in trailer units towed behind each vehicle. It was an ingenious, Heath Robinson-like arrangement which was successful in saving more than three million gallons of diesel oil and petrol, but the scheme also had serious disadvantages. Transport writer John Price, who rode on these buses regularly as a schoolboy during the war, remembered them well some years later:

> The most unforgettable feature was the smell. The trailer, with its firebox, anthracite hopper, water tank and cooler, produced the gas from activated anthracite and water, and the smell was that which you get from throwing water or wet slack on to a hot boiler fire.

> Secondly, there was the performance: a gas bus was quieter than a normal one, but decidedly sluggish in getting away, and seemed positively unable to re-start on a hill; the only way with a hill was to rush them.

To everyone's relief, improvements in the availability of fuel supplies, coupled with operational difficulties in operating producer gas systems, led to its abandonment in the autumn of 1944.

In 1939, just before the outbreak of war, London Transport had developed, in partnership with manufacturer AEC, its most sophisticated double deck bus design, the RT type. Only 150 of these were built in the early months of the war before commercial vehicle production was suspended and nearly all bus building and maintenance facilities were turned over to war work. It became increasingly difficult to keep older vehicles in service without regular overhaul and most of the buses damaged by enemy action in the Blitz could not easily be either repaired or replaced.

Although the proportion of London buses and coaches destroyed in the bombing was quite small, at 166 out of a total of about 6,400, there were over 4000 cases recorded as 'more than superficial damage'. This meant that, in effect, the majority of buses suffered at least some bomb damage, quite often windows broken by blast or flying debris. Even when unscathed, the effect of simply being left to run without body overhaul, or even a repaint, often caused what was to prove quite serious deterioration in the wooden body framing.

From 1942, the Government allowed the manufacture of new buses to a rigid 'austerity' specification. London Transport received 435 Guy Arab double-deckers built in Wolverhampton in 1942–6. Many of these arrived in a grim brown-and-yellow colour scheme and the earlier ones had no upper-deck rear windows. The first batch had sprung leather seats but most later austerity vehicles entered service with wooden slatted seating. This decidedly basic public transport was a long way from the comfortable AEC buses manufactured in Southall and Park Royal that Londoners were used to.

London Transport not only transported and sheltered both civilians and military personnel; it also made an important contribution to the war effort through its workshops. After experience gained in servicing Spitfires and Hurricanes in the summer of 1940, London Transport joined forces with four motor companies to set up the London Aircraft Production Group to manufacture Handley Page Halifax heavy bombers for the Ministry of Aircraft Production.

Four thousand staff were involved in this work, which was carried out at Chiswick, Aldenham and Leavesden. Over a four year period more than 700 bombers were completed by a workforce of whom 80 per cent had no previous engineering experience. More than half of them were women. Valuable lessons were learned in the use of precision engineering, interchangeable parts and lightweight materials such as aluminium, all of which contributed to the next new bus design for London, the Routemaster, in the 1950s.

The contribution of London Transport's various 'backroom' road, rail and building departments to military engineering reached a peak in the months leading up to the Allied invasion of Europe in June 1944. As D-Day approached, London Transport buses conveyed six infantry divisions to their ships and assault craft at the Channel ports. Over the next few weeks many of them were required again to transfer returning army casualties from trains to hospitals.

By this time London was under attack from a sinister new weapon, the V1 flying bomb. The heaviest V1 assaults were between June and August 1944, but from September the Germans began launching their more powerful V2 rocket bombs as well, and continued to hit London until the end of March 1945. Damage was much less serious than during the Blitz of 1940–41, but the final months of bombing prompted a new wave of evacuation from London. It also contributed to a new reduction in London Transport's passenger carrying levels, which had increased in 1942–3 with greater mobilisation for war work and the arrival of US Forces in Britain.

By 1945 fares had gone up by 10 per cent but costs had soared by 45 per cent. When VE (Victory in Europe) Day dawned on 8 May, London Transport could proudly claim to have successfully 'carried on' throughout the worst periods of the six-year war, but it was clear that serious new challenges lay ahead.

ARMISTICE OBSERVED

James Agate

Although there was no ceremony in Whitehall today all the buses stopped at eleven o'clock, and people stood still in the streets.

Journal entry – 11 November 1939

WAR-TORN LONDON RE-LIT

F T Lockwood

Bus lighting restored. How strange it seems to see the buses well lit, upstairs and down, headlights on as required. The streets will look like fairyland when the lamps go on again at full power.

Diaries – 27 April 1945

7 POST-WAR PASSENGERS AND THE WINDRUSH GENERATION

After six years of war and the hell of the Blitz, London was a shattered wreck, and prefabs were hastily erected in their thousands to accommodate those left homeless by the bombing. If austerity reigned supreme, with rationing not ending until 1954, it was also a period of optimism. The Labour government, having been voted in on a landslide, set about nationalising industries, creating the Welfare State and the NHS and embarked on ambitious rebuilding schemes. Its swansong would be the Festival of Britain, staged on the South Bank in 1951. A tonic to the nation after five years of privation, it was a showcase for modern design featuring the space age-y Skylon, the Dome of Discovery, the Royal Festival Hall and, outside the festival site, the Lansbury Estate in Poplar. But as austerity gave way to the New Elizabethan age of Never-Had-It-So-Good affluence, London Transport, in particular, was faced with severe labour shortages.

The arrival on the HMS *Windrush* carrying with it 492 passengers from the Caribbean is widely seen as a pivotal moment in the country becoming a more multicultural society. But London Transport played its own part in this story when in 1956 it began to recruit staff directly from Barbados.

LT Recruitment Officer Charlie Gomm interviews the first batch of Caribbean applicants for jobs with London Transport, Barbados 1956

AN OVERSEAS VISITOR
BOARDS A BUS

Ranjee Shahani

I mounted a bus. I went on the top deck, which in those days was open to all the winds of heaven. It was bitterly cold, and the seat were both cold and hard, but I bore these discomforts like a good Buddhist (a feeling which, perhaps, is not widely different from 'being British'). I wanted an unimpeded view of London, of which as yet I had only the remote knowledge received from books read thousands of miles away.

When I looked at the houses extending before and behind me in unending rows I asked myself: 'Is it possible that the English all live in tenements, jostled together in apartments? Where are the bungalows, the detached residences, the spaciousness, the signs of dignity and leisure, for was not the impression given to Indians just that which had been reflected by those who stood for Government.'

In Calcutta, in Delhi and Bombay, I have seen in the centre of the city beautiful houses standing in large grounds. From Grosvenor square to Fleet street there was no such graceful sight to be seen. Only mass on mass of bricks and mortar... The torrent of traffic sweeping by my bus, at most times in two directions, terrified me. It looked as though I had landed in a world of iron and steel.

from The Amazing English *(1948)*

THE BUS THAT DIDN'T STOP

Travis Elborough

On 30 December 1952, a No 78 double-decker bus had to make a daring leap over a 3-foot gap, after a watchman failed to ring the bell to announce that Tower Bridge was opening.

The driver Albert Gunston told *The Times* newspaper: 'I had to keep going, otherwise we should have been in the water. I suddenly saw the road in front of me appeared to be sinking.'

You can still catch a No 78 bus over Tower Bridge, but automated traffic lights and gates make it impossible for accidents like that to happen today.

from Tower Bridge, the Official Guidebook

MATT MONRO

The singing bus driver

Michelle Monro

His next job stayed with him for the rest of his life. He was compelled to forsake the microphone for a steering wheel. He had met up with Gordon Holland an old schoolmate of his in Hornsey Café. At his suggestion, Terry went over to the London Transport Depot at Manor House and signed up as a driver for Holloway Garage. Being only five foot six inches tall he had quite a unique way of passing his test at Chiswick. The driving test was taken in a single-decker bus with a crash gearbox. He found that once seated he couldn't reach the clutch pedal. Each time he had to change gear he had to stand, rather like a jockey urging on his mount. It was only after they had passed him that he was told he could screw the seat down to accommodate his smaller frame.

Because of the driving test incident Terry gained the nickname of Titch. London Transport hired the aspiring singer and put him on a weekly wage of £9.00. Allocated his bus badge, N46052, he took out the No 27 Highgate – Teddington route and at times, to cover other colleague's holidays, he also worked the No 14 route from Putney Bridge to Hornsey Rise. Both Terry and his regular conductor Nellie Mitchell had to be up at 4.00 am to take the bus out at 5.00 am. Driving the bus during the day he sought to establish himself as a band singer in the evenings. He sang at a pub called The Favourite in Hornsey Rise and also filled in with a Saturday night gig with Harry Pitch's band at the Hornsey Town Hall. They would then pass the hat around for him and there might be a couple of quid in it at the end. The trio finally asked him to do it properly for a fee of 32s 6d a night.

> My brother Chris and I used to frequent the Favourite pub
> in Hornsey Rise, which was the terminus for the No 14
> bus. They only had piano and drums but we both used to
> get up and give a song. We thought we were good. We
> realised Terry was well known in the pub because whenever
> he entered, whoever was next to be called to give a song
> had to wait until Terry had sung. On the first occasion we
> grumbled about the unfairness of this, but it was explained
> that Terry only had a limited amount of time because

he had to get back in his bus. When we heard him sing,
all our objections evaporated. He was so good that we
used to make a point of going to the pub just to listen to
him. He was a very nice, modest man, a great artiste – no
gimmicks, no show, just a wonderful voice and personality.
– George Skelly

His given name Terry Parsons and pseudonyms Terry Fitzgerald and Al Jordan had not been particularly lucky for the singer/bus driver, but another name change [to Matt Monro] was just around the corner.

Whilst Terry was working on the buses, bass player Spike Heaty sent a forgotten recording from Green's Playhouse Glasgow to Winifred Atwell, one of the biggest musical acts of the 1950s with a series of boogie-woogie and ragtime hits. She was also an accomplished rag pianist and Decca Record's most successful artist. Terry's mother, Alice, had received a note from the Decca Recording Company addressed to her son, politely telling him that the record submitted had been unsuccessful. A couple of weeks later she received another letter telling her son that on Winifred Atwell's recommendation they had re-visited the disc and that they wanted to see him. Strangely it seemed that if Winnie had faith in this young man's relaxed style perhaps they were wrong.

Impressed by the young singer's demo Winnie had also sent a cable to the flat asking Terry to come and see her at the London Palladium where she was appearing. Terry arrived at the theatre in time to catch most of the Trinidadian's act. Her stage persona was of a gentle, rather aristocratic woman who came alive at the piano and her dazzling smile literally lit up the stage. Winnie's husband and manager, former stage comedian Lew Levisohn, who was vital in shaping her career as a variety star, watched from the wings.

Winnie and Lew made a business out of nurturing new stage and music talent and Terry was next in line. Terry chatted with the couple, the outcome of which was an audition for the young singer at Decca with Dick Rowe, Winnie's recording manager. The label shared Ms Atwell's zeal so much they took the practically unheard-of step of launching a new singer with an LP and a recording contract. The usual practice would have been a single disc release. Terry left that night with not just a recording contract with Decca but also a management agreement with Lew Levisohn.

On September 17 1956, Terry Parsons signed a contract with Decca for one year with two one-year options. He was so broke that the record company bought him a navy-blue tonic suit and a plaid shirt, which were to be taken out of future royalties. He still used his two shirts and four starched collars which were the only decent clothes he owned. Decca also bought him shoes with 'lifts' and an overcoat.

Less than six weeks after signing the new recording contract Terry was booked in the studios to cut his debut album, *Blue and Sentimental*, with the Malcolm Lockyer Orchestra. Terry, who was still driving his No 27 bus, turned up at the studios to record his first professional disc. It was a chilly miserable Sunday and Terry's temperature was not helped by a grade-A attack of nerves. Partly to keep himself warm and partly to have the comfort of familiar things he kept on his heavy blue serge bus driver's jacket.

from The Singer's Singer: The Life and Music of Matt Monro *(2010)*

SMALL CHANGE

The bus driver from Barbados

Sam Selvon

One time a fellar name Small Change get a work with London Transport. Small Change not really his name, but that is how all the boys know him as. I mean, you could know a fellar good, owe him money, or he owe you, go all about with him, and the both of you good, good friends, and yet if a day don't come when it necessary to know what his true name is, he would be dead and you still calling him Small Change.

Small Change hail from Barbados. You know where Barbados is? You don't? Well that is your hard luck. Anyway you must be read in the papers about how London Transport send men down there in the West Indies to get fellars to work on the tube and bus, and it look as if they like Barbadians, because they didn't go to any other islands: they just get some boys from Little England – that is what they call Barbados down there – and bring them up to work the transport.

At the time Small Change was working on a barge what used to go to the big shops and bring in goods. He used to handle a oar so big that two-three fellars had to handle one oar. When Small Change get the wire that they recruiting fellars to go to England and work, he left the barge same time and went home and put on some clean clothes and went to the office where they was recruiting fellars.

'Can you drive?' they ask Change.

'Me? Drive?' Change smile and try and make his face look like he driving a bus ever since he born. 'I was born behind a wheel.'

'Have you got a license?'

'Yes but not right here. I could go back home for it, though, if you want.'

'Driving in London isn't like driving in Barbados, you know.' The Englishman lean back in his chair, smoking a Lighthouse, which is the Bardadian equivalent to a Woods. Change didn't deign say anything to that, he just wait.

'How about your education?'

'Codrington College,' Change say. Change never went to school, but he call the name of one of the best college in that part of the world and hoped for the best.

'Have you got any recommendations?'

'No, but I could get some if you want.'

Well in the end Change find himself on ship going to England. I mean, when you have ambition you have to play boldface and brazen, otherwise you get no place at all...

Anyway, Change come to London city, with Alipang, All-Fours, Catch-as-Catch-Can, Jackfish and a set of other fellars what get work with London Transport. (I am sure you must be see All-Fours already — he have a work conducting in a bus, he only have eight fingers in all.)

... Of course, when the ship reach England it wasn't long before they find Change don't know anything about driving. In the garage a test tell him to move a bus, and Change get in as cool as anything, sit down, start the engine, and throw in a reverse gear by mistake and back the bus up against the wall and give it a big dent right where it had an advertisement for binoculars, besides breaking up the glass in the back window where does have the names of the places where the bus going to.

Afterwards Jackfish tell him: 'Man I warn you all the time I teaching on the ship, that these buses in London funny. And you mean you didn't know how to put in a reverse?'

'The buses really funny', Change say. 'Upstairs and downstairs, and I don't too like the view when you sit down in the driver seat'.

Jackfish say: 'You better try conducting old man.'

So Change say he prefer to conduct instead of drive, and they put him on a course to learn the ropes. Everything they teach Change, went in one ear and out the other. Change not paying any particular attention: he studying a little thing that he get in with down by the Elephant, where he living. When Changes get in with this thing she ask him: 'Can you rock 'n' roll?

'Can I rock 'n' roll!' Change repeat. 'Child, that dance out of fashion where I come from, we used to do that two years ago. The latest thing now is hip 'n' hit. You mean to say is only now you all doing rock 'n' roll in London?'

'Hip 'n' hit? the blonde say, puzzled. 'What's that?'

'I'll show you Saturday night, when we go dancing,' Change say.

So while the transport people trying to learn Change how to conduct, Change studying some kind of newfangled step, and when elevenses come he went to the other boys and tell them how he have to invent a new dance else the West Indies would be let down.

Catch-as-Catch-Can who used to lime out regularly at all the dances it have in Barbados, tell Change to take it easy.

'You want to learn some new steps?' Catch say. 'Give me a beat.'

So Change sit down on the platform on a bus and start to beat the side, and Alipang finish drinking tea and hitting the empty cup with the spoon, while Jackfish keeping time on the bar it have what you does hold on to when you going in the bus. And Catch dancing some fancy steps, a kind of Gene Kelly mixup with some mambo and samba and some real carnival 'break-away', which is what they call the dancing the people dance in the islands when is carnival time.

'This bus have a good tone', Change say, looking up to see what number it is, as if the number make a difference.

So Change get up and start to do as Catch was doing, and Catch saying no, not that way, and showing him how.

Them other English fellars gather around enjoying the slackness, because you know how they themselves cargoo, they don't know how to shake a leg or how to get hep, until a fellar who was in charge finish his tea and come and say: 'All right fellows, break it up.'

Change get a 196 bus to conduct, from Tufnell Park in the north to Norwood Junction in the south. The first morning he went to work, the bus get about a quarter-mile from the garage before Change realise that he left all his tickets behind. He had was to ring the bell and stop the bus and go out and tell the driver what happen. This time so all them people hustling to get to work and want to know what happening: in the end they had to get out and wait for another bus while the driver drive back to the garage for Change to collect the tickets.

Meantime he learning all the teddy boys and teddy girls in the Elephant to dance 'hip 'n' hit', until it become a real craze south of the river. It was ruction in the town when the teddies start up this new dance that Change introduce, and pretty soon everybody forget about rock 'n' roll and start to concentrate on hip 'n' hit, and old Change figuring out if he can't make something on the side by giving lessons after work...

from the short story 'Working the Transport',
first published in Ways of Sunlight *(1957)*

YOU REMIND ME OF SOMEBODY

Donald Hinds

Turning up at the Labour Exchange I can still remember the excitement (or was it confusion?) among the clerks when I presented my Jamaica Local Examination Certificate. There was excitement/confusion because they had never seen one before. However, eventually the clerk suggested that I might wish to be tested for a job as a London Transport Executive Bus Conductor. It sounded very grand.

My boyhood dream of growing up and driving the most powerful American truck had not abandoned me. I had been on London buses in the few days since arriving from Jamaica, but had not seen any black conductors. Were I successful at the interview, I would not be driving an American truck or even a London bus, but conducting on one was the next best thing, or so I thought.

I was sent to the London Transport Recruitment Office adjacent to Baker Street tube station. The preliminaries successfully cleared, a fortnight after training at Chiswick and later at Camberwell Garage, I was posted to Brixton London Transport Garage at Streatham Hill where I was to become the fifth or sixth black bus conductor in the company. There, I was let loose on the already suspicious passengers who depended on routes 57, 96 and 109 on weekdays, and the 133 on Sundays. I remained in post from September 1955 until January 1965; exactly 9 years and 4 months...

Within two weeks or so of starting work, the cleaner at the garage, a large old woman approached me in front of the other workers and announced that I reminded her of someone. I asked who and volunteered Harry Belafonte, whose handsome profile was seen in *Carmen Jones* and other films; or it might be Frank Worrell, the immaculate cricket player. I went as far as to mention Paul Robeson, whose great voice and physique had been thrilling women and theatre-goers for decades. She shook her head in annoyance; she couldn't quite place who it was I was supposed to resemble.

A week or so slipped by before she broached the subject again. Then, one day she approached me with great elation. 'I remember!' she shouted as she waddled closer to me.

'Really! Who is it?'

Driver and conductors gathered around for the great announcement.

'You remind me of the golliwog on Robertson's strawberry jam jar!'

She delivered her statement with the timing of a music hall comedian, and waddled off with her brush and cleaning bucket.

I do not recall any of the conductors or drivers making any comment, neither did I, but it was years before I could face another jar of Robertson's jam.

Since there were few blacks (coloureds) behind the counters in shops and stores, I generally thought that the black bus conductors and Underground workers were the acceptable face of black migrants. However, a daily uniform of clean shirt and tie and well-creased trousers rarely extracted a polite response from passengers that being the British way.

But our presence wasn't lost on fellow immigrants, who would assume we knew of rooms to let, or how they could get to The Telephone Manufacturing Company or to PB Cow's of Streatham. Those were two employers who had an insatiable need for immigrant labour.

from When I came to England: An Oral History
of Life in 1950s & 1960s Britain *(2001)*

MADE OF STEEL

Edwin Myers

I arrived in England on a very cold morning in January 1961. As soon as I landed, Oh, God, I wanted to go back! What I saw I didn't believe because from the airport — it wasn't called Heathrow — it was London Airport at the time. It was a dim morning and I couldn't believe that this was England, the Mother Country I had envisaged...

I went to Manor House to London Transport for a job. I did all the preliminaries; filled in the papers and then the bloke said to me, 'Sorry, your application wasn't successful.'

I said, 'Why, what happened to it?'

He said, 'It's not successful.'

I said all right then, so I left from there and I went down the tube and went to Griffin House, same London Transport, did the same thing and the manager said, 'All right, come back Monday morning.' I'd got the job.

I stayed on the buses for years doing, different jobs. Then I packed the buses up for a time and I went to the factory for a year. I went back to building for another year, and then back to London Transport.

I enjoyed London Transport, to be honest, because you were your own boss; your own guv'nor. I spent 27 years with them. I was offered driving and I turned it down; I preferred to do conducting. When I'm conducting, I'm me own boss. When I'm driving, I'm everybody's boss: I'm responsible for the passengers behind me and the pedestrians on the road; everybody. And that's confinement. Conducting now, I was relaxed, you know, I could do what I wanted to do: chat up a bird, go collect a fare.

Promotion was there for me but I didn't want it. I liked things the way they were. Personally, I never found any prejudice. They called me 'black' and I was proud, because, that's what I am. If they'd called me 'white', I would have been upset.

One morning, on the buses, it was very cold and I sat blowing into my hands to warm up, and this woman said, 'Oh conductor, do you feel the cold?'

I said, 'No, I'm made of steel.'

Then she was upset and started calling me a 'black bastard', but it didn't bother me.

also from When I came to England: An Oral History of Life in 1950s & 1960s Britain

AN UNCOMFORTABLE COMMUTE

E R Braithwaite

The crowded red double-decker bus inched its way through the snarl of traffic in Aldgate. It was almost as if it was reluctant to get rid of the overload of noisy, earthy charwomen it had collected on its run through the city – thick-armed, bovine women, huge-breasted, with heavy bodies irrevocably distorted by frequent childbearing, faces pink and slightly damp from their early labours, the warm May morning and their own energy. There was a look of indestructibility about them, from the tip of each tinted head in its gaudy headscarf, tightly tie to expose one or two firmly fastened curls, to the solid legs and large feet which seemed rooted to the earth.

The women carried large heavy shopping-bags, and in the ripe mixture of odours which accompanied them, the predominant one hinted at a good haul of fish or fishy things. They reminded me somehow of the peasants in a book by Steinbeck: they were of the city, but they dressed like peasants, they looked like peasants, and they talked like peasants. Their cows were motor-driven milk floats; their tools were mop and pail and kneeling pad; their farms a forest of steel and concrete. In spite of the hairgrips and headscarves, they had their own kind of dignity.

They joshed and chivvied each other and the conductor in an endless stream of lewdly suggestive remarks and retorts, quite careless of being overheard by me – a Negro, and the only other male on the bus. The conductor, a lively, quick-witted fellow, seemed to know them all well enough to address them on personal terms, and kept them in noisy good humour with a stream of quips and pleasantries to which they made reply in kind. Sex seemed little more than a joke to them, a conversation piece which alternated with their comments on the weather, and their vividly detailed discussions on their actual or imagined ailments.

I sat sandwiched between a window and a very large woman whose great dimpled arms hugged her shopping bag in her lap. She kept up a ribald duet with a crony sitting immediately in front of her.

'What've got for the old Man's dinner, Gert?'

Gert's square body remained ponderously immobile, but she tuned her head around as far as her massive neck would permit and rejoined:

'He'll be lucky to get bread and dripping today, he will.'

'He can't do much good on bread and dripping, Gert.'

'Feeding him on steak and chicken won't make no difference neither, Rose. Never mind, he keeps me back warm.'

All this was said in a tone intentionally loud enough to entertain everyone, and the women showed their appreciation by cackling loudly, rocking their bodies as much as the crowding permitted. Rose turned her head to look fleetingly as me, then leaned forward to whisper rather audibly to Gert.

'Wouldn't mind having this lot in me stocking for Christmas, Gert.'

The chuckle which accompanied this remark shook every ounce of her like an ague, and I could feel it being conducted through the bus to me. Again Gert was forced to perform the trick of rotating her head against the uncompromisingly thick neck; her beady eyes slanted backwards to bring me into orbit. She retorted, not so loudly.

'Aw, give over Rose, you wouldn't know what to do with it, you've been a widow for too long.'

'Speak for yourself. Gert', Rose replied gaily. ''S like riding a bicycle, you never forget how. You wouldn't credit it, but I figure I could teach him a thing or two.'

'Hark at her,' Gert enjoined the bus at large, who were sharing delightedly in this byplay. 'Never mind Rose, I'll send Alfie round to see you one of these nights; he's not too bad when he gets around to it.'

Unable to resist the amusement I felt, I smiled inwardly at the essential naturalness of those folk who were an integral part of one of the world's greatest cities and at the same time as common as hayseeds. There they sat, large and vigorous, the bulwark of the adventurous.

The smile must have shown on my face, for Rose glanced at me in some surprise, then leaned forward to whisper to her neighbour and soon there was a chain reaction of whispers and giggles and nudgings, as if they were somewhat surprised to discover that I had understood every word. I felt sure they could not care one way or the other; these people who had lived too intimately with poverty and danger and death would not be easily embarrassed.

The bus swung around Gardiner's Corner and along Commercial Road. Its pace was quicker now, and the chit-chat began to flag as other thoughts intervened. At each stop now they were disembarking, returning to their homes in the strange, rather forbidding deep tangle of narrow streets and alley-ways which led off from the main thoroughfare in a disordered unpremeditated pattern. Through the windows I watched the fleeting panorama of dingy shopfronts and cafés with brave large superscriptions telling of faraway places. The long Commercial Road lay straight ahead, fluttering like an international maypole with the name ribbons of Greece and Israel, Poland and China, Germany and Belgium, India and Russia, and many others; Semmelweiss and Smaile, Shultz and Chin-Yen, Smith, Seibt and Litobarki.

The bus eased to a stop. Rose shifted her shopping bag off her lap and with a grunt levered her ponderous body upright; she smiled broadly at me, and with a cheery 'Ta Gert, ta girls,' she waddled toward the exit while I eased my shoulders in relief from the confining pressure of her body. God, what a huge woman.

As the bus moved slowly on, a bright-eyed little boy in a school cap and blazer paused momentarily beside the vacant seat and then quickly moved a little way on in courteous deference to a slim, smartly dressed woman who followed behind. As I looked up she smiled her thanks to him and was preparing to sit when her eye met mine. Surprise flickered briefly on her face as she straightened up and moved forward to stand in the narrow aisle beside the boy, who looked up at her with a puzzled expression.

The conductor approached with his cheery 'Any more fares, please, free ride only after midnight'. He had been keeping the charwomen entertained with such witticisms throughout the journey. The woman reached into her bag, and the conductor casually remarked as he took her fare: 'Empty seat behind you, lady.'

She received her ticket with a murmured 'Thank you', but gave no sign that she had heard him.

'Seat here for you, lady.'

The conductor indicated the vacant place with a turn of his head and moved on to examine the boy's school pass and exchange a word with the youngster. On his way back he paused to look at the woman, who returned his gaze with the cool effrontery of a patrician.

'No standing on the bus, lady.'

The conductor's voice was deliberately louder, with an angry rasp to it; the charladies twisted and craned their necks in an effort to discover the reason for his sudden brusqueness. The slim woman remained standing, cool, remote, undismayed by the conductor's threatening attitude or the pointedly hostile glances directed at her by the women: in their immediate sympathy and solidarity with the conductor against someone who was obviously not of their class. My quick anger at the woman's undisguised prejudice was surprisingly tinctured by a certain admiration for her fearless, superior attitude; she was more than a match for them. What a superior bitch! She looked at the conductor straight in the eye and round her mouth I could discern the muscular twitchings of a suppressed smile. I guesses she was secretly enjoying herself. What a smooth, elegant, superior bitch!

Just ahead I saw a nameplate on a building, New Road. I quickly rose and said to the conductor, 'Next stop, please.' He gave me an odd disapproving stare, as if I had in some way betrayed him by leaving before he could have a real set-to with the woman; I sensed that he would have liked to try and humiliate her, even to putting her off the bus. He pulled the bell-cord and the bus jerked to a stop, and as I stepped off the platform I saw the women take the seat I had just vacated, stiff-backed and unruffled. By leaving I had done the conductor a favour, I thought. He'd never get the better of that female.

from To Sir, with Love *(1959)*

A NERVOUS BUS DRIVER

Kenneth Williams

Rehearsed Kingsway 10.30. Got the No 1 bus home. I sat behind the driver and saw that he was young, handsome and incredibly blonde: I particularly noticed it: then at Warren Street I realised he wasn't using the indicator to turn left, so I banged on the glass & signalled the direction. He turned round, acknowledged it with a nod, and did as I bid. After, the conductress, said 'That was good of you, love, to keep your eye on him – I was upstairs getting the fares you see & he doesn't know this route at all – he's been switched from Catford, you know – only country buses – and he's not used to the West End at all – all this traffic makes him nervous.'

Kenneth Williams' diary, 21 September 1965

8 BETTER BY DESIGN

As a city London has developed, for the most part, organically, and, despite some valiant efforts, to no pre-ordained pattern or great plan. But if anything has ever supplied a sense of order and coherence to this unreal and unruly city and its outer suburbs then it was the comprehensive identity of its public transport network, forged by the London Passenger Transport Board. Following its creation in 1933 and under the stewardship of its first Chief Executive, Frank Pick, the man who gave the Underground its roundel, Beck's tube map and posters by Man Ray, London Transport would make Greater London look and feel like a singular city. Combining functional operation with crisp modern design, its work continued in the post-war period with the creation of a Brutalist masterpiece of a bus garage and one of most-loved passenger road vehicles ever built.

DESIGNING LONDON'S BUSES

Greg Votolato

As London motorised in the early 20th century and many sorts of passenger vehicles jostled in its streets, a few of them acquired what we now call iconic status; the black taxi cab, the black Rolls-Royce limousine, and towering above them all, the red double-decker bus. A more conspicuous vehicle could hardly be imagined, its body a riot of decorative information and imagery, its interior as comfortable as current technology would allow.

Over the past hundred years, successive generations of engineers and designers, together, refined the city's buses, trolleys and tube trains. They provided Londoners not only a safe and effortless journey but one that was pleasurable, given the high volume of traffic and the diversity of travellers, including rich, poor, workers, tourists, old, young, individuals or groups. Outstanding among them, architect Charles Holden, known for his 'plain living and high thinking', designed Underground station buildings, bus shelters and garages that expressed not only London Transport's (LT) corporate identity but also the identity of London, itself, modern and sophisticated. Textile designer Enid Marx, typographer Edward Johnston, poster artist Edward McKnight Kauffer and industrial designer Douglas Scott all created elements of the service that communicated civic pride through the refined appearance of this public amenity.

Equally important were the products of many anonymous designers who devised such elements as liveries, branded ephemera, and uniforms or badges for drivers and conductors. Despite the prominence often given to the names of well-known individuals, designers rarely work alone, particularly in relation to complex products such as the London bus. When all this design activity was working harmoniously to the drumbeat of an enlightened management, London Transport rivalled or exceeded the coherence of other great urban transport systems such as those of New York and Paris. And in few other cities did the motorbus become such a prominent instrument of modern city life.

At first, design was in the hands primarily of engineers who laboured just to make vehicles start and stop reliably. Even Frank Searle, Chief Motor Engineer of the London General Omnibus Company (LGOC), who is credited with designing London's first standardised bus, the B-Type of 1910, was assisted substantially by a creative engineer Walter James Iden, who became Works Manager overseeing B-Type production. Its steel-and-wood-sandwich frame, engine and running gear were built in the LGOC service garage at Walthamstow, while the timber bodies were constructed at various factories around London and elsewhere, using the coach-building skills of the horse-bus era. Only in the 1920s, when the process of building LGOC buses was brought together at a new plant in Chiswick, did motorbus design break fully with that of the horse-drawn omnibus and engineers begin to collaborate more closely with body designers.

Historians of London Transport have recognised how the company's early managers, who consolidated 165 independent companies into a single operating company between around 1900 and 1933, employed designers to create a corporate image that enhanced the esprit de corps of the newly merged work force while giving the passengers an impression of the whole system as progressive, efficient and attractive. Railway manager Albert Stanley (Lord Ashfield), transport administrator Frank Pick and industrial designer Christian Barman are among the most significant figures in that process of unification expressed through enlightened design patronage within the 'big picture' of corporate objectives.

Their importance typically overshadows the work of engineering teams and, for example, specialist coach builders working anonymously.

Other, external forces influenced the design evolution of the London bus. During the 1920s, the police exerted a conservative influence over the development of the bus, holding back permission to roof the upper decks and to introduce balloon tires, until they were eventually satisfied that such improvements to comfort would not compromise safety. Politicians too have profoundly influenced the shape and nature of the London bus. Transport Minister Barbara Castle's support for one-man operated, single-deck buses in the 1960s contributed to the demise of purpose-designed AEC vehicles. And since 2000, successive Mayors of London have advocated alternative typologies; generic, articulated buses versus traditional double-deckers, with or without conductors.

Those professional designers, who made the most creative and recognisable contributions to LT design, established a benchmark for quality over a century.

Alongside the unification of London's transport system, the modern concept of a design profession was also developing during the late 1920s and early 1930s to bring visual coherence to manufacturing companies, civic institutions and service providers. In the case of LT, managers recognised how 'designers for industry' could provide clear and highly visible indicators of emerging civic values embodied in public transport.

Some of the best work in the history of transport design was executed soon after the creation in 1933 of London Transport (1933–2000) under the socially aware design ethic of Chief Executive Frank Pick (1878–1941) and communicated through his design decisions, facilitated by his Presidencies of the Design and Industries Association (1932–34) and the Council for Art and Industry (1934–39). The entire urban population could see and feel the effects of the corporation's aims in the tube stations, Underground trains, and a new generation of buses, which began entering service shortly before the outbreak of World War II. Beginning in 1935, Pick was assisted by Christian Barman who, as the company's Publicity Officer, coordinated advertising, information, signage and street furniture including bus shelters and benches, implementing Pick's ambitions for the presentation of London Transport.

Pick's coordinated design strategy is evident in a comparison between the 1938 tube stock, designed under the direction of William Sebastian Graff-Baker, LT's chief mechanical engineer for railways, and the RT (Regent Three) bus, of which only a small number entered service before war delayed its wider introduction. Production of a refined RT began in 1946, after which nearly 7,000 were delivered before its replacement, the Routemaster (RM), appeared in 1954.

Comparing even two such different types of vehicle reveals the determination of LT management to employ a consistent aesthetic across its services to bind together Londoners' overall transport experience. Thus, new train carriages and new buses bore the same DNA, with their general appearance and character as precisely aligned as their routes and termini.

Although the morphology of the tubular, single-deck Underground train, its electric motors located underneath the car, differs significantly from the shape of the double-deck London bus, with its internal combustion engine located in front, their styling from the late 1930s declared their kinship. As a result, passengers transferring from the imposing architecture of tube stations to buses, their infrastructure marked only by the lightest of shelters, street furniture or signage, would nevertheless experience an aesthetically seamless journey from their point of departure to the final destination.

Designed jointly by London Transport and the manufacturers, Associated Equipment Company (AEC), the RT bus retained the basic layout of earlier London buses, a design approach expressing Frank Pick's preference for evolution through refinement. Significantly, LT's chief mechanical engineer for buses was Albert Arthur 'Bill' Durrant, who had been in charge of bus policy since 1933 and had links with the LGOC going back to 1919, when the first post-war buses, Models K and S, were on the drawing boards. Yet the RT stood out as a modern design with its smooth,

Prototype Routemaster
RM1 photographed
during pre-service trials
at Golders Green in 1956

streamlined body, bright interior and comfortable tubular steel seats. It was economical due to its lightweight construction and reliable diesel engine, while driving was made easier and safer by improved sight-lines, air-pressure brakes and Wilson pre-select gearbox. This was the long-serving 'father' of the more celebrated Routemaster, with many remaining in use until the late 1970s. Its overall concept and elegant details, inside and out, resulted from the design team's consideration of the vehicle's fitness for purpose and Pick's vision of a product that embodied the functionalist design criteria of London Transport.

In the early 1950s, with Bill Durrant still in charge of bus design and a mandate to replace the remaining trolley buses in London, the RT's successor was developed to achieve unprecedented performance and comfort. This would become the Routemaster, engineered by Durrant protégé Colin Curtis, and styled by the versatile Douglas Scott, an alumnus of the pioneering Raymond Loewy industrial design practice.

Their brief was to build a vehicle that would offer the comfort of a high-class automobile, economy demanded by post-war fuel shortages, and greater passenger capacity than the RT. This was an all-new vehicle of monocoque, aluminium construction, with power-assisted steering, independent suspension, hydraulic brakes, automatic transmission and saloon heating. Yet, Scott's styling closely followed the appearance of the RT, inside and out, confirming LT's evolutionary design philosophy.

Although London Transport ran more than twice as many RT than RM buses over their combined lifetime, the RM became most iconic, possibly because its design was the ultimate refinement of a long evolutionary process, but also because it was the last of its species.

Pick's continuous modernisation process and his insistence on quality deeply influenced the corporation's reputation for emblematic products, images and architecture, executed at every scale, from that of Adie, Button and Partners' mammoth Stockwell Bus Garage of 1952 to the classic 'Push Once' Bakelite bell button. Such timeless elements of LT design are still recognised and revered today, confirming their enduring significance in London's global image.

With rapidly increasing private car use in the capital during the 1960s and 1970s, followed by privatisation of London bus services in the 1990s, the once glorious and democratic London bus came to be seen as transport for the disadvantaged. Private operating companies stopped ordering custom designed vehicles for use in the metropolis, turning instead to major international manufacturers such as Mercedes-Benz and Volvo to fill their fleets with generic vehicles. The ghosts of buses past, however, still haunted those fleets of brick-shaped double-deckers and articulated, single-deck, 'bendy-buses', promoted on the basis of their 100 per cent accessible interiors. Most continued to be painted at least 80 per cent red. And to further satisfy public expectations, their interiors were decorated with reminders of London bus history such as the patterned moquette upholstery used since the Type B.

During the period of decline in London bus services much industry design expertise was lost. Colin Curtis lamented the demise of the former LT experimental workshop in Chiswick where he and his design engineering team tested prototypes of the RM in the 1950s.

When he died in 2012, Transport for London had recently ordered 800 of the New Routemaster (aka New Bus for London, NBfL), engineered and built by Wrightbus of Northern Ireland and styled in the London design studio of Thomas Heatherwick. Given his long experience working in the LT design ethos of Pick and Durrant, Curtis viewed the new vehicle as more a political vanity project than a solution to London's current transport requirements.

Nevertheless, the dreary, inappropriate generic buses of the previous 20 years fuelled a widespread desire for a bus, based on the persistent image of the historic red double-decker, to reassert the proud tradition of public transportation in London, a desire partially satisfied by the NBfL. This coincided with a rise in passenger numbers, as the private car lost its lustre in town and the opening up of Overground rail services, coordinated with bus and tube lines, increased the usefulness of public transportation in the outer travel zones of Greater London. London's long bus routes always required a vehicle more comfortable for seated passengers than the more recent mass transporters, such as the Mercedes Citaro, designed to be packed with standing passengers over shorter routes in smaller cities.

Although Heatherwick's designers were given a brief laden with nostalgia for the by-gone days of bus conductors, RMS *Queen Mary* and the Empire, their visual reinterpretation of the London bus had merit by recalling the high design standards of earlier, bespoke vehicles.

The sleek surfaces and rounded junctions of its main elevations created a distinctive profile consistent with LT design traditions, harking back to the Type B, while the interior detailing, finishes and colour palette appeared luxurious and comfortable, with traces of Art Deco styling.

However, when its provision for conductors was finally deemed unsustainable, the design of the NBfL, with its three sets of doors and two staircases, proved to be overblown. As a result, a modestly reduced prototype, labelled SRM, was developed, retaining the sophisticated styling of the Heatherwick design, scaled down to operate as a driver-only vehicle with two door-sets and one staircase.

If tested successfully, SRM could be produced by Wrightbus on a generic Volvo chassis to reduce cost, ease maintenance and yet still provide Londoners and visitors to the capital with a public service vehicle designed to respect both its users and the specific urban context in which it operates. Relying increasingly on buses for all types of journey, London passengers deserve more than just a high capacity transporter. They are also entitled to a handsome joyride vehicle suitable for days out and nights on the town.

GREEN LINE AND
COUNTRY AREA SERVICES

Taking modern design into the countryside

James Hulme

London Transport's commitment to good design and a clear identity for its services influenced towns and villages well beyond the limits of the metropolitan area. For many years, the incursions made by Green Line coaches and LT Country Area buses in London's hinterland were a feature of daily life for millions across the Home Counties. The amazing reach of these services brought LT's corporate image to the country lanes and picturesque market places of Horsham, Guildford, Aylesbury and High Wycombe, the brave New Towns of Hemel Hempstead, Crawley and Harlow; green buses met the international liners and river traffic at Tilbury and Gravesend. Those who never ventured into London could benefit from the benign influence of LT's vision – at once benevolent and convenient, enticing and reassuring.

Those with even a passing interest the development of 20th-century London will be aware of the comprehensive and creative new identity forged for the capital's transport operations after their absorption into a single entity, the London Passenger Transport Board, in 1933. Part of the remit of this new body, London Transport, was to rethink the presentation and promotion of a large and disparate network. The thoroughness with which LT approached all aspects of communication and its 'house style' led the organisation to become a major patron of commercial art and industrial design, across a range of disciplines from graphic art, typography, vehicle design and architecture. At the height of its influence, from the mid-1930s to the 1960s, LT was one of the foremost promoters of fresh, modern design anywhere, attracting international acclaim for its vision. This was largely due to the influence its visionary Chief Executive and Vice Chairman, Frank Pick.

Pick's passionate commitment to good design and a strong identity for London's transport system led to the successful development of the concept and image of a Greater London. He made sure that the outward expansion of the tube, bus and trolleybus network was accompanied by expressive modern architecture, the sleek design of vehicles, a consistent

DOUBLE - DECK

GREEN LINE COACH

This is the new luxurious DOUBLE-DECK COACH, which is being introduced over the coming months on eight of the busiest routes, including some serving New Towns.

These features set a new standard in Green Line comfort:

- Panoramic top-deck views as you go, from wide-view windows.
- 57 comfortably foam-cushioned seats to cut the queues.
- Fluorescent lighting for reading and fresh-air heating on both decks.
- Power-operated doors to keep the weather out.

The new coaches will run on Routes 715 (Hertford-London-Guildford) and 715ᴬ (Hertford - London) from August 29.

Details of timetables will be shown on coach stops.

FOR ALL ENQUIRIES please telephone ABBey 1234.

1962 poster advertising the new double decker Routemaster Green Line Coach (RMC) to operate on routes 715 and 715a between Hertford, London and Guildford

corporate identity (notably in the use of colour and the 'roundel' motif) and eye-catching posters and other promotional material that extolled the virtues of the new suburbs and promoted travel generally. As well as being encouraged to live in leafy outlying districts, artful graphic images encouraged Londoners to pursue country walks, visit distant attractions, or indulge in shopping expeditions (all outside peak hours). Art historian Nicholas Pevsner said that Pick saw in every detail a 'visual propaganda' to promote public transport in London and improve surroundings as a whole. By any analysis this was art as public good.

Pick's strong relationships with the best designers of the day, including architect Charles Holden, cemented his strategy to create a strong and enduring identity through innovative and consistent design. Despite his early death in 1941, his influence and legacy endures to this day on the modern network in the Edward Johnston typeface, the roundel, the groundbreaking architecture so suited to its purpose, and the overall simplicity and clarity of the LT style. The ambition and foresightedness of this vision for London's public transport at this time furthermore carried a social message, signalling a commitment and investment by the government in beneficial public works, a notable precursor to the postwar Welfare State.

Pick's efforts and the achievements of his design team in unifying LT's visual identity is justly celebrated today. Most accounts of this exciting period of public patronage focus on the urban and suburban network, but its visual impact and success was equally strong in the places served by LT's Country Area and Green Line coach operations. With the cessation of almost all of these green-branded services today, it is hard to appreciate just how far Pick's urbane, art-led, visionary aesthetics impacted on outlying towns and countryside well beyond the formal boundaries of the city. Until the winding down of the outer operations in the 1970s, LT's readily identifiable symbolism – its propaganda of democracy – was evident in places up to 30 miles from central London.

Of course, this expansive vision encompassed not only promotion but the quality and efficiency of service provision. In the central area a massive investment programme during the 1930s brought tubes, buses, trams, and trolleybuses into an interconnected system covering city and suburbs. Beyond the central area, a broad band of country encircling the capital was also seen as an important part of LT's remit. Here, the onus was on keeping out competition from rival provincial operators, and offering a level of service that brought country towns and rural districts closer to London through a reliable feeder network.

Green Line coach services had been inaugurated in the late 1920s, in direct competition with railways for commuter traffic. Original coinage of the name is attributed to Arthur Hawkins, Managing Director of the East Surrey Company, who initiated his semi-fast commuter service from Redhill and Reigate to Northumberland Avenue in 1928. The name stuck, and the Green Line coach operation enjoyed consistent investment and expansion under LT to become the prestige service of the Country Area. These premier, cross-London services demanded flagship vehicles – some of London's best buses were developed for Green Line routes. Investment in the distinctive green coaches as well as local buses would become LT's chief manifestation across their Country Area. This bus and coach network was of course more than the vehicles themselves – depots, route terminals, signage and roadside shelters all came under the scrutiny of Pick's design team and contributed to a readily identifiable and visually rich, whole.

The design language that linked services in both the city and hinterland had a sophisticated simplicity. The principle motifs developed for LT's identity had their Country Area or Green Line equivalents. The roundel (logo) and the Johnson typeface were universally employed; the gilt-lettered legend that flashed from the side of buses at Piccadilly Circus was also to be seen down green lanes. Red had been the colour chosen for London buses as far back as 1908 by the London General Omnibus Company. As the Country Area system developed, the delightfully simple device differentiating country buses from their town equivalents was the substitution of a sharply contrasting Lincoln Green for this bright Bus Red. The variation in colour was applied to not only the buses but at stops and shelters, on timetables and publicity, imparting an identity for the Country Area, at once part of the LT network but distinct from Central operations. As every student of art knows, red and green are oppositional, complementary colours – the dramatic optical effect wherever town and country networks met was quite sensational.

The evolution of vehicle design was a field in which both Central and Country Area passengers enjoyed the fruits of continuous research and development by LT's design team. In the early days buses remained boxy in profile, design innovations were slower to appear than modish architecture or graphics. Notwithstanding, the somewhat raffish Q-Class of 1934 had streamline styling that was the bus team's riposte to Holden's architecture, and was distinctly ahead of its time with a front entrance rather than a traditional half-cab and rear platform. While the double-decker version never got past a handful of prototypes, a single-decker variant made it into commercial production, and the side-engined, full-fronted AEC/Park Royal-bodied Q class entered service in December 1936. LT ordered 200 of these 32-seat buses, their generally good performance making them a hit on both central and country services – there was also a Green Line coach incarnation. In 1939 the Leyland Tiger Flat Engined Coach (also for the Green Line) took innovation a step further with an underfloor engine allowing for a 'streamlined' radiator by the half cab, complete with a roundel device framing the water cap. The curvaceous appearance of the whole took vehicle styling to unprecedented heights – a bus version, the REC, brought the streamline dream to street corners.

The gradual evolution of LT buses for both town and country took on again after the interruption of World War II. One of the first fruits was the RT, debuted just before the war and produced in large numbers as part of the network's postwar reconstruction. The RT was as slim and graceful as a double-decker bus could be, with its tall swept-back front and graceful curves in both vertical and horizontal lines. The RT had its green-coloured variant for Country Area services, though it would be some time before the Green Line had a double-decker designed for its own needs. Meanwhile the RF single-decker, a truly radical departure of 1951 and the precursor to the Routemaster, proved eminently adaptable to the rural network – 21 were delivered for Green Line services, forming the backbone of the service throughout the 1950s. The RF's elegant, classic good looks, probably the most refined of all London buses, were by Douglas Scott, who would go on to style the Routemaster. Scott, like LT designers before him, was concerned with softening the box-like appearance of a bus by utilising radiused curves for all visible corners – roof and body line, window and door surrounds, handrails and seat backs internally. The external livery was crisp, internally colours were muted; the burgundy panels, yellow roof and green window surrounds complemented the tartan seat moquette. Small but vital details – bell pushes, poster housings, lettering, headlamps and sidelamps – all clearly belonged to the LT house style. The exposed circular ceiling bulbs with their soft glow were a particular joy of this period, albeit a magnet for petty theft!

The RF, which also had a ubiquitous Central area variant, embodied the glory days of the Country network after the war, when ridership rose from 25 million passengers in 1947 to all-time heights of 36 million in 1957, 1959, and 1960. To a great extent these statistics can be attributed to the Abercrombie Plan and the decantation of London's population to the postwar New Towns, the radical dispersal through slum clearance of inner city populations to the brave new world of garden estates represented at Harlow and Stevenage, Crawley and Hemel Hempstead. Before mass car ownership, before the A40 and the Mini, the appearance of an RF at a bleak bus stop would have reassured the housewife with New Town blues that civilisation was still within reach. When these places were productive industrial centres in their own right, the green buses vied with bicycles as the principle means of getting to factory or office.

At this point the much-loved Routemaster enters the story of London's transport. Its design was a team effort, with its most important feature – the integrated body with an aluminium alloy frame – an outcome of technology first developed for World War II bombers. Squaring up to increased competition from the private car, the bus was the first to utilise coil springs and shock absorbers for suspension, housed in separate front and rear running units. The quality of ride as a result was a revelation to the bus passenger, an important consideration on the longer country routes. One of the four prototype Routemasters – CRL4 – demonstrated a coach option and this began trials on 14 June 1957. These having been successfully completed, of the production Routemaster got underway. Green Line passenger numbers in the years up to 1960 proving ample justification for the commissioning of 68 Routemaster Coaches (RMC); these entered service in 1962.

Their introduction was the high-water mark of the whole LT Country Area endeavour. The RMC was the deluxe Routemaster, several notches up on its city street sister, with fewer seats (57), deeper cushions, luggage racks above the windows, an electrically operated door enclosing the draughty rear platform, and fluorescent lighting completing the passenger experience. A more powerful engine, auxiliary fuel tanks and distinctive angled double headlamps meant the RMC was a singular force on the road, highly suitable for those climbs into the Chilterns or North Downs. A raised roundel placed centrally between upper and lower decks (later altered to a transfer below the first window) confirmed this as a senior member of the LT fleet. Equally striking was the absence of all advertising – a distinction held only by Green Line services. The popularity of the RMC with passengers and staff led to the commissioning of a further 43 coaches in 1964, this time to a longer 30-foot wheelbase; the mighty RCL was the outcome, the ultimate symbol of the Green Line and a matchless vehicle providing unsurpassed service to the outer districts.

It was indeed downhill from this point. With reliability challenged by worsening traffic conditions when private cars began to swarm London like flies, improvements to rail services further tapping traffic, passenger receipts began to fall dramatically and service cuts exacerbated a swift decline. In 1970, LT's Country Area buses were transferred to the state-owned National Bus Company (NBC) as London Country Bus Services. The aging vehicles would no longer be serviced at the state-of-the-art Aldenham Works, with London Country establishing its own overhaul facility at Tinsley Green near Crawley. After NBC took control, it set about modernising its fleet with vehicle purchases including more off-the-peg rear-engined buses to replace London Transport standard RTs and

Routemasters. The virtuous circle of high-quality design fostering excellent service and passenger loyalty was broken.

Southeastern England is an unmitigated hell of traffic today, and you will search in vain for a roadside green roundel. Without indulging nostalgia, it is hard to avoid bitter regret for the Government policies and personal choices that have to the abandonment of a transport system developed entirely for the public good, leaving us at the mercy of mayhem on our modern roads. London Transport's 'green' network may have left little legacy, but its memory should be recalled by all those who hope for civilised society.

POSTER MASTERS
AND ROUTEMASTERS

Naomi Games

Before the age of television and film advertising, posters on hoardings and on railway platforms were designed to catch the imagination of the passing public. There was less traffic on the streets and life moved at a slower pace. A new poster in the 1930s was an event and fresh ones appeared at regular intervals. This was the art gallery for the men and women on the street and they could easily and cheaply buy a poster to decorate their homes.

My father, the designer Abram Games, realised early on in his career that posters are seen fleetingly and must be legible from a distance. 'If ideas do not work an inch high, they are never going to work.' he said. He kept his designs simple but impossible to ignore. The message was given quickly and once intrigued, the viewer would participate in helping the design fulfil its purpose. He regarded the poster more as an efficient machine than a picture, and the designer as more of an engineer than a painter.

It was thanks to the enlightened Frank Pick, Chief Executive of the London Passenger Transport Board between 1933 to 1940, and Christian Barman, Publicity Officer at LPTB from 1935, that young aspiring designers such as Games were given the opportunity to launch their careers. They were delighted to find that their client gave them freedom to develop their ideas and rarely intervened in their designs. For over 155 years, artists have been designing posters for London Transport. Many striking posters for the London Underground have been commissioned but only a few were published to promote the use of the London bus, nor indeed do they feature a bus; such is still often the case today.

My father worked in a cold studio at our family home and his three young children, frequent visitors and persistent telephone calls often distracted him from concentrating on his commissions. Games never learnt nor ever wished to drive a car. He was a proud Londoner and travelled by public transport. His favoured mode of getting around was to ride on the top deck of a bus so he could puff on his pipe, and there he was unlikely to be disturbed. From his pockets he produced scraps of paper and a pencil, and thought his time and journey wasted if he hadn't scribbled down six

'By bus to the pictures to-night' by Tom Eckersley and Eric Lombers, 1935

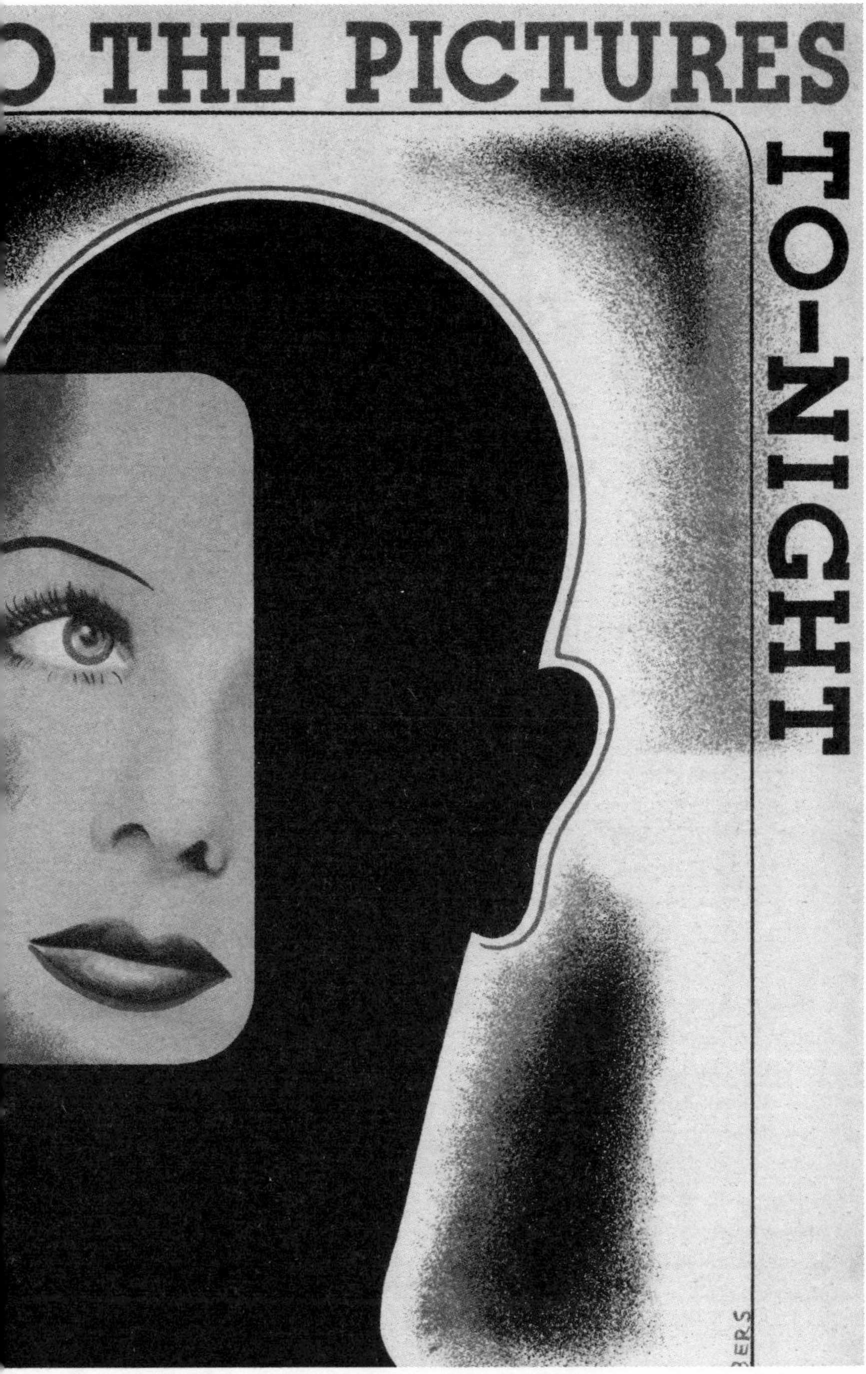
THE PICTURES
TO-NIGHT

ideas before reaching his destination. On a bus journey in 1956, he was contemplating a design for a new Guinness poster. He soon realised that he had no paper in his pockets but his bus ticket was blank on the reverse, so he could draw on it! By the time he jumped off the open-decked Routemaster bus, he had conceived his five-times, internationally award-winning Guinness 'G' poster. He said, 'I should have paid London Transport rent. I never get disturbed on buses or tube trains, but sometimes I'm so busy concentrating, I overshoot my stop.'

Games designed numerous posters for the London Underground and for Coach and Sightseeing Tours, but only one of his LT posters celebrates the bus. However, he designed the curious 'Bus Target Twins' for LT's commercial advertising department. These were used to fill the panels on the front and back of a bus when no advertising was forthcoming. He designed another poster featuring a colourful 'swinging 60s' inspired bus. The now-defunct British Bus and Coach Council published 'Carfree, Carefree' in 1967.

My father regularly walked his family through the City of London to explore its tiny streets and new places of interest were often discovered. When he was commissioned by Bryce Beaumont to design his 1968 'Sightsee London' poster he was determined to incorporate as many of the city's greatest buildings as possible. He drew umpteen progressive sketches and challenged his children to identify the sights, which in the final poster formed the shape of a bus.

When he won the competition to design the 1951 Festival of Britain symbol it was a great fillip to Games's career. This 'tonic to the nation' was a party to which everyone was invited. He must have been thrilled to see his ubiquitous 'Britannia' symbol adorn the four new RT buses departing for a tour of Europe in 1950. They were to play a vital role in promoting the Festival and its exciting and numerous events held nationwide.

Tom Eckersley and Abram Games, both born in 1914, were friends as well as colleagues. Lancashire-born Eckersley had attended Royal Technical College School of Art, Salford in 1930 at the age of 16, winning the Heywood medal for 'best student' in 1934. After graduating in the same year, he moved to London in search of design work with fellow Lancastrian, Eric Lombers who was also born in 1914. Their fathers generously gave them allowances. The Principal at Salford, Harold Rhodes, recommended the Eckersley–Lombers partnership to Frank Pick, his fellow committee member on the Council for Art and Industry. Pick and Christian Barman asked them to submit samples of their work. They were so impressed they gave them a commission. The young designers never looked back.

ROUND LONDON SIGHTSEEING TOUR. Two hours, twenty miles, of the City and West End. From Buckingham Palace Road (near Victoria Station). Every day, hourly 10 00 - 16 00 (not 13 00). Fare 6/- (child 3/-). Seats not bookable.

'Sightsee London' poster for London Transport by Abram Games, 1968

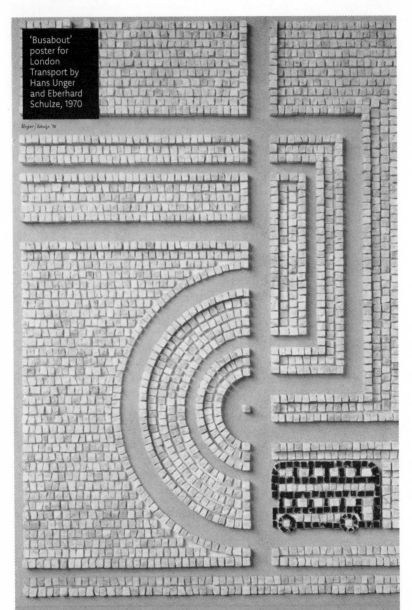

'Busabout' poster for London Transport by Hans Unger and Eberhard Schulze, 1970

BUSABOUT The London red bus, its top deck high above the traffic, is your i grandstand view-point, for historic buildings, places of interest and the endlessly entertai hubbub of the teeming streets. A Red Bus Rover ticket gives you a day's travel-as-you-pl on 1,500 miles of red bus routes and costs 7/– (child 3/6). A leaflet gives details. Another le 'London from a Bus Top' suggests a lot of ways to use it. Ask at any London Transport Tr Enquiry office or write to the Public Relations Officer, 55 Broadway, S.W.1.

BY LONDON TRANSPORT ⊖

In 1935 an airbrushed, hand-lettered panel poster, 'By Bus to the Pictures tonight' was published. It was designed to encourage the public to visit their new local suburban cinemas. The same stylised red bus also featured on the panel posters 'Aldershot Tattoo' and 'to Hire' which the duo designed a year later. Like Games, they had noticed posters by Edward McKnight Kauffer, Hans Schleger and AM Cassandre and they all readily admitted that they were greatly were influenced by their work. Eckersley– Lombers continued to work for the London Passenger Transport Board, as well as for the great patrons of the poster: Shell-Mex, the General Post Office and the Royal Society for the Prevention of Accidents.

By 1940 the war had intervened. Eckersley became a cartographer in the Royal Air Force, while Lombers joined the Army. They briefly worked together again in 1945, but Eckersley soon established a successful freelance practice, working on his own. He continued to design several posters for London Transport but only one, designed in 1969, was to promote travel by bus. 'See London by Bus, Round Sightseeing Tour' is a beautiful, simple collage but there is no bus in sight. Like Games, Eckersley designed a poster, 'Relax by Bus, you're carfree, carefree' for the British Bus and Coach Council, which was published in 1974.

Most of the artists who designed posters for London Transport knew each other. They formed lifelong friendships and generously shared clients. Hans Unger was part of this design family and lived near Games and Eckersley in North London. Unlike Games and Eckersley, Unger was an émigré, settling permanently in Britain in 1948. He was born in Germany in 1915 and originally studied medicine but soon realised that, as he was Jewish, he would have to flee Nazi Germany for fear of his life. He travelled to South Africa in 1936 and became a designer on the *Cape Times*.

When war began in 1939, Unger volunteered for the South African Army and became a gunner. Four years later, while defending Tobruk in Libya, the Germans captured and sent him to a prisoner-of-war camp in occupied Italy. He made a heroic escape, walking across the frozen Pyrenees into Spain then Portugal in 1943–4. Unfortunately, Unger suffered frostbite and lost some of his toes. He returned to his unit in South Africa but was invalided out of the Army. Aware that his work prospects would be better in Britain he arrived in London in 1948. His reputation as a top poster artist was quickly established and soon his distinctive signature appeared on posters for the General Post Office, the 'Ideal Home' exhibition, the *Observer*, British Rail and London Transport.

In 1959 he set up a studio with German-born Eberhard Schulze to produce mosaics and stained-glass windows. Unger had learnt the required techniques while visiting traditional studios in Italy. The two friends fused stained glass and ceramic, which they combined with traditional Venetian glass smalti, and they experimented with new materials and processes. Numerous commissioned mosaic murals were produced for corporate and public buildings and their stained-glass windows were installed in many churches in the United Kingdom and the United States. Unger designed the projects and he and Schulze carried through the technical side. Both men signed the three-dimensional work and Unger continued to design his posters, sometimes incorporating mosaics into the image. One such poster was the exceptional and unusual 'Busabout' Unger and Schulze designed in 1970. Although colour was an important aspect of his work, Unger kept the glass mosaic monochromatic so that the little red bus traveling through the maze of London's streets would be the highlight of the piece. Thankfully the original mosaic artwork is preserved in the London Transport Museum's archive.

A few other bus posters are worthy of a mention, though little is known about the artists. John Lobban worked as a commercial illustrator in Britain during the 1950s. He designed posters for London Transport from 1956 to 1960, including a series of cartoon-style posters for LT, each depicting a black-outline character with a roundel for a head and a body comprised of a placard pronouncing 'Hop on a Bus'.

Like Lobban, much of Harry Stevens' work was cartoon-like. He designed posters for London Transport from 1960 to 1978. Stevens was born in Manchester in 1919. From the age of fourteen he worked for a local printing firm where he was employed as a designer. During the war he joined the Army. He was not only a designer, but also a painter.

Victor Galbraith designed posters and leaflets for London Transport from 1957 to 1966 when he emigrated to Australia. In 1959 he designed a painterly 'Sightseeing Bus Tour' poster and a year later he produced another depicting a colourful patchwork bus in front of London's historic sights.

I know that should my father still be alive, he would happily 'hop on a bus' and get excited sitting on the top deck of a Routemaster, appreciating the view of London from the windows. I always do.

MY PAEAN TO LONDON'S MOST IMPORTANT BUILDING

Will Self

This evening at the Royal Academy I will be proposing to an informed audience and a panel of architectural experts that Stockwell Bus Garage, far from being a dull lump of municipal concrete, is in fact London's most important building.

Perhaps I should qualify this: Stockwell Bus Garage is London's most important building to me. It isn't a merely subjective judgment on my part. However, I do accept that it has yet to reside alongside the National Gallery, the Natural History Museum or the Gherkin on an Acropolis of acknowledged regard. I hope to change that.

The building itself, while indeed comprising a mass of grey-beige concrete, is no undistinguished rectilinear block. In fact the 120-metre-long roof is supported by 10 extremely shallow arched ribs, in between which are cantilevered barrel vaults, and along the uppermost edge of each vault run large skylights.

The overall effect – seen best from Lansdowne Way – is of a series of monumental whales' backs, as if a pod of these leviathans had been frozen in mid-motion as they coursed through the choppy brick seas of inner-London suburbia.

Designed by Adie, Button & Partners, the whale-back roof was a solution to the post-war steel shortage. Garages of this type were usually built with large numbers of steel trusses, but by using only reinforced concrete, the architects and engineer AE Beer succeeded in covering a colossal floor area – 6,814 square metres – without any obstructive pillars.

At the time of its opening in 1952, Stockwell Garage had the largest unsupported area under a single roof in Europe. Far from being a dull workaday building, this is architecture as vaulting ambition.

We tend to pride ourselves in this city on having it all: every architectural style from Gothic to postmodern and back again. But the truth is that central London is an overwhelmingly Victorian city upon which the impact of Modernism has been largely baleful because of limited to low-cost public housing and low-spec office blocks.

A line of RT-type buses dwarfed by the expanse of the new Stockwell Bus Garage, designed by Adie, Button & Partners, in 1953 – at the time the largest unsupported single-span roof in Europe

Stockwell Bus Garage is different: this is Modernism at its best, a triumphant attempt to show that form and function can be beautifully integrated through what were then the most advanced civil engineering techniques.

But its aesthetic merits are not the only reason why the garage is so important. Museums, art galleries and office buildings are all very well but there are sound reasons for believing that for a building to be truly important it must embody the city's functional life. We aren't all art lovers or plastic piano players but we all ride on the bus and quite a lot of us work on them.

And that's my final point about the Stockwell Garage: beginning in 1948, there has been a relation between immigrants from the Caribbean and London's buses. The changing ethnic composition of inner London is the most significant sociological change the city has seen in the past half-century, and the garage embodies this.

I've lived around the corner from it for the past 15 years and every time I walk past it I'm further moved: sometimes, of an evening, seeing the herd of double-deckers queuing for admission, I'm driven to think of the vast distances they've traversed that day, linking the entirety of London together, then finally returning home to their spiritual home, this temple of public transportation.

Evening Standard, *14 March 2011*

RT-type bus in the street near St Paul's, 1952

A BUS RETIRES

LONDON'S most famous bus, the 40-year-old RT, made its final run last Saturday, and received a big send-off.

Watched by hundreds of people, a calvalcade of RTs left London Transport's Barking garage to make their final run over the 62 route to Ilford and Barkingside. This is London Transport's last route to be worked by RTs and 200 enthusiasts had booked to go on this last run.

The cavalcade was led by RT1 (now in private hands), the very first production model, followed by six London Transport RTs and several other privately-owned examples.

It returned to Barking garage shortly after 6pm to be given a cheering reception by the patiently waiting crowd.

As one enthusiast put it, 'the end of an era.'

The RT (Regent Three) first entered service with London Transport in 1939, and with its narrow, upright radiator grill and half-cab became one of London's best-known sights and a tourist attraction in its own right.

About 7,000 were built and with a 40-year history the RT was London's longest serving bus.

Commercial Motors, *13th April 1979*

⑨ PRIVATISATION AND BEYOND

———————

The following piece was originally written by the distinguished transport historian, writer and politican Christian Wolmar in September 1992, as Londoners looked forward with mixed emotions to the imminent sell-off of bus operations – the most profound change to the way in which the system operated since it was brought under public control nearly 60 years previously. Not everything turned out exactly as he or anyone else had anticipated, and below the original text is his recent response to what he had first written a quarter of a century earlier.

Greater London Council poster on Stoke Newington Road, 1984

COME IN NUMBER 9 YOUR TIME IS UP

If the Transport Bill becomes law, services will be cut.
Kill the Bill. Phone 633 4400   ⊖ GLC

HOLD TIGHT ON THE CLAPHAM OMNIBUS

Next stop, privatisation

Christian Wolmar

London's buses are not always red any more. Some are yellow, blue, off-white or even grey-green. But despite what many passengers might think, the routes have not been privatised.

London Transport remains the sole operator of buses within the capital, and it determines the routes and the frequency of bus services before putting them out to tender. Much as the Government would love to see London's buses deregulated and in private hands, it will be some time before that arrives – 1995 is the latest forecast.

The bewildering variety of coloured buses that can now be seen fighting through the London traffic is the result of a process of putting routes out to tender that has been gathering pace for seven years. London Buses is big business, with a turnover of some £550m per year, and 4 million passengers a day. Subsidy is now down to about 20 per cent of costs.

Contracting out started, with government encouragement, in 1985, when Route 81, from Hounslow to Slough, became the first to be put out to tender and the contract was won by a small coach operator, Len Wright Travel, later called London Buslines. The idea was, of course, to reduce costs to London Buses by imposing competitive pressures both on routes put out to tender and those retained in-house. About 250 of London Buses' 400 routes have been put out to tender but this only represents 40 per cent of mileage, because the shorter and smaller routes were offered first.

Nick Newton, general manager of London Transport's Tendered Bus Division, says that at first London Transport had to ensure that there were potential operators ready to bid for the contracts. 'We started with small outer-suburban routes because there were more likely to be existing operators interested in providing services.'

They then moved to large outer suburban, inner suburban and eventually central London routes. Three years ago Route 24, which runs from Hampstead Heath to Pimlico via Parliament Square, became the first route passing through central London to be put out to tender. The £3m annual contract was won by Grey-Green. Next month there will be another landmark, when tenders are received for Route 19, the first 'crewed' route (with both driver and conductor). Of the 253 routes put out to tender so far, just over half the contracts – and 55 per cent of the mileage – have been won by bids from the 10 large London Buses subsidiaries, such as Selkent, Leaside and others, whose logos now adorn red buses.

However, Mr Newton says that savings have been made both on contracts won in-house and on those won by private firms: 'The average saving in costs is around 15 per cent.' Routes were also selected for contracting out on the basis of their previous performance. Those that were losing the most money or had poor reliability were put out to tender first, because they were thought to offer the most scope for improvement.

The financial performance of a route is, in fact, immaterial to the operators, although there are penalties if a contracter fails to provide the required mileage or frequency of service. The contractor only bids to operate the route, and hands over all the revenue each month to London Transport. London Transport provides electronic ticket machines and has an extensive inspection system aimed at ensuring that revenue does not go astray. The 17 private operators are generally pleased with the way the system runs, although they would like their contracts to last longer than the currently normal two or three years.

If the operator has correctly calculated the costs, then providing a bus service without concern for the revenue is, as John Pycroft, managing director of Grey-Green, which is the third-largest private operator, with 120 buses and 13 routes, puts it, 'a nice little earner'. However, he adds: 'We deserve it because we have invested heavily and we have worked hard to keep costs down.' As Grey-Green does not have access to LT garages, it has to do 93,000 miles a year of empty running on the 24 route alone to get the buses from Hampstead Heath to its Stamford Hill depot. This major cost disadvantage compared to LT must be offset by greater efficiency elsewhere.

The private operators have kept their costs down by challenging long established union practices, so that drivers spend more time 'wheel-turning rather than sitting on their bottoms at the depot', as Mr Newton put it. The unions argue that wages have been forced down by the introduction of competition. Mr Newton believes that take-home pay has been largely unaffected but that staff now have to work harder or longer to get it.

The staff has to be flexible. Mr Pycroft says: 'We are not fettered by 60 years of union agreements. If there's a shortage of drivers, the supervisors and inspectors will volunteer to drive the buses.' Grey-Green's staff are, nevertheless, still unionised. 'You wouldn't get that in London Transport. We have also set up a system which allows those who want to work longer hours and others who want short hours to do so, rather than employing everybody on the same basis.'

So far the impact of all this, apart from the change in colour of the buses and an improvement in performance, has been minimal on passengers. The contracting-out process is something of a prelude to the real revolution, when deregulation and privatisation could bring much greater changes. The Government has been notably hesitant over deregulation of London's bus routes. Measures were expected to be announced in the Queen's Speech after the general election, but they were postponed, with priority being given to rail and coal privatisation instead.

Outside London, buses were deregulated in 1985 and the outcome is still a matter of fierce political controversy. The Government points to a 19 per cent increase in bus mileage, but detractors say that the 16 per cent fall in passengers is the more significant figure. Legislation is now expected in the next Parliament and this would be implemented in 1995.

The shape of privatisation has been largely decided. A London Bus Executive will be created and the bus subsidiaries will be privatised. Price Waterhouse is due to report to the Government next month on whether the 10 large bus subsidiaries can be privatised before deregulation, as LT is seeking. It will also report on how an interim contracting-out regime would work. The key phrase in last year's consultation paper is: 'The Government takes the view that the present system is planning-led and that central planning, however expertly it may be conducted, is not an acceptable substitute for the free play of market forces.' Those are words to strike terror into the hearts of London Transport's management and also, more surprisingly, into those of some of the potential operators.

As Mr Pycroft of Grey-Green says: 'I don't think either the industry or passengers will benefit from unfettered competition. Outside London, you can't even get a combined bus timetable because operators are not keen to advertise each other's services. Usage will undoubtedly decline.'

He will, nevertheless, be in there vying for some of the routes.

The Independent, Monday 14 September 1992

The idea that bus privatisation would stimulate small firms into running services soon ran into the hard reality that the big beasts in the industry quickly dominated the field. Thankfully, London buses all became red again, thanks to ministerial direction – which was important not just because it was an iconic colour associated with London, but also because it was an important marketing tool. Londoners knew what a bus should look like.

The break up of London Buses undoubtedly put pressure on wages and constrained union activity, which was one of its key purposes. Since most of the costs of running the services are the wages, there have been some savings for Transport for London but at the loss of quality control and a dedicated long-term workforce committed to public service.

Christian Wolmar, June 2018

10 RED BUS REQUIEM

The last Routemaster bus, less a vehicle than an icon for London, its image still reproduced on picture postcards, guidebooks, tea towels and bags and badges today, made its final journey from Marble Arch to Streatham on Route 159 on 9 December 2005 — just two months shy of the 50th anniversary of its maiden voyage. The decision to axe it from regular service and its eventual passing caused a good deal of soul searching across the capital.

STANDING ORDERS

Magnus Mills

Years ago someone decreed that these buses should have five standing passengers and no more. This was both for safety reasons and to give the conductor room to move round and collect fares.

Which seems reasonable. This is not how the passengers see it.

People desperate to get home from work don't say 'Ah, this bus already has five standing passengers: I'll wait for the next one'. They see room for another 10 or 15 at least, so they keep clambering aboard. And nothing is going to stop them.

The first time I experienced this was outside Brixton Underground station. Brixton is at the end of the Victoria Line and a train had just come in. The blokes in the station must have opened all the ticket barriers at once, because this great crowd surged out of the entrance. I looked back through the glass and the conductor's face had gone pale. Then he disappeared in a sea of bodies. The bus rocked under the onslaught. The cab bounced up and down. It was a bit like being inside one of those coin-operated Postman Pat vans you put children in to keep them quiet for five minutes. It took a long time for the conductor to get everybody sorted out and to get going again. Some conductors are more ruthless: they just hit the bell and hope for the best. That's why buses at busy stops line up with their noses sticking out into the traffic as if they are on a starting grid. It's so they can make a quick getaway. There are certain times of day when it seems that any vehicle painted red and parked by the side of the road is likely to be boarded by people with a wild 'take me home' look in their eyes. This is probably why fire engines keep to the back streets. If it's red it must be a bus: get on and then find out where it's going.

If it's a one-person operated bus, take a good book, 'cos you'll be a long time getting home. Whoever thought of putting these buses on the same roads as Routemasters?

Six o'clock in the evening and we've just loaded our people and we're ready to go. We're behind a driver-operated bus and he's just closed his doors and started to pull out, so I move off. Then a woman runs up and knocks on his door. I will him to ignore her, but he doesn't. He stops again and I'm trapped. I can see through his bus. She staggers on board. She's been running. She looks in her bag. She puts it down. She tries her pockets.

She speaks to the driver. Time passes. I thought she was looking for her bus pass, but perhaps I was wrong.

Maybe she's negotiating to buy the bus. Maybe she's a terrorist. I close my eyes. Eventually his engine roars and he's away. But by now my conductor has been swamped. I look back. He's trying to explain about five standing passengers...

Of course, passengers will say it's all very well for me to go on about being swamped and all that, but all they seem to see are buses hurtling past without stopping at all. Well, it never ceases to amaze me that people will stand for ages at a bus-stop and then when the bus comes not stick their hand out. Only the white stops are compulsory; the reds are request only. Do people who work in offices answer phones that aren't ringing?

The odd thing is that the white stops are not located where they are because they are more likely to have passengers standing at them. It is so that the brakes get tested from time to time. This is to keep the Metropolitan Police happy. Therefore a stop on a bend near a hospital may be red, so that people have to be alert to catch the bus when their minds are on other things. Meanwhile, a stop hardly used by anyone, say in Park Lane, might be white.

If a policeman sees a bus fail to make a halt at a white bus stop, he is supposed to take appropriate action. So next time a driver leaves you behind at a stop, have him arrested.

The Independent, *27 June 1994*

A bus passes on Turnpike Lane, 1983

DEATH OF THE ROUTEMASTER

Andrew Martin

I was riding down Oxford Street on a No 12 Routemaster. As we passed HMV records, I remembered that I wanted to buy a certain CD so I jumped off the bus and did so.

Oh dear, my first Routemaster anecdote seems a bit on the short side. Maybe I should add that no British bus produced since the Routemaster would have allowed me to do this.

Here's another No 12 story... When I first came to London 20 years ago, I stepped on board one – again on Oxford Street – and saw the actor Edward Fox sitting on the lower deck. He looked ferociously dapper, like Edward VIII, a part he had recently played on TV, and yet the bus was not upstaged. It matched him for style, and these two icons blazed forth London-ness, Britishness and elegance in a very pleasing double act. Only the Routemaster would have done this. If you don't believe me, try to imagine Edward Fox sitting on one of the new bendy buses (those mobile bungalows), held prisoner in effect by a grumpy, over-worked driver. It is just not possible.

But even in those days, there was a shadow over the Routemasters. The buses were deemed dangerous; it was frequently pointed out that their celebrated 'open access' rear platforms were less accessible for the disabled.

The last No 12 Routemaster ran on 5 November 2004. The following day the bendies were to take over. All along the 12 route, from Shepherd's Bush to South Croydon, there were bus fans in ones and twos taking photographs, making notes for their own impenetrable purposes, but mainly just sitting on the top decks and looking sad.

Other bus fans were gathered on a traffic island at Marble Arch. I asked one of them – a man photographing a 12 as it rumbled by – 'What's so special about the Routemaster?'

'Good design,' he said, concentrating on his photography. '...Step on, step off says it all really.' I got talking to another man on the traffic island, Terry Hopkins. The afternoon was drawing on, and the first fireworks could be heard above the traffic roar.

'Bonfire night', said Terry, as another 12 rolled past, '...it's quite appropriate really.'

I shouted up to the passing driver: 'Sad day for you?'

'You bet', he called back. I then watched a well-dressed woman walk into heavy traffic to board one of the 12's. In our sanctimonious modern climate it seemed a reckless act. What if the health and safety police had been watching?

I boarded the next 12 to be heading in a westerly direction. Amongst those waiting at a stop in Queensway was a man eating from a packet of Jammy Dodgers, and a vicar. It seemed a paradigm of Britishness: a last flicker before we're all submerged into something new and vaguely continental.

Two Americans also boarded at the stop. They were Rich and Gale, from Tampa, Florida. I told them this had been the year of death for this type of bus; that they had already been lost to nine routes in 2004, and that this was the last day of the Routemaster on this particular route, and that the remainder would go in 2005. 'Oh wow,' Rich said to Gale, 'already we're into history!' Then Rich had a further thought. 'You know, to be honest,' he said, 'I like these buses better than the ones we have at home, and they're famous... Why are they going?'

I told him that was a very good question.

Early London buses had looked as though a horse ought to be harnessed to them. But by the time of the STL type (1930s), the humane equation had been formulated: enclosed cab for the driver, balanced by an open access platform at the rear for passengers.

Between 1954 and 1957, London Transport and the Associated Equipment Company produced four prototype Routemasters. The bus was the late product of the golden age of public transport. London Transport was still allowed to build its own buses, for instance, whereas its successor, Transport for London, merely stipulates the types to be used by the private companies now running the services.

But the car was already threatening, so the aim of the Routemaster was to give as good a ride as a car, with warm air heating, and sophisticated suspension. The Routemaster employed lightweight aluminium that made for fuel economy but was at the same time strong enough to allow integral construction. There was no separate chassis, in other words. And all parts were completely interchangeable for ease and speed of maintenance. You could replace one end without replacing the other.

The bus was originally going to be called the 'Road Master' but that was thought too unfriendly, and the Routemaster *does* project benignity with its modest, melted-looking bonnet. It was beautifully lit, with low-wattage, half sunken bulbs, and a colour scheme officially described as 'Burgundy lining panels, Chinese green windows surrounds and Sung yellow ceilings.' This is why a Routemaster in traditional garb (because they've been re-decorated by the colourblind for years) looks like a welcoming lantern on London's streets, roast-chestnut seller's brazier, a mellow public house with the bus conductor as publican.

The first Routemaster hit the streets in 1956, and by 1968, the final total of 2,760 had been built. My 'own' Routemaster was the 36 (due to be discontinued in January), on which I regularly travelled between the West End and Camberwell. I particularly enjoyed travelling on the open platform... There you were, standing next to a pole in the open air – it was like being still at the bus stop, *and yet you were still moving.* I enjoyed the freedom of being able to choose when I got off, the power that comes with decision making. You're on the bus but only conditionally so. You can come and go. You're free, rakish, elusive, enigmatic.

I enjoyed the way that, if you'd just missed your Routemaster, you might have a second bite at the cherry, should it stop a moment later at a red light. I enjoyed the sight of the driver from the lower deck: from the passenger's point of view he was decapitated, and you mainly saw his back and elbows, making him look awe-inspiringly like an automaton. I enjoyed walking up the curved stairs, and the first surprising glimpse of the top deck: will it be smoky and boisterous, or will there be just one slumped existentialist on the front seat? The bus, with its lambent glow, the surly but reliable growl of its engine (and its conductor) was one of the few aspects of the city that made sense in my early London years.

The first bus to follow the Routemaster was the Daimler Fleetline. It was not a success, but it set the template for double-deckers that followed. I can't be bothered to differentiate between them: they're one-man operated, with interiors strip-lit like a hypermarket, and all the aerodynamic élan of a wardrobe.

Routemaster withdrawals began in 1982, when 1,500 were taken out of service. Many were bought by bus companies outside of London, or by private individuals. The Routemaster Association, comprising 150 people who own Routemasters, is like a band that tours Britain playing oldies. (They'll pitch up in a town with their buses and run routes as they used to be in the old days, before cash-strapped depression settled over the services.)

By the mid-90s, there were 600 Routemasters left working in London, with engines adapted to meet modern emission standards. When Ken Livingstone stood for Mayor in 2000, he presented himself as the friend of the bus. 'The Routemaster bus will be saved and given a new lease of life by London Mayor Ken Livingstone' enthused the *Evening Standard* in August of that year.

Livingstone had set himself the task of overcoming prejudice against bus travel, and probably reasoned a good start would be to keep the one bus people actually liked. He also sought to promote tourism in London, and he accepted that the Routemaster was a beacon for the city, a 'London icon', as he put it in 2001, boasting that he had 'kept his promise' on Routemasters, he introduced an extra 150 conductors, and returned to service a further 50 of the buses that had been mothballed.

Then came a small but ominous event. In August 2003, Route 15 (Paddington to East Ham) was converted from Routemaster to one-person operation. 'That has us all worried,' says Steven Wood of the Routemaster Association. The march of the mobile wardrobes (albeit fully accessible ones, with ramps and/or low floors) resumed. Between 2002 and 2003 something happened in Ken Livingstone's head and nobody knows what since he doesn't talk about it. Mr Wood's own theory is that the advent of CCTV on buses would allow Ken Livingstone to say that conductors had now been superseded — if he were ever persuaded to discuss the matter.

But who is ever reassured by the presence of CCTV? To most people it represents simply a promise that, if you are attacked, the events will be nicely caught on camera, so that somewhere down the line, a reporter can write: 'Police today released CCTV images of... [Insert details of your worst urban nightmare]'.

Leave alone for now the usefulness of having a conductor about the place, to ask directions of, to moan at; to remind you that transport is a human business. Of course, conductors must be paid for, but then so must new one-man buses. A bendy bus costs £200,000; and they are known to some low-life types as 'freebie buses.' It is not the driver's job to check that travelcards are being carried; or that tickets have been purchased from the machines at stops, which in any case often do not work. And what are the chances of meeting an inspector?

The other arguments for the new TfL position are as follows. Bendy buses can carry more people, and are therefore cheaper to run; passengers are twice as likely to be injured boarding or leaving a Routemaster as compared to other buses; the Disability Discrimination Act requires a bus fleet accessible to everyone by 2017; Routemasters are old and falling apart.

It is ridiculously easy to counter these, which I assume is why TfL wouldn't grant me an interview. To begin with expense of running. Bendy buss can carry 140 passengers, 60 more than most Routemasters, but only 49 of that 140 will have seats. If you catch a bendy in the rush hour, you tend to be resigned to standing. Routemasters also travel more miles to the gallon than bendy buses.

Let's accept the contention that more people are injured on Routemasters. Apparently three people a year are killed getting on or off them. But I expect three people a year are killed by walking into lampposts while looking at attractive members of the opposite sex; or by eating soup. Perhaps the bendys can be boarded even more quickly than the Routemasters. But they're long – like a corridor on the move – that they often have to manoeuvre, or wait, before settling at a stop. And besides, it's fun to sit on the top deck, to be high up. Ask any child sitting on its father's shoulders.

The strongest argument of the abolitionists concerns access for the disabled, especially for those in wheelchairs. One thousand of those six million journeys are made by wheelchair users. Must Londoners have horrible buses on account of those one thousand journeys? No. In his second mayoral campaign for the Conservatives, Steve Norris suggested building a new version of the Routemaster, one with an open platform that be lowered if necessary. This would be overseen by our old friend the conductor, who would be on hand to provide any other assistance required. (Help the Aged told me that a fully accessible son-of-Routemaster 'would be popular with many elderly people.')

Another London politician, incidentally, said this: 'Re-introduction of conductors is a priority. We should also retain the existing Routemaster fleet until a modern Routemaster can be designed.' That was Ken Livingstone, speaking in 1998, and what was once plan is now that of the preservationists: work towards a new Routemaster (the mere couple of hundred bendies now in service don't have to be the future); meanwhile retain the existing ones, most of which run along transport corridors already covered over most of their distances by fully accessible buses.

Instead of discussing these matters, TfL sent me some press releases in which TfL employees congratulate themselves on introducing the new bendy buses on various routes. 'Interviews with passengers', are adduced to show high satisfaction with the bendies. In the case of the 73 route (Tottenham to Victoria), which lost its Routemasters in September 2004, London Buses Performance director, Clare Kavanagh, is quoted as saying: 'The new accessible vehicles will be particularly welcomed by people with children in buggies, those with mobility difficulties, and people with lots of shopping.' No mention of the 500-signature petition that was got up to keep 73 a Routemaster route. No mention either, of the near 10,000 signatures on the Save the Routemaster petition on the internet.

At the time of writing, the only consolation being offered to followers of the Routemaster is vague talk of a 'heritage route', along which a few survivors will run in a parodic sort of way for the benefit of tourists.

I have a musician friend – the baritone, and *Autocar* subscriber, Andrew Williams – who loves the Routemasters. He puts them in the same category of his favourite car, the Lamborghini Countach. 'The No 11 is the classic', he says, categorically. (Or did, because it went in October 2003). He boycotts the bendy buses in London, but not elsewhere. 'If you arrive at Luxembourg central station, among all the signs saying Metz, St Petersburg, Moscow, and you see one of the blue bendy buses going by it's wonderful, because it symbolises continental Europe. But I have this nightmare where I got to sleep in London, wake up and see a street with bendy buses... And I have no idea where I am.' Andrew once asked me to close my eyes and picture a new Routemaster. 'What do you see?' he asked, 'What do you see?'

Just think, Ken Livingstone, if instead of giving us some bendy buses, you'd revived the Routemaster. Think of the sheer theatre of the unveiling, the publicity for yourself and London, the boost to tourism and bus-riding, the reaffirmation of the capital's identity. On top of the good work you've already done for London's buses, this would be deification; instead of being condemned you would have been congratulated for your consistency, your denial of administrative climate not so nannyish as mawkish, managerial and just plain boring. And your publicity people would not have to adduce dubious customer satisfaction surveys to prove that your decision had been a good idea, because we would all already know it was.

Ken, it's not too late.

Daily Telegraph, *1 January 2005*

TO THE WORLD'S END

Cathi Unsworth

On the day Red Ken killed the Routemaster, they showed an old film on TV. *To the World's End* it was called, a requiem for the people's bus and the route that it took, through Camden Town and Chalk Farm, Swiss Cottage and Kilburn, Westbourne Park and Kensington High Street. It finished up in Chelsea, where some old boy and his old dear ran a sweet shop and were having a party on the King's Road. Local kids came and he gave them sherbet dabs and lemonade and they laughed in the sun of a late summer afternoon. I know it was Chelsea, but it seemed like a different world.

All of it did, truth to be told. Camden Town looked shabby; boarded up houses, dreary brickwork crumbling into browns and greys, the hump of Dingwalls Dance Hall across the lock and ripped flyposters of bands long forgotten. But the Greeks were having a wedding and inside their Orthodox Church it was a riot of colour and dancing; they were proud of their traditions, proud of their heritage. There was soul and stability, family and feasting behind those chipped bricks, dirty panes and neglected streets.

Up in Swiss Cottage, an elderly Jewish emigré played his piano and dreamed of the Vienna where he'd spent his youth. No way back for him now, except through the key of memory. On Kilburn High Road, a strong-faced, red-haired Irish woman played bingo and drank half a stout, laughing that since her old man dropped dead she'd had a lot more fun.

On Westbourne Grove, earnest young men fasted for the poor at St Mary's of the Angels. A couple of policewomen patrolled Kensington Market, looking for truants amid the punk clothes and slot machines. A little girl skipped home from school onto Ladbroke Grove, to help out at her Grandma's hairdressers. In between, the film crew talked to the bus conductor, who looked like Arthur Scargill, only not an Arthur Scargill you'd recognise but a happy and relaxed one.

Bus conductors, yeah? Another thing we don't need no more.

All of it got to me; I have to admit it. But what really did it was the allotments up on Adelaide Road. Hundreds of them there was, all the way up the hill, like we was suddenly in the countryside. Growing beans and raspberries, marrows and tomatoes, rhubarb and asparagus, right there on the road to Chalk Farm station. What is there now is row upon row of brown, square, ugly flats, a couple of tower blocks taking out the view of

Belsize Park behind, shielding the millionaires from what goes on on the 31 bus route these days.

Yeah, it was my bus route, as it was in 1986. Whoever would have thought that Thatcher's Britain could look like halcyon days?

Whoever had never been on the 31 these days, I suppose.

Chelsea and Kensington, that's still all right, well kept by the Tories for the toffs and tourists. Where it changes, and changes suddenly, is when you get down the end of Chepstow Road and turn left on to Westbourne Park Road, where the first, early-bird nutters of the day join you, throwing their fare down with red-rimmed eyes that strafe through you like a knife.

Then you do a right down Great Western Road, and that's where all the fun begins, that's where the nerve centre of our operation stands, a brown-brick megalith on the shore of the Grand Union Canal. A confusion of automobiles around the entrance, buses pulling in and out, the controllers in their yellow vests with their walkie-talkies, making up orders, changing shifts, stopping for a natter about last night's footie while the passengers grow restless, packed already onto the single-decker that has replaced the mighty Routemaster. This is where the real nutters live, mate. The bus drivers.

You, the passenger, might feel uncomfortable enough already in your sticky green and purple upholstered seat, made to face the skinny bloke in front of you who's twitching 'cos the Methadone is wearing off and you've got no newspaper to hide behind, trying to avoid his darting eyes. Or even worse, you could just be hanging from the bright yellow pole in the middle of the bus, your arm already coming away from its socket, swaying precariously and trying not to bang into the pram at your feet and the three generations of women staring back at you, willing you to fall into their little Kyle so they can have a proper row. But you have to wait here, at Westbourne Park, 'cos bus drivers don't like to be rushed, and some of the newer ones might not even realise they're supposed to swap over with your departing driver right now, they might still be in the works canteen drooling over today's Stunna while blanking out what lies ahead. You have to wait until there's an army of angry housewives waiting across the Harrow Road on Elgin Ave, wait for them to shove their way on, squalling and hollering, telling you to get your fat arse out of the way and stop taking up all that room.

At least you don't know what happened on that seat you've managed to grab for yourself last Wednesday lunchtime with Smiffy and Earl and that tart they picked up on the Five Corners. You are blissfully ignorant that this bus is a love machine when it's out of service and it's a small mercy really you don't know what they done with her, inspired by what they'd been watching earlier in the common room. Only a heavy dose of pornography can get your bus driver through the action adventure of the rest of his day.

Wankers, eh?

With the screaming, bickering housewives aboard, you turn left onto Chippenham Road, a little stretch of Queen's Park that's started to go upmarket, before you veer away quickly onto Kilburn Park Road and the first of many vast vistas of 1960s town planning hell that pockmark the rest of the route. Two distinct types of bastard tend to board the bus here. Firstly the rowing, alcoholic couple, dirty bags of clothes, grey battered faces and chainsaw voices cultivated by a million Rothmans and a dark brown sea of Special Brew.

'Don't you fackin' touch me you dirty cunt!' she'll say as she tries to push him over, oblivious to the onboard audience who suddenly prick up their ears, perceiving the presence of somebody madder than themselves.

'I'll fackin' stab you you dried-up old bitch!' will be his quaint reply.

Well you'll be lucky to get Richard and Liz, as it goes, because the second type is infinitely worse. These are the ones who start the mutinies and riots. The teenage rebels, the baggy-arsed outriders of the Kilburn apocalypse, wearing their hoods over their eyes, one trouser leg rolled up, reeking of hydroponic skunk weed and telling you:

'Don't have to pay, I'm 15 innit?'

The driver has three clear choices at this juncture. Does he:

Drive on, wearily resigned to his fate of being mocked and scorned by the general public?

Demand some proof, stop the bus and provoke the rest of the passengers into a frenzy of screaming and recrimination, schoolgirls shrilly proclaiming they know he's 15, cos he's in their class, yeah? Fed up commuters already late for work offering to pay the fare themselves if you'll only get a bloody move on?

Offer him outside and punch his fucking lights out?

'Cos he won't have no Arthur Scargill to help him, now will he?

The answer, my friends, is clearly A, if you have a whole day ahead of you and just want to make it as quiet a one as possible. Option B is tempting if you have a sadistic streak, as some of my kind do, and actively enjoy the acute discomfort of your trapped audience. But personally, there's only so many thrills I can take. Option C is, of course, the preferred one, but only if it really is the Alamo and you don't mind losing what little you have left.

Anyway, you're only on Kilburn Park Road, there is still all of Rudolph Road, Cambridge Avenue and the swing over the High Road to go, and here, as the traffic piles up around the endless roadworks, you will have more than enough fresh challenges to face.

By the time you descend down Belsize Road, at least six angry men will have threatened your life and a further ten, maybe 12, schoolchildren spat at your feet in disgust. At least the housewives have disgorged themselves in Kilburn, to be replaced by a frailer type of pensioner, the thin shadow of the strong-faced Irishwoman, perhaps, no more laughs to be found since they closed down the bingo and changed it into an Alpha Course Centre.

And on you'll roll through more planners' dream homes, stacked up the whole way along Belsize Road. Did the architects seek to punish those that were exiled from St John's Wood and Hampstead by purposefully designing the most humiliating blocks of unloved concrete that they could possibly imagine to dump here? Did they light a fat cigar and laugh that they were really gonna get paid for this, then turn to pore over the map, putting more red dots down across the allotments of Adelaide Road?

But such thoughts disappear under more pressing considerations as you point your steel steed towards the junction of Swiss Cottage. You've already let on more than you should, and by the way, how is that seat smelling up at the back now? But here's another danger spot, another flashpoint where it could all go horribly wrong. As you pull up on the end of Hillgrove Road, your radio may crackle to life with the unwelcome news that you're running so late the controller wants you to stop here and go back to the garage. A bonus for any Sadian driver, granted. But to face the wrath of the punters, some of whom are by now half an hour late, as you force them to pile off onto the pavement with still two miles between them and their final destination, you need a countenance of stone and ears that can go selectively deaf. Then what do you do if they all stage a mutiny, which has happened in the past, and refuse to budge unless you drive on?

Well you drive on, don't you?

There's only so much a bloke can take.

But if you're lucky, now you're on the final stretch and as you wing it past the Odeon, laughing to yourself at the banners that proclaim SWISS COTTAGE IS HAPPENING, you strain your ears for the ghost of a melody played on an old Baby Grand. Hear it in your head as you sail down Adelaide Road, where all that is left of those wonderful allotments is a line of Scots pines, swaying in the breeze to an unheard Viennese waltz.

Down into Camden, no longer all broken down and derelict, but done up like a dog's dinner with garish papier maché effigies of boots and guitars; Dingwalls Dance Hall now Jongeulers comedy club and the last Greek family you remember from the Olympic café now forced out by fucking Starbucks and the rest of the trade of overpriced nothing.

For a moment here, you are safe. For a moment you can shut the doors and read the paper, catch some moments for yourself before you head back through it all over again.

Only, that day, I didn't. The day after they showed that film.

I mean, I made it through my shift, through the short winter's day. But I couldn't stop thinking about what it had been like. About all of them people then. The young ones with life in their eyes, the old ones who could still laugh at the world, the hopeful ones in between who had found something for themselves in London that they couldn't get nowhere else.

And the rows of beans up on Adelaide Road.

As darkness fell, I had nearly made it. Chalk Farm Road was chocka, thanks to the roadworks by the tube, and there was already about two busloads pushed on there, laden down with their shopping and their woes. No one pitied the poor bus driver as the jabbbering line of schoolchildren punched their way past everyone else, eyeing up who was stupid enough to use a mobile they could snatch, to bag the back seats and furtively pass packages of weed and fuck knows what else to each other. No one pitied me and I was past caring about them, so that even when some Hampstead matron, a little off course from her familiar environs, demanded to know what I was going to do about them, I found myself just giving her the finger and driving on.

'Did you see that?' she screeched. 'He made an obscene gesture! What's your number driver, I'm reporting you?'

I started to laugh then, that Viennese waltz playing louder in my head.

'Six six six,' I replied and blanked her out, all the way up Adelaide Road. Blanked everything else out and all. The sound of the bells, the calls of 'Driver!' 'Driver, what the fuck you doing man? You some kind of mad man?' 'Stop the fucking bus now!' Blanked out the faces pressed against my bullet proof glass screen all the way to Swiss Cottage, when I finally pulled up to a shuddering halt and flashed the internal lights.

'Right,' I informed them, 'you can all get off here now. This bus is no longer in service.'

Oh how they screamed and yelled and cursed and banged their fists against my unbreakable shield. Oh how they plotted my demise, my lynching, my immediate dismissal. But they did all finally get off, and I could hardly stop myself from laughing as I drove away, unencumbered. Back through the concrete columns of Belsize Road, back across Kilburn High

Road and down Kilburn Park Road, the NOT IN SERVICE banner on the front of my bus allowing me to pass with impunity, ignore the crowds of angry yet impotent passengers queued up at every stop in between. Until I found myself back on Chippenham Road.

There's a nice old boozer on the corner there, The Chippenham it's called. It wasn't in the film about the Routemaster, but it is about the only thing I could think of what hasn't changed since 1986. I left the stupid little bus there, abandoned it outside, and strode into the bar a free man. Ordered myself a pint and drank myself back through it, back to the allotments on Adelaide Road. Back to the World's End.

END OF THE LINE

Ian Jack

There are no more Routemaster buses on route 38 from Victoria to Clapton Pond. The last one ran last night. As of today, only one Routemaster route runs in London – the 159 from Marble Arch to Streatham. When that ends on December 9, there will be no more buses with conductors as well as drivers, and with open rear platforms that you can jump on and off. The London bus conductor will join the crossing-sweeper and the old-iron collector as a defunct personality. Just as I have never heard the cry 'Cherry ripe, who'll buy my sweet cherries?', my grandchildren will never hear 'This stop for the British Museum!', 'Room on top!', or (my favourite) 'Highbury Corner for Highbury tube and all international destinations!'.

London was the last preserve of the bus conductor in Britain, and, for all I know, the world. I suspect that Blackpool trams may still have conductors, but buses there and everywhere else ditched them long ago. In the early 1980s, a London woman once gave me her definition of provincial cities: 'They're all Chelsea Girl boutiques and one-man operated buses.' That was before provincial cities turned their disused mills into art galleries, and also before a few canny entrepreneurs saw money in the government's deregulation of bus services and set old London buses to work in places such as Paisley and Perth: an Indian summer of bus conducting, which came quickly to an end when 'competition' proved really to mean private rather than municipal monopolies. No need to pay two wages when you can get away with paying one.

Conductors, or rather conductresses, were a memorable feature of my youth. A big blue double-decker came to our village every half-hour, where, helped by the conductress blowing a whistle, it did a reverse next to the Albert Hotel and then stood with its engine switched off before the journey back to town. Driver and conductress would sit on the back seats that ran parallel to the passageway and share a flask of tea. This being Fife and not Sicily, the conversation was quiet and understated – what I remember is the silence of a stilled bus and the illegal drift of cigarette smoke on the bottom deck – and what little animation there was usually came from the conductress who, being a woman and having to deal with the public, had been given a licence to talk.

We knew their names: Big Ella, Sadie, Maggie. Ella was probably my father's favourite. He was a big confectionery man and Ella, too, liked her sweets. She would dip into the offered bag and dig out a Callard and Bowser treacle toffee, heedless of the results on a body that was already doing battle with her thick uniform and the straps that held her leather money bag and the ticket machine. She had a big voice. Before the stop near the pier, her call of 'Ferryboat!' would ring up the stairs, right to the front seats on the top deck. Once, she told us, she'd opened her back door at home to call the cat in and shouted 'Ferryboat!' by mistake. The bottom deck laughed at that.

I shall miss London conductors and their Routemasters, which are such well-designed and beautiful objects. Riding with my son on the No 38 to Clapton Pond last weekend – a farewell trip – I couldn't help thinking how both belonged to a more civilised and orderly metropolitan era, before the disintegration of the bus queue and the coming of the CCTV camera and the warnings about unattended objects. Earlier this year on another of my local buses, the 43, a man on the upper deck was stabbed to death when he objected to a fellow passenger throwing take-away chips at his girlfriend. No wonder, then, that the drivers-cum-faretakers are protected from their passengers by a strong screen, with help available by two-way radio. In my memory, the most that Big Ella and Sadie had to worry about was a man who had stayed too long in the Volunteer Arms singing 'The Yellow Rose of Texas' on the last bus home.

The Guardian, *29 October 2005*

QUEEN OF THE ROAD

Iain Sinclair

To be waiting at a bus stop for your connections, mid-morning work abandoned, is a rare privilege. You have to understand the pressure TfL employees are under, squeezed from above by accountants, to arrive within seconds of the stipulated time, up there in lights, above the shelter. Get ahead of yourself and you are obliged to dawdle, taking in the view, ignoring restless clients carving up seats, munching, shouting into mobiles, hefting outsize rucksacks. The white middle classes no longer use public transport, outside the early City shunt. They power-walk, pump-cycle, pile into high-wheeled Chelsea tractors or tax-avoiding electric dune buggies. If the driver of the 242, bladder bursting, is held in the Dalston Lane gridlock, he'll have to gun it past the next few stops. Cross his legs. Park up, risking everything, to acid-irrigate a convenient garden. Or ring for the wife, as happened to one prostate sufferer, to bring down a change of trousers.

To say that these men – women too – are unappreciated is to state the obvious. Like Eichmann in Jerusalem, they are prisoners in perspex cages designed to frustrate the ire of fare-dodgers, the vocationally disgruntled, new girl gangs. Rappers of counterfeit coins who block your airholes with gum. A mob who insist on riding 50 or 60 yards, from one stop to the next. It has become a class issue: the wealthier you are, the further you walk in order to avoid viral democracy. The yatter, the multitongued babble. Window seats are protected by large persons challenging you to get past them. *Respect.* Respect: an invisible but electric exclusion zone.

BUS STOP: that frequently ignored command. The street is so quiet I begin to think it has been closed off for one of Danny Boyle's post-apocalyptic fantasises. I can hear a man shouting: 'Give me the keys. Give me the fucking keys.' A house on the south side of Graham Road. Right next to the Turkish Cypriot Cultural Association (Education Counselling). And then a woman, her screams. No twitch at the dirty muslin curtains.

The screaming stops, the muslin moves and a tall slim black man in a white vest glares at me. We're in a *Rear Window* scenario, the snoop and the potentially misinterpreted drama. Should I act? I'm not stupid enough to use the camera. Years ago, innocent of Hackney ways, I intervened when a child was smashing milk bottles and positioning the jagged shards beneath the wheels of the parked cars of schoolteachers. His mother, in conversation, looked on indulgently. Now it would be different: I would stand trial for my reckless challenge, no question. I'd find myself on the register, featured in the *Gazette*. We'd have to leave London. In the 1960s, I copped a tirade of motherly abuse: wait-till-my-bloke-comes-home. Hearts of gold, those tigerish mums. That night, my first car, a distressed red Mini, was battered into a heap of scrap. A sound ecological gesture that brought me into the age of the bicycle.

The 242 draws up. The driver, who rang me to advise of his imminent arrival, is a veteran of this route. I present my orange holder with the Hackney Freedom Pass, the sole reward for survival in the borough. I hang, trying to talk through the perforated screen, as the vehicle accelerates to recover time lost in a confrontation with a black youth who flashed a Video Library card and then jumped off, promising retribution, when challenged. This was nothing, the driver reckoned. What he can't get used to is the way some of them spit, so venomously and accurately, through the constellation of holes in the perspex.

He recalled the final night-run in a 38, that much-lamented casualty of Ken Livingstone's bendy-bus fetish. As he cruised down Dalston Lane, alongside the burnt-out reefs of Georgian terrace, the abandoned family businesses, he heard a loud pop. His conductor was on the floor. Buses, in those over-financed days, still had conductors. This one, trembling slightly, said that he had dodged a random bullet. Which passed 'literally' through the vehicle, leaving a star-shaped exit wound. A bandit salute to the 38, queen of the road, Dalston Lane to Victoria Station. Our passport to the wider world.

from Hackney That Rose-Red Empire: A Confidential Report *(2009)*

THE BASTARDS ON THE BUS

Geoff Nicholson

Dr Martin Bax, the paediatrician, editor, novelist, and pal of J G Ballard, is fond of quoting a bit of research done in the early 1950s charting the number of heart attacks suffered by bus drivers as compared with bus conductors. The conductors had far, far fewer.

The study posited that it had nothing to do with stress: driving in London was considered to create much the same level of stress as dealing with the London public on board a bus. So it had to be something to do with exercise. The study observed that the bus driver, in his cab, was sitting down throughout his shift, whereas the bus conductor was on his feet, constantly running up and down the stairs to collect fares. This exercise, it was concluded, kept the conductor fit and offered protection against heart disease.

I wouldn't question the research, and it seems pretty obvious today, but certainly my memory is that although bus conductors may have been heart-healthy, that didn't by any means solve all their problems.

I was once on the end of a very unpleasant experience while travelling on a Routemaster heading north along Tottenham Court Road. I remember it like this. I was sitting upstairs, at the front, and when the moment came, I stood up to make my way to the back of the bus, and pressed the button that rang the bell, signalling to the driver that I wanted to get off at the next stop. However, at almost – but not exactly – the same moment, the bus conductor, who was standing at the rear of the upper deck, by the top of the stairs, also pressed a bell – thereby creating two rings, a signal that the bus should keep going.

It was perfectly clear what had happened, and I imagine it must have happened more than once in the history of London Transport, but the conductor didn't understand, or pretended not to. He was thrown into a fury, and as I approached him, making my way to the stairs to descend, he started shouting at me, saying it was strictly forbidden for passengers to give the bus a starting signal. I explained, not very gently, that this wasn't at all what I'd done. I'd only pressed the bell once. If I'd pressed the bell twice then there would have been three rings – obviously. And if he didn't understand that then he was a very stupid man.

I'm not sure that he understood my point about the bell, but he definitely understood that I'd called him stupid. I'd only done it in response to his anger, and since I imagined terse exchanges between conductors and passengers might also have happened more than once in the history of London Transport, I assumed it was no big deal, and that as the end of things. I was wrong. I went past him and started to descend the stairs in order to get off the bus, which meant that at some point my head was inevitably at the same level as the conductor's foot, at which point he aimed a vicious kick towards my face.

He missed, but only just, and clearly he hadn't intended to miss. I hurried down the stairs, got the hell out of there, got off the bus and stood in Tottenham Court Road as the bus pulled away, surprised more than anything else. I really hadn't expected that a bus conductor would try to assault me. A fellow passenger who'd got off at the same time and had seen what happened said I should call the police, at least make an official complain to London Transport.

I didn't, because I was pretty sure no good would come of it, and after all I hadn't actually been assaulted. I shrugged it off, and said something along the lines of, 'The poor bastard must have a miserable enough life without me making it worse,' a comment that even at the time I realised cut in several directions. I'm sure this was the sensible thing to do, but from time to time I've thought that I might have grabbed that flailing foot as it came towards me, and pulled on it, in which case I'd have dragged the conductor down the stairs after me, but I'm sure even less good would have come of that.

That, as I say, is how I remember it. However, the editors of this volume tell me my memory must be false, that the configuration of the Routemaster would have made this incident impossible. They tell me there is only one button to press upstairs and the sound it creates is a buzz. This distinguishes it from the downstairs button which creates a ring, and the two are therefore easily distinguishable. Now, it is possible I suppose that I pressed the buzzer upstairs as the conductor pressed the bell downstairs but that couldn't be construed as a signal to the driver to keep going, and in that case the conductor surely had no reason to be angry. It is, I suppose conceivable that my hand slipped and I accidentally pressed the buzzer twice; that surely would have incensed the conductor but if I'd done that I'm pretty sure I'd have 'fessed up and not incensed the conductor by calling him stupid. The truth is no longer out there, although it seems we can say that life on the Routemaster can play strange tricks.

In any case I had clearly plugged into that conductor's reservoir of simmering rage, which was perhaps common among conductors. My memories of another occasion, and in which I was less directly involved (and in which the vagaries of my memory are less likely to spoil a good story), suggest this was often the case. I was again upstairs on a Routemaster, this time heading west along Oxford Street. The traffic was heavy and the bus moved slowly; it might have been quicker to walk. The conductor was a youngish, plump, soft, melancholy lad, and I could hear that he'd got into some kind of altercation with a small group of young teenagers downstairs. From my place up top I couldn't follow the argument, and definitely didn't know how it had started, but at some point I heard the conductor tell the kids to get off the bus. Perhaps surprisingly, they did, not without some backchat and low-level abuse, but they did descend from the bus onto the pavement of Oxford Street.

If there had been less traffic and the bus had gone on its way, the kids would have been left behind, and all would have been well. But the bus was moving quite literally at walking pace, and the kids walked alongside, every now and then hopping back on to the bus platform to hurl more abuse and mockery at the conductor. Any time he tried to assert what little authority he had, the kids got off the bus again and continued walking along Oxford Street next to the bus, and so the process continued.

The kids would surely have got bored with this sooner or later, but the conductor's feeble responses only spurred them on. Who knows how long it might have continued, but when the bus got as far as Selfridges the conductor brought things to an end. He'd had enough. He was actually in tears by now, and he packed up his ticket machine and announced to the passengers, 'That's it. I've had enough. I'm jacking in this job.' Somehow, we knew he meant it. He went and had a word with the driver who turned off the bus's engine and lights, and we just sat there. The conductor's young tormentors disappeared into the crowded street.

It was hard to know what was going to happen next. Would the conductor have a change of heart now that the kids had gone? That didn't seem likely. Would London Transport send out a replacement crew? Well possibly, but who knew how long that was going to take? Gradually in dribs and drabs, all the passengers trooped off the bus. The conductor was now standing on the platform, still looking horribly upset, but his tears had dried and, although his head was down and he looked defeated, he had somehow acquired a strange, quiet dignity, a captain on his doomed vessel.

Of course, I had to go past him in order to get off the bus, and so I decided to say something that had been said to me by older and wiser men when I too had been stuck in horrible, miserable jobs. 'Hey,' I said, 'don't let the bastards get you down.'

It was, I suppose, a stupid and redundant thing to say; he obviously had let the bastards get him down. But at least this time I wasn't one of the bastards.

RED BUS, SILVER SCREEN

Barry Curtis

The red double-decker bus is an icon that physically resembles itself, a part of childhood that is a continuing presence in adulthood. It is a symbol of 'Britishness', in particular, of London, embellishing postcards, posters, tourist literature. It has woven through the streets following familiar and unvarying routes that stretch back beyond living memory. It seems supremely 'natural' – in its essential 'omnibus' form, with historical associations to earlier horse-drawn transport, the enclosure of the roof space occurred as a kind of organic process. The two-storey structure means that it is implicated in other conventions – it resembles a house with a staircase and an upper floor that is more 'private' and withdrawn. The 'conductor' is a presence, somewhere between a landlord and a host. The bus figures as a vehicle of regulated commuting as well as a theatre of sociability and aggression. The 'night bus' mediates between the moods of the entertainment venues that lie along the route, light-hearted encounters and grim performances of alienation.

For the purposes of this essay, the double-decker bus is intimately associated with London. It is always red, always available and frozen in time, at the point when the platform is a performative space of entries and exits. It is an everyday reality, maintaining regulated routes – the maintenance of headway, complex logistics, servicing and protocols. It is both an intensely familiar and a surreal object – a vehicle of wonder that becomes evident when sharing front, upper deck seats with tourists and excited children.

There is a kind of futility in thinking about buses in films. The bus features, in some way, in every film set in London – as a background presence or, instrumentally, as a means of transporting characters and staging encounters. I will look at a few almost arbitrarily chosen films, that seem to me to amplify and engage with aspects of the 'double-decker experience'. The upper-deck view has a particular filmic quality; it is position of natural authority, but also an alienated point of view that provides unusual perspectives and intimate glimpses into other vehicles and first-floor windows. The position of detachment and privilege was exploited by early film-makers – one short film included in Patrick Keiller's compilation of *fin de siècle* films *City of the Future* is a slow progression through an inner suburb of London in the early years of the 20th century, a tracking shot filmed by mounting a camera on the top deck, a view that is available to any ticket holder.

The athletic accessing of passing buses was part of the iconography of 'Swinging London'. The bus figures in the early paintings of pop artist Alan Jones, who demonstrated how it can be reduced to a simple iconic format, and of course it appeared on *Time* magazine's famous 1966 cover of Swinging London, indicating the ways in which the London bus condensed meanings that were central to the idea of a liberated, youthful city open to influences from the States, Continental Europe and the mysterious privileged values of an older Britain.

The film *Summer Holiday* (dir. Peter Yates) was released in January 1963, intended to capitalise on the success of *The Young Ones*, Cliff Richard's previous 'musical', released in 1961 and the second-most popular British movie of that year. It was filmed in Cinemascope and Technicolour.

The simple, picaresque plot involved Don (Cliff Richard) and his friends, who are bus mechanics at the London Transport bus overhaul works in Aldenham, Herts. Don persuades London Transport to lend them an RT double-decker. The bus is converted in a montage of scenes into a holiday home which they intend to drive to the south of France. The structure of the bus is revealed in a sequence of shots through the chassis of the deconstructed interior, and the accompanying song which counts down the days anatomises the attributes 'like a beauty queen', 'as tough as an army tank' and 'like a first-class hotel'. The head-on tracking of the No 9 bus driving down a tree-lined French road with 'characteristically French' pedestrians and cyclists waving and registering their surprise is supplemented with shots of Cliff, singing the title song, framed by the emphatically red side window and windscreen. The 'Englishness' of the adventure is reinforced by the comic incompetence of the boys, and by cups of tea being made en route and passed to the driver.

Throughout the film, which involves an encounter with three English girls and a runaway girl masquerading as boy, the bus is a suggestive but chastely shared domestic space. It acts as a proscenium and backdrop for musical performances. It is re-routed, by the plot, to Athens. Richard reminisced in an interview (*Daily Telegraph,* 20 September 2008) 'At the time to watch it was to blast into a world that was not meant for us'. 1963 was a time when this kind of ad hoc adventure wasn't imaginable to most young working-class Britons. The incongruity of a London bus passing by the Parthenon was a vivid commentary on the opening up of new horizons and possibilities for acculturation and upward mobility. The bus becomes a complex signifier of familiarity projected into an expanded field of experience – The Beatles 'Magical Mystery Tour' (1967) deployed a similarly archetypal British 'coach tour'.

Just one year after the release of *Summer Holiday*, Ken Kesey converted a 1939 'International Harvester' school bus to carry his 'Pranksters' on a filmed cross-country tour of the USA (not released as film, but featuring in a documentary in 2008)*. The bus was named 'Further'. The 'trip', inspired by Kerouac, became a metaphor for self discovery and, in the case of *Summer Holiday*, a very mild form of anti-authoritarianism. Nomadic architecture was widely explored in the early 60s as a harbinger of a new society, inspired by Buckminster Fuller and the writings of the Situationists. It is just possible to see vestigial elements of this fantasy in the mise en scene of *Summer Holiday* – the conventional double-decker bus transformed into the fantasy of a liberated bus, no longer scheduled transport, and an inspiration for many young people to make their own way to the Continent without the comforting environment of the No 9. In a 'punk' subversion of the sunny mood of the film, in the 1980s TV comedy *The Young Ones*† the last episode ends with the cast singing titles from *Summer Holiday* and driving a No 73 over a cliff, into a quarry.

The bus is very much at the centre of *Summer Holiday* – a London bus alienated from its usual functions and routines. In *The Ipcress File* (Sidney J Furie, 1965) the bus appears fleetingly as a kind of epiphany at a moment of emotional intensity. Harry Palmer works for British intelligence, in a subordinate, routine role. The author of the 1962 book on which the film was based, Len Deighton, intended Palmer to be a realistic riposte to the extravagantly luxurious and libidinous lifestyle of James Bond‡. Played by a young Michael Caine, Palmer is involved in a complexly plotted world of counter-espionage and is confined and tortured (subliminally 'brainwashed') in a grim prison. Abrupt restrictions to the budget of the film, which was originally intended to include sequences in Beirut and Cape Canaveral, meant that the 'Albanian' prison sequences had already been constructed at Pinewood. Palmer violently overcomes the Albanian-speaking guards and escapes from the dungeon, leaving the viewers anticipating Palmer's difficulties in escaping from 'the East' – however, he runs down an alley and, as he reaches its end, his first sight is a red double-decker – a memorable moment of relief and security.

This is double-decker as Gestalt – a testimony to the condensed meaning of the red double-decker bus. However, there are other moments in the film that the bus is metaphorically invoked. A relatively inexperienced director, Furie worked with the Czechoslovakian

* An account of this 'trip' featured in Tom Wolfe's *The Electric Kool Aid Acid Test* (1968)
† titled *Summer Holiday*
‡ Producer Harry Salzman had already made the first three Bond films using the same production team, including Ken Adam and John Barry

cinematographer Otto Heller, using a strategy of creating a sense of claustrophobia and ambiguity by shooting through foreground obstacles and existing frames – in more than 100 instances frames-within-frames are created – featuring shots through telephone boxes and windscreens. This was an early use of a technique that is now very widely employed, especially in Netflix series. In *The Ipcress File*, it replicates the experience of seeing London through the frame of a vehicle – the surprisingly unfamiliar points of view that are vividly experienced in moving within a bus.

In *28 Days Later* (dir. Danny Boyle, 2002), the film opens with a confusing montage of glitchy shots on surveillance screens showing riots, scenes of street fighting and confusion. The sequences are being watched by a chimpanzee, constrained by straps and electrodes in a laboratory. The opening sequence is poorly lit, almost monochrome, following animal activists releasing the caged chimps in the laboratory. A researcher warns them that they are infected with 'Rage' – the activists persist, release a chimp and it attacks them in a montage of confusing fragments, accompanied by screeches and the sound of clashing mesh barriers. There is a cut to an eye opening, in extreme close up – the camera draws back to reveals a silent, abandoned hospital room, a naked man lying on the bed. He releases himself from the drips that are attached to his body, wandering through deserted rooms in violent disarray. In ominous silence we see him, wearing 'scrubs', wandering along the Embankment and across Westminster Bridge. As he approaches the Cenotaph in Whitehall, the point of view cuts to a shot framed by the smashed rear window of a red double-decker bus. There is a partial shot of the bus lying on its side, followed by a crane shot of the same bus, showing that it is diagonally positioned across the road. This functions as a clear sign that some kind of catastrophe has happened. The legendary stability of buses, their patient normality, has been disrupted, and we can assume that the natural order of things has been overthrown.

In the third of the cycle of Harry Potter films: *The Prisoner of Azkaban* (dir. Alfonso Cuaron, 2004), Harry sits on the kerb of a street in Palmer's Green, North London. A nearby playground is ominously active – a roundabout turns, swings swing – a horror film trope for restless spirits – a giant hound emerges from the foliage – Harry, confused and scared, wields his wand and is distracted by two deep blasts of a horn, accompanied by comic tuba music – a purple bus pulls up with a conductor standing on the platform. The conductor announces that the 'Knight bus' provides 'emergency transport for the stranded witch or wizard'. He urges Harry on board and helps him with his trunk. From Harry's point of view, the lower deck is a row of beds with snoring occupants. A further two decks loom above an internal well with a massive chandelier lighting the interior.

The conductor dispenses a ticket. His message to the driver is relayed by a shrunken head, the bus accelerates and throws Harry onto a bed — we see a shot of it careering around a corner, from Harry's point of view, the beds swaying and the chandelier swinging. The bus passes other vehicles, including 'normal' buses and narrowly avoids collisions — we learn that it is invisible to the non-magical 'muggles'. It stops abruptly, within inches, to allow an elderly woman with a walking frame to cross the road. Crossing Lambeth Bridge the driver, guided by the shrunken head, sees two red double-deckers approaching side by side; he pulls a lever, the bus morphs to a fraction of its width, and squeezes between them. As it leaves Harry outside the Leaky Cauldron, it accelerates and vanishes.

The chaotic scene — the animated conductor, the sleeping passengers in what seems very like an NHS hospital ward, and the hazardous driving by an apparently visually challenged driver, is surreally reminiscent of many people's experience of the pleasantly chaotic and sporadically intimidating 'night bus' service. Conflating the 'emergency' service with a different zone of perception is dramatically funny. The absurdity, to some visitors to London, of a two-storey bus is compounded by adding another deck, although both upper decks only serve to accommodate the enormous decorative light fitting. This is a whimsical fantasy rendition, but it conjures with some of the mythic and magical dimensions of a ubiquitous, reliable force of transport.

Finally, I consider another imaginary incarnation of the double-decker, as redeeming life saver. The film *Cockneys v Zombies* (dir. Matthias Hoene 2012) is about two brothers who carry out a bank robbery to secure the funds to prevent their grandfather's 'Bows and Bells Old Peoples' Home' from being redeveloped by a corrupt property company. Laced with 'cockney' themes, it was released in Olympic year. There is a thematic emphasis on the redevelopment of London as a kind of plague/invasion, and although the zombies include West Ham and Millwall football fans (still fighting in their undead state), there is a strong suggestion that the real enemy is gentrification.

Having stolen two and a half million pounds — the outcome of an embezzlement arrangement between bank and developers — the young robbers and friends have to rescue the inmates of the Home. They realise that there is no room in their car and their feisty female cousin hotwires a Routemaster (205); another young woman is left with the bus during the rescue attempt and drives away, only to return just in time to save the encircled rescuers — and rescued — in an iconic moment of arrival. The bus provides moments of sociability and exposition, intermittently interrupted by the need to shoot zombies as they climb aboard the platform. As well as being an indomitable symbol of London-ness, the bus is deployed as a weapon as it runs over and brushes aside crowds of the undead. If there is a 'message' in a film that manages to exploit a number of genres simultaneously, it is that there is a continuity in London culture that has survived tragedies and disasters and the rather optimistic suggestion that this will prevail in the future. The Routemaster is the vehicle of desire that combines a sense of rugged irresponsibility and acts as an 'omnibus' capable defying the forces of disorder and carrying Londoners to safety.

11 **A 7/7 STORY**

On 7 July 2005, in the worst single terrorist atrocity on British soil, four suicide bombers with rucksacks mounted attacks in London, detonating three devices on the Underground and the fourth on the top deck of a No 30 bus travelling through Tavistock Square. 52 people were killed and hundreds more injured. What follows is a fiction based on that day's events.

THE COMMUTE

Linda Mannheim

That morning she rode the Northern Line to the Central Line. At Tottenham Court Road, where she usually changed trains, she left the station instead. She interrupted her trip for a swim at the leisure centre three times a week. The outdoor pool there was heated, and she liked it best in winter, when mist rose from the surface, when her bare feet became so cold on the concrete path between the building and the water that she had to run. That morning it was not cold. July had just begun, but the sky was sadly grey; the pool was grimy around the edges. It started to rain soon after she'd begun to swim and when the other swimmers went inside, she was happy to have the pool to herself. She liked to look at the shabby 1960s tower blocks that surrounded the pool, at the single potted palm tree. Like her, it was not from there. The pool was a perfectly ridiculous place to swim, ugly and always in need of cleaning, but it was one of the few places in the middle of the city where she didn't have to watch herself, could forget everything except floating.

Lately, she is tired of crowds, of the crush of her commute, of stepping over duffel bags left on train floors, of tourists who hesitate before getting on escalators, of delayed trains, routes that aren't running, and stations evacuated because something's left sitting on a platform. She has lived in London for more than a year now, but the evacuations from the tube make her feel she does not know anything. When she emerges on unfamiliar streets, she always has to take time to find the bus she needs, is always slightly panicked when she tells work that she will be late again.

She is late a lot. She is always overly optimistic about public transport, about making connections.

This morning though, she will be on time. She walks back to Tottenham Court Road Station after her swim; it is only 9.30. She will have time to get a sandwich on the way, make up for the breakfast she skipped, reach the office by ten (when the 'core hours' begin). But when she reaches the damp and pee-smelling entrance to the station, she sees a crowd bustling out. The station is being evacuated. 'The Underground is being shut down,' a man in a transit worker's jacket explains.

'The entire Underground?' she asks.

'Power surge,' he tells her.

What a fucking hopeless system, she thinks – its equipment old and rusty, the trains never replaced. She wonders what will happen when the Olympics come.

On the street everyone is wandering to the bus stops. She listens to the people on their mobiles: 'Yeah, a power cut. I don't know. I'll get there soon as I can.'

Now she'll be late for work, won't have breakfast. She glances into one of the coffee shops. Jammed, not worth going in. But she finds a bus stop where she can get a bus going to Bethnal Green, and she is pleased that she's found it without having to ask anyone.

The first buses that come are swarmed by people as soon as they stop, crowds waiting to board then filling the top and bottom. But when the 8 arrives almost no one is left and the upper level holds just a scattering of silent and tense looking commuters. She takes a seat next to the window and looks down on the prettily packaged West End Streets. The West End always makes her feel as if she's entered an illustration in a children's book, is walking through a world where everything's staged, but the East End feels like home to her – chaotic, broken, loud. She'll be at least 15 minutes late for work. The traffic inches ahead, stops. The passengers shift restlessly, but they do not speak to one another. And then she hears a sound: snorting, wild and hungry, as if someone is gobbling air. She turns around. A red-face man in a windbreaker, unshaven and wearing a baseball cap, has an ecstatic grin on his face. His smile widens suddenly – he notices that she's looked. 'The war is wrong!' he calls out. 'Tony Benn said so! Tony Benn said–'. She can't understand all of what he says; his exclamations don't fit together. He's raving, switches accents, snorts. He speaks like an American. Has he intuited where she's from?

She tries to focus on the unmoving traffic out the window, will it into motion. She tries to think about what a good first scene this would be in a movie, a set up for a Hollywood morality tale or meet-cute comedy. But the man's exclamations seem to surround her, block escape. 'Labour's no good!' he screams. 'Labour's not going to help us now!' he laughs.

She picks up the newspaper she hasn't been able to read, puts it in her bag, and steps into the aisle. Near the front, there's a seat next to a business-suited older man, but she has to pause for a minute so he can move his briefcase. The raving continues: 'Blair! Who's Blair? He's the one that got us into this war!' She tries to make eye contact with the business-suited suited man next to her, but he looks away. Finally, across the aisle, a woman with straight brown hair and a mumsy dress turns and raises her eyebrows: they smile at one another briefly then look away again.

Behind her, a mobile phone chirps. Then a man's voice: 'Yeah, I'm on the bus.' She turns. A suburban boy in his twenties is dressed in a leather jacket and beat up jeans; he's striving for a messiness that doesn't come natural to him. He has a Nokia pressed to his ear; his eyes first lighten with comprehension, then widen with alarm. 'Two explosions? Where?'

Everyone has heard it. The passengers glance at each other briefly, but they do not speak. No one will confess to eavesdropping. 'Are you sure?' the man asks. Then again, 'Are you sure?' He gets off the phone, fidgets uncomfortably. No one asks him for details, and he does not offer information to anyone.

Well of course there were explosions. Every time an Underground station is evacuated, you wonder if it's the real thing this time instead of someone forgetting their luggage. The posters on the Underground show an abandoned rucksack and a plea: Two ways to find out if it's suspicious: Call 999. The other doesn't bear thinking about. The drama of it annoyed her. She preferred the other one: If you see an unattended package don't touch, check with other passengers, inform station staff or dial 999. Everyone poked fun at the misplaced commas in those posters, how they seemed to say: If you see an unattended package, don't do anything at all.

The bus lurches ahead and she pulls her phone out of her bag and dials the number for work, but she only gets the answerphone, the out-of-hours message. Someone should be in by now — unless one of the young people they work with has had a crisis. She leaves a message explaining the delay, the problem with trains — sheepish, apologetic (again).

There were no more pronouncements about the war, no fast-forwarded analyses of New Labour, no snorting. She looks over her shoulder: the raving lunatic is gone. The business-suited man stands and she moves her knees to the side so he can get out too. Dozens of people get off at Liverpool Street Station. And, finally, they reach the East End, a landscape of normalcy: Cyber Kitchen and Paradise Cottage, the shabby storefronts erected after Second World War bombings had destroyed what was there before. She alights on Cambridge Heath Road, turns down Old Ford Road and then walks through the gated entrance to what was once a settlement house, a Georgian hulk of a building. And when she punches the code into the lock and opens the door, she realises, no one who should be there is there; it's dim, empty. She flicks on the light, climbs the stairs to an office filled with used furniture, and tosses her bag on the desk. Behind her, the door opens just a bit. Shy, plump Huma pokes her head inside. 'Hey,' she says to Huma. 'Did you hear something about the transport this morning?'

'My husband drove me,' Huma says. 'The Underground was shut.'

'Did you hear something about explosions?'

'Some bombs went off.'

'Bombs?'

The door opens again and this time, Yvette appears. She's wearing black jeans, a black jumper, and a black knit cap – like a nightclub version of a cat burglar. 'They made us get out of the Underground!' Yvette announces, outraged. 'I walked here from Stratford! In these!' She hoists her foot onto the chairseat, shows her black, high heeled boots. 'I couldn't even get a taxi!'

'Some bombs went off,' Huma says quickly.

Yvette's lowers her eyebrow. Is Huma sure?

Her phone pings. A text arrives with a green glow: *Are u ok?*

A message from Richard, who has become like an uncle to her, bear big and always hunched over with concern.

Yes, she texts back. *Made it to B Green. Are you Okay?*

Yes, we may hv to review this evng – rng u th afternn.

She texts Ivan, who is supposed to gets his chemo treatment at Bart's that day.

I'm at home, safe, he texts back.

And then: a cacophony of phone calls, texts.

Are   you   okay?

Ok roads closed here no-one in or out.

The radio is background noise, *The Guardian*'s webpage a blur, obsessively refreshed. Bombs have gone off. There are rumours about Stratford and Canary Wharf, rumours about hundreds of people killed.

Are you okay?

Where are you?

She remembers the day after the World Trade Center attack, the grounded airplanes and silent skies and immediate talk of revenge. She was not in New York; but longed to be there, back in the beat-up part of the city where she'd grown up. She'd moved to Miami two years before, a place where everyone seemed to be some kind of exile. So there was something eerie about seeing New York on television that night: the smoke and flames, the twisted steel, and the stunned expressions of the witnesses. In South Beach, the tourists and overhyped entrepreneurs existed in another world; they sat in cafes on Lincoln Road, walked down to the beach eating ice cream, exited air-conditioned shops in comically glossy halter dresses and white trousers. A man in a sharply ironed polo shirt predicted: 'There's gonna be a lot more opportunity here now. People are gonna be scared to go to New York after this.' He had on Ray Bans, looked past the man he was talking to like a distracted cocktail party guest.

On a lamp-post, there was a poster showing Osama Bin Laden in the crosshairs of a rifle. She imagined someone sitting at their computer on the day of the attack, dragging and dropping the image of the crosshairs over the image of Osama Bin Laden, carrying their graphic to Kinko's late at night and copying it onto oversized paper, walking and laughing with their friend while they taped up notices. She reached up and pulled down the poster, wadded it up, and threw it in a trash can, glaring at the middle-aged woman who watched her. Then she walked to where a second poster was, ripped that one down, and threw it away also. She kept going until she could not find any more posters.

She flew back to New York three weeks later, needing to see it again, needing to see the people she knew there. The airport was filled with boys in military uniforms; they sat on the floor next to their duffel bags, their phones plugged into the wall sockets so they could get in last calls. Some seemed frozen in disbelief, imagining what was to come; some had tears streaking down their faces. The older men in uniforms were waiting in the train stations, automatics held ready. They nodded when you passed, as if to tell you: This is for your own good, honey. She resigned herself to the bag searches, the pat down searches. We're just trying to protect you, ma'am. In Arizona, an aircraft mechanic told friends he was 'going to go out and shoot some towel-heads' and murdered a Sikh gas station owner. In Seattle two teenage boys had set fire to a mosque. In Chicago, a middle-aged man threatened to blow up a grocery store owned by Muslims. Then came Operation Enduring Freedom, announcements about the War on Terror, the Patriot Act.

She walks out to a quiet spot in the hall and phones Safiye.

Safiye reminds her of someone from New York — loud, in a constant state of outrage, unedited — but she is from Istanbul. She has henna-red hair, wears carefully ripped and restitched skirts she buys in shops off Brick Lane, biker boots, an old leather jacket. They get roaring drunk together on weekends, talk about the oddities of England.

As soon as she hears Safiye's voice, she finds herself weeping.

'I know about the bombings,' Safiye says. 'But I don't know why you're so emotional. People here don't know what to do when something like this happens. They're shutting everything down now. Do you have somewhere to stay? You should come to my house.'

Of course it's going to be impossible to get home without the Underground.

By one o'clock, the office shuts. Safiye is in Leyton — 15 minutes on the Underground, but she has no idea how to get there by bus.

Just come. 55 or 48 comes to bakers arms, Safiye texts. *Then 10 min walk.*

Huma walks with her to the bus stop. Sirens spin through the air. Central London buses have been taken off route, they've heard. But the 55 approaches. She and Huma hug one another goodbye and she climbs on. The bus is packed, people standing, leaning away to let her through. She climbs the stairs, peering around for an upper level seat. She sees a spare place and sets herself down with her bag on her lap. The bus goes, lurches, stops. She has no idea what route it's taking. She panics for a moment, thinking she might be going in the wrong direction. But she's not. And slowly, they edge ahead. There is nothing to do on this bus but look out at the slow-moving traffic, the bustling streets. What will change? Everything will change after this. Everyone on the bus is silent, tense. She thinks of pulling out the newspaper she bought that morning, then remembers its headlines will be about London winning the right to host the 2012 Olympics – obscenely irrelevant news.

She starts to text again:

I'm on my way to Safiye's. I thnk it will be a while before I can get back home.

And then a transit cop appears in a yellow jacket. What a time to check tickets, she thinks. They can't be serious.

'Anyone got any bags nearby that aren't theirs?' asks the cop, standing at the front of the aisle. 'Anyone got anything rolling around their feet?' He sounds like a tour guide, congenial under pressure, smiling every now and then.

They're checking the bus for bombs, she texts Safiye.

Take a cab, says the text she gets back.

But she knows there won't be any cabs. And the bus is moving again. It's moving slowly, but it moves. Then it stops. Everyone gets out. She follows the crowd and finds herself in front of a soot-streaked Victorian pub, looks up and sees a green rail bridge. Cars nose one another as they move into the traffic jam. Nothing is familiar. She asks a stout older woman with a short Afro if she knows Safiye's street and is directed down the road and told, 'Oh, it's a long way from here.' She asks and she walks and she asks and she walks until an hour later, she has reached Safiye's street and she knocks on Safiye's door and Safiye answers it.

*

They sit in the overgrown back garden, in wobbly plastic chairs, and they smoke roll ups, drink bad red wine. She looks at the lights moving slowly across the sky, grateful to see that planes are still flying. She has tried to phone the people she should phone in America, but it is impossible to get through. She remembers, suddenly, that she still has a wet swimming costume wadded up in a Sainsburys carrier bag, stuck into the bottom of her shoulder bag.

They'd picked up the wine, some parsley, and some tomatoes in the corner shop. A small television on in the corner showed people gathered outside the entrance to an Underground station, Tony Blair speaking at the G8 lectern, a helicopter landing in a field at Gleneagles. Behind the counter a group of men were debating one another in Turkish. No, not really debating – agreeing with one another, topping one another's statements.

'They think English people are making too much of the bombings,' Safiye explained, once they were back on the street. 'You get used to this in Turkey. And those guys are Kurds, so they're really used to it.'

She sleeps on a mattress they've brought into the front room. She is wearing an old t-shirt of Safiye's, is curled beneath an old satin duvet. The light from passing cars illuminating the room every now and then, the sound of wheels against asphalt reassuring her.

The next morning, she hears the TV, pulls on her trousers, finds Safiye watching it in the kitchen. Safiye pours them coffee. They sit there watching, eating toast.

On the little TV set, there's an image of a bus – the No 30 for Hackney Wick – with its top blown off, the roof a roll of red metal rolled up in front of it. The other bombs had gone off on the Underground, but this – the bus bombing – had happened after the Underground was shut, an hour later than the other bombings. And she finds it such a strange sight – the bus blown apart in central London – that her throat closes. The newsreader tells them that some of the rumours from the day before were wrong – there weren't six places bombed, but three Underground stations and this bus. Then there are images of nearby streets very early in the morning. The streets look quieter than usual, but there are a few people out. They appear before the camera, microphone in front of them. A newspaper deliveryman explains, 'I feel very very bad about the people who were killed. My heart goes out to them. But, I also think that, when you live in a free society, you have to risk this happening. So we're going to have to risk this happening.'

And she feels weirdly, unexpectedly, reassured. There is no talk of reordering life, of redoubling security, of revenge.

Safiye gets a text on her phone and announces: 'The transport's running again.'

12 WRITING THE ROUTES

London buses have had numbers for their routes since the Vanguard Bus Company, taking its cue from the German Baedeker guide book to the capital, first introduced them on its vehicles in 1906. For many of us, these numbered routes become intimately intertwined with our experiences of the city as a whole, governing where we go, what we see and what we subsequently remember about the places have visited in London over the years, as tourists, commuters or residents.

THE REASONING BEHIND THE NUMBERS OF THE ROUTES

Mark Hadfield

Last week I was waiting for the bus and wondered why they are numbered as they are, and why some have letters in front of a number.

I emailed the following note to TfL:

> *I just have a simple question that I'm hoping you can explain to me. Most buses are a number, but some are letters and numbers. So I catch the No 55 to work. But I also see the C2 when I'm around Old Street.*
>
> *I'm just wondering can you explain the number system to me please? And also, who decides which number goes on which route?*
>
> *Thanks*

Well, yesterday I received this response:

> *We appreciate the importance of route numbers to London's bus passengers. They might be described as the shop window by which passengers recognise a route. In some cases — particularly with regard the long-established routes — a particular number may even evoke affection.*
>
> *The numbering of London's bus routes has evolved slowly since the earliest days of regular bus operation in the capital. In a few instances, it is possible to trace the lineage of sections of existing routes back to their identically numbered predecessors from horse-drawn days. You may be interested to know that in 2 years time one London bus route will incontrovertibly reach its centenary. Route 24 first started operating between Pimlico and Hampstead Heath under The General Omnibus Company in 1911, and since then the route has been subject only to minor changes to accommodate one-way systems.*

There is a tradition for route planners within Transport
for London and its forerunner organisations deliberately
to respect the past by re-using numbers that have local
historic associations. That is the case with route 55 that
you mention. It was first introduced between Central
London and Leyton during a major service re-organisation
around 40 years ago. Its number was a deliberate echo
of a trolleybus route 555 that had run along Old Street to
Hackney and beyond some years previously, and also of
the tram route 55 that the trolleybus had replaced.

London Transport operated the capital's buses in various
guises between 1933 and 1984. Until 1970 the organisation
also had responsibility for routes in a doughnut-like ring of
the outer surrounding countryside. The routes that served
this area utilised numbers between 300 and 499, and 800
between and 899, with the 700 series set aside for Green
Line coaches. With the resulting pressure on available
numbers for new routes in the Central area (operated by
red buses), in 1968 London Transport first started using the
system of prefix numbers that continues to this day. The idea
is that the prefix letter should designate the place around
which the routes cluster — P for Peckham in the case of
routes P4, P5, and P13; E for Ealing in the case of series E1 to
E11, for instance. The C in C2 stands for Central. The prefix
'N', however, denotes a night bus.

Now, with over 700 routes within Greater London alone, it is
necessary for us to maintain this system. When we introduce
a new route — or make alterations to an existing route by
splitting it — the last digit or digits of the historic 'parent'
route are used wherever possible, so that passengers might
associate the incoming route with its predecessor. This was
the case in 2003, for instance, when route 414 was chosen
as the number for the new route between Maida Hill and
Putney Bridge, which was intended to augment historic
route 14 south of Hyde Park Corner.

email exchange originally published on That Gormandizer Man blog, 12 March 2009

On a No 73
bus in 1983

GLIMPSES THROUGH THE WINDOW OF A NUMBER 73 BUS

Roger Mills

The No 73 took me everywhere I ever wanted to go. A bus as an educational tool. And during the late 1960s and early 1970s the only thing I was interested in being educated about was an *alternative* London.

If every bus route tells a story, the No 73 from beginning to end is one of cultural enlightenment. I grew up in Stoke Newington, northeast London, when it was still a working-class district. Its face was one of respectability and industriousness, albeit carrying a slightly peeved expression after 1965 when it was subsumed into the more boisterous borough of Hackney. A good place but not the most thrilling. Excitement was elsewhere, and the 73 bus was the device to get there.

On Saturdays, the ultimate destination listed on the front of the red double-decker was RICHMOND, which sounded like an impossibly far-off place. Was that even in London? A memory related to the name was submerged somewhere in my mind. Often I rode the route with friends, other times, with perhaps the smell of a spring morning in my nostrils, I would set off on my own, just to see where it took me.

Leaping on to the back platform I would make my way upstairs. And always take the front seat on the left. The conductor's *ting-ting* of the bell was an unlikely fanfare for the promise of adventure to come.

The bus set off from Stoke Newington Common. I didn't know then that young Mod-turned-Hippie-turned-Glam-Rock-megastar, Marc Bolan, had grown up there just round the corner to me. But I was aware of the literary associations connected with Church Street, which the bus then lurched into; Daniel Defoe lived in a house there and the American writer of macabre short stories, Edgar Allen Poe, attended a school a little further along. Both residences have long vanished. As passengers began to clatter of the stairs of the bus, the air thickened with cigarette smoke.

It took an age for the bus to crawl into Islington's Essex Road and if you look at a map you'll see that that a long time was spent getting not very far at all, the route hugging the edge of old Stokey as if it didn't really want to leave. So why didn't I take a tube instead? The answer is that there wasn't one! There was once a theory that Stoke Newington would never be colonised by the middle class because the transport links were so rubbish. That idea was demolished with the arrival of teachers and social workers and all manner of bright young 'creatives' in their wake.

Then, it was Islington that was the up-and-coming cultural hub, the junction at the Angel providing access to the King's Head Theatre on Upper Street, a Victorian pub with a theatre in a back room which had served as a boxing ring and pool hall, and Camden Passage, a narrow lane carrying the exotic scent of the 60s, lined with fancy-looking shops flogging antiques, vintage clothing and bric-á-brac; all of it fascinating, none of it affordable.

The Scala was an independent picture house in the shadow of King's Cross Station, where the bus moved on to. Here, I was introduced the occult-inspired *magick* cinema of American outsider Kenneth Anger, and attended regular all-nighters. The area had acquired something of a reputation in those days. I went to a showing of John Schlesinger's *Midnight Cowboy* one summer evening; the events in the street while going in, what happened on the screen, and the real-life scenes outside after the film had finished, all ravelling into a seamless, down-at-heel whole.

The stone masks of comedy and tragedy above the entrance to the Royal Academy of Dramatic Arts are well-viewed from the upper deck of the 73 as it moves through Bloomsbury before cautiously chugging past Harry Hyam's monster, the Centre Point building — a 33-storey finger raised to the rest of London — stacked uncomfortably close to the second-hand book-buyer's paradise of Charing Cross Road. Then into the already run-down eastern end of Oxford Street. Richard Branson's Virgin Records store stood on the corner, the stench of 'sell-out' apparent from the minute they stopped selling bootleg discs.

Two places that I travelled to frequently with my mates were on tributary roads running off Europe's busiest shopping street: the Marquee Club on Wardour Street, and the bookshop, Dark They Were, and Golden Eyed, on Berwick Street. The former, having started as a jazz club was by the early 1970s the place to go for loud and sweaty rock bands, and the latter, named after a Ray Bradbury short story, was always packed with a legion of long-haired men — they were mostly men — wearing army surplus greatcoats, rummaging through shelf upon shelf of SF and Fantasy paperbacks and imported American 'underground' comics.

From my vantage point at the top front of the bus I always managed to pick out the same middle-aged man, wearing the sort of cap championed by the young Bob Dylan, hoisting a long pole with a mysterious message on the placard attached to it. It remained constant, with slight grammar-busting variations down the years:

LESS LUST

FROM LESS

PROTEIN:

LESS FISH

BIRD, MEAT

CHEESE

EGG; BEANS

PEAS; NUTS

and SITTING

For a few pence, Stanley Green also supplied a self-printed booklet explaining his message. But as I never bought one, I never found out what it was. Another regular fixture on hot sunny afternoons were the robed and dancing shaven-headed devotees of the Radha Krishna Temple who would snake between the shoppers at alarming speed, clanging finger cymbals and chanting the Hare Krishna Mantra, later put onto record by Beatle George Harrison.

Beyond Regent Street, the more classy end of Oxford Street asserted itself, emphasised by sculptor Barbara Hepworth's *Winged Figure* perched on the outside of the John Lewis department store, before the bus approached Marble Arch and Hyde Park corner. After being overlooked from the very start of journey by residential and commercial buildings, the open air and blinding light freed up by the large expanse of flat park before me was exhilarating. So too were the times listening to the crackpots and anarchists spouting their opinions at Speakers' Corner, and one glorious sun-baked Saturday in July watching the Rolling Stones perform free amongst long-haired hippies and Hell's Angels.

From there, the 73 bus curled into Park Lane and Knightsbridge at speed, my fingers gripping the back of the seat in front of me as if I were being spun in a slingshot fairground attraction: the Hilton Hotel, Harrods, and little mews flats of the type inhabited by Roger Moore's TV *Saint*. They breathe a different air there.

I got to see a lot of major bands at the Albert Hall a little farther along the route. Rock was getting too big for clubs like the Marquee, and stadium venues hadn't yet appeared. Then one day we found out about Kensington Market, a set of indoor stalls with all sort of hippie gear being sold by girls so pretty that I was too intimidated to approach them. Future Queen Supremo Freddie Mercury sold tat here.

That was usually as far as me and my mates got. But I had an unexplained ache to complete the 73 route from beginning to end on my own. It was no whim, more a calling: destination as destiny. On Saturdays the route finished at Richmond, so I was perplexed to find out on the crisp autumn Sunday afternoon of my sojourn it was extended to Hounslow via Twickenham.

When I crushed the coppers into the conductor's hand, telling him that I wanted to go the whole way, he gave me a curious look as the long paper tongue rolled out of the ticket machine hanging round his neck.

After Kensington Market, I found myself moving into unfamiliar territory.

The bus passed Derry & Tom's department store, its fabulous roof garden something I knew only from the dystopian novel, *A Cure for Cancer*, featuring counter-culture, shape-shifting agent of anarchy, Jerry Cornelius. In Michael Moorcock's imagination the gardens come under machine gun attack from a hovering copter, the branches of its fruit trees whipping back and forth under the thrashing rotors. When I actually got to visit this elevated retreat years later and wander through its Tudor Courts and Spanish Garden I was a little disappointed to find no evidence of bullet holes in the Moorish pergolas.

Apart from the imperial structure of the Olympia Stadium looming up impressively to my right there was nothing comparable thereafter to make an impression, lacking as I was knowledge of cultural markers on the route from then on. Miles of endless tarmac were gobbled up beneath the wheels of the bus as the sky darkened. I felt, rather than saw, the oppressiveness of the looming Hammersmith flyover as the No 73 passed beneath it. Lights were being switched on in expensive houses, bright eyes charting my progress and shiny black doors like mouths seeming to ask what business I had in this part of the city.

Other passengers on more justifiable journeys came and went. The bus filled up and emptied out. The conductor must have been wondering if I was setting up home permanently on the top deck. The driver probably thought I'd died up there.

Passing over Kew Bridge and the flat, chill waters flowing beneath it I realised that I had started my journey far too late on this November day, not realising just how long it would take. Richmond just didn't *seem* like a far-off place, it *was* a far-off place.

That memory I had of Richmond, I realised, was not my own; but washed up from the underground river of the rock-and-roll collective mind. Somewhere in the distance the Thames lapped at the shores of Eel Pie Island where the Island Hotel had once harboured bands at the hard-edged rhythm and blues end of the scale. That was in Richmond, wasn't it? Or further along in Twickenham? What I did know was that The Who had long since embarked for world fame, so I wasn't expecting a guitar-smashing and amp-shredding rendition of 'My Generation' as a reward at the end of my journey — even if I were able to locate it in what was now the pitch-black evening. I began to worry about the time.

I decided to disembark at Richmond where I, the last surviving passenger, staggered off the bus through the haze of a day's accumulated nicotine. I realised that I had no idea of an alternative return journey home other than by the same means. The very thought was exhausting. But that's what I had to do, arriving home late in the cold wintery night.

I can't claim that I actually made the route from beginning to end; they kept changing the destination. In the same way, I never got to fully engage with that other London I was looking for. I was so enamoured by the changes going on about me I had never thought about the ultimate destination. But I'll always treasure those glimpses through the window of a No 73 bus.

FAMOUS STOPS

Dickon Edwards

According to *Heat* Magazine, there's yet another reality TV show coming up called *Fame Academy*. Apparently it's a cross between *Popstars* and *Big Brother*. And the house the contestants will be in is... up the road from me. In Highgate Village, near The Flask pub, 'next to Sting's house'.

I had no idea Sting lived near me. In eight years of living here, I've never seen him ONCE at the 134 bus stop.

He must take the 210.

Diary, 17 September 2002

AHMED ON THE 274

Elizabeth Wilson

For a long time I lived in Camden Square. Adjacent Agar Grove marked one of many complex boundaries between the gentrified and the unreconstructed corners of this backwater and along it the 274 bus operated an almost door to door service from my house to Selfridges. It bustled me past Primrose Hill, round the top of Regent's Park and down Baker Street to the emporium and its hollow promises of desires fulfilled.

A single storey cross-town route, the 274 felt more like a countryside route than an inner-city journey. There were the same familiar faces week after week, year after year. There was the bony, red haired, ill-tempered old Irishman, always solitary, never smiling, a refugee from the years when the mansions in my square, now gentrified to within an inch of their lives, were rooming houses for Irish railway workers. Agar Town was described by Dickens in *Dombey and Son*, when the railways were being built in the 1840s and the railways still coil across and under every part of Camden.

There was the once-beautiful 80-year-old whose startling sapphire eyes were set in a crab-apple face. There was my daughter's friend's mother from the 'bad' estate. There was the neighbour whose post kept being mis-delivered to my door. There were school kids who forgot their ID and pensioners who clutched their bus passes. They greeted the driver when they got on and thanked him as they left and in between they chatted to friends and cooed at babies in buggies.

The journey took in several tourist attractions. It was punctuated by flurries of activity as families were decanted outside the Zoo. During the cricket season it filled up with big men in blazers who shouted across the aisle about the test match before getting out at Lords. On Fridays, Muslims alighted and thronged the pavement outside the mosque. At Baker Street a long queue of tourists outside 221B Baker Street, fictional home of the fictional detective, Sherlock Holmes, waited patiently to view the fake home of a person who never existed.

Baker Street was also the stop for Madame Tussauds and it was here that I first noticed The Driver – when he actually *left the bus* to direct some tourists to the wax works. Passengers became restless as they saw him disappear round the corner, followed by a trusting Japanese family.

How little noticed are the drivers who ferry the masses around town, but now I really looked at this one and saw a hook-nosed, wild-eyed brigand with an untamed beard and spotless white cap. 'It's part of the service,' he grinned. 'Apologies for the wait.'

Somehow no-one minded.

I began to realise that everyone knew him. 'Oh yes, the one with the beard! Ahmed! He's a character!' So fellow passengers even knew his name!

He wasn't the sort of driver that piously refuses to let you out at the lights or accelerates as soon as they see a pedestrian approaching a crossing. He halted by the curb if he saw a puffing, flailing figure desperately, hopelessly hoping to beat the bus to the next stop. He greeted each person as they got on the bus and cried: 'Go carefully!' and 'Have a nice day!' when they left.

Once I failed to notice him when I boarded the bus, but as we approached Selfridges I saw it was he and walked down to the front to say hello. He had noticed me, it seemed. 'I could tell you were lost in your dreams.'

'My favourite tennis player just won a tournament.' This was 2009 when I was a big Roger Federer fan and the Swiss star was beginning to regain his rightful status after the previous dreadful year when Nadal had beaten him at Wimbledon.

'Roger Federer!' cried the driver. 'He played really well.'

Hearing this, a woman behind me stood up. 'I'm from Switzerland,' she said. 'Wasn't it wonderful! He needed that.' The Swiss player had just beaten Nadal on clay – a rare event.

The traffic stalled and the three of us talked tennis and Federer until we reached the Selfridges stop. I was surprised the driver knew so much about the sport. The Swiss lady and I shook hands on the pavement. 'Take care now!' shouted the driver. 'Don't max out your credit card!'

The neighbour whose post was regularly delivered to me (she was No 9 in a nearby road, I in the square: 'The postman seems to think No 9 any old road is good enough,' she said) coincided with me at the bus stop.

'I wonder if it will be Ahmed today,' she said. 'You know, I think we should put him in for an MBE. The other day there was a crowd of boys who got on the bus and they were behaving really badly. It was getting quite unpleasant. But *he* just gave them a bag of sweets he fished out and told them to hand the sweets round to all the passengers. And they did and the whole thing calmed down. He made them feel important. Everyone was laughing and smiling.'

We gathered a number of testimonials and filled out the form. It was months before we heard back and were very disappointed to be unsuccessful. Surely a more imaginative committee – or whoever decides these things – would have understood that Ahmed improved the experience of daily life just as much as a lollipop lady or Dusty Springfield.

A few years later I moved away from the Square to a different part of Camden. I'd dreaded losing my 274 taxi to Selfridges, but then the department store moved startlingly up-market, (bespoke tailoring and Balenciaga instead of Toast and Shirin Guild) so I didn't miss it as much as I'd expected. Now a different little 'country' bus, the 214, ambled down from the self-satisfied heights of Highgate to deposit me outside the British Library.

The stop by the Heath was a gathering place of sorts with a new set of familiar faces: the woman in her 30s who always dressed in 1940s vintage; the friendly American; the retired psychiatrist from the next road, the Labour Party stalwart. Mid-afternoon was the time of the school girls attired in kilts, ties and blazers, their uniform a public expression of some weird English attempt to recruit them to the armed forces or compulsory lesbianism.

As passengers waited, they watched the dog owners making for the Heath. The dogs came in every hue and pattern. There were red setters, Dalmatians in their showy black and white, snuffling pugs, vivacious poodles, loping greyhounds, Rhodesian ridgebacks, cockapoos and labradoodles. The owners by contrast formed a drab army in their uniform of dingy nylon puffa jackets, jeans (skinny for the under 50s, baggy for the over 70s) and anoraks, pretensions to style and elegance having migrated to their colourful pets.

One day I climbed onto the bus, self-absorbed as usual. Only as we stopped and started through the permanent traffic holdup of the Kentish Town Road, did I notice the driver waving and calling out to passers-by. He seemed to know everyone.

Ahmed!

'You're stalking me!' he cried in manic glee, with his wild cackle of laughter.

'It could be the other way round,' I said. 'How lovely to see you.'

And so I rode on Ahmed's magic bus once more. He lifted the bus ride from drab routine into a 'day out', borne along by his hilarity. Sometimes he pretended the bus wasn't going to stop. On one occasion he saw me running to catch it, waited until I'd reached the door, then drove off, only to stop again a yard further up the curb. Another day it was: 'this stop's closed, madam' to the woman waiting to get out, before startling her a second time by opening the doors after all. Whatever he did it was always to make the passengers laugh, even the bad jokes: 'Beware of pickpockets. They're operating in this area. I know – I'm their boss.'

I wondered if his wife found him a bit of a handful.

'Drive carefully Ahmed. No cowboy stuff!' I said when I got off the bus. It was not that he ever drove badly, but I half expected him one day to turn the tables and drive us all away to a mystery destination. I liked to imagine a hint of danger, an undercurrent to his manic glee. I liked to imagine him a modern Pied Piper who would one day entice his busload to follow him into the unknown. With his flashing black eyes and white teeth, his untamed beard and Muslim cap he could have been the lord of misrule. I even wondered if one day he might join the ghost riders in the sky with their hot breath and flashing eyes eternally galloping through the clouds in pursuit of the devil.

But that was too fanciful and missed the whole point of Ahmed. Ahmed's mission was to raise his passengers' spirits, to make real the empty cliché of 'have a nice day'. The unexpected moments when he startled us was as when a child is tossed into the air in fun. It was always party time on Ahmed's bus. It was a celebration of everyday life. Often on other buses I saw my fellow passengers lost in careworn indifference or retreated myself into glum introspection. Then the bus ride dwindled to an empty interlude between two places, one of life's intermissions. Ahmed brought the bus ride alive and with Ahmed at the wheel every moment was worth living.

SIGHTSEEING DRINKING GAME

Patrice Lawrence

Bailey was 20 minutes early and he hadn't even been walking that fast. Dad said when he and Mum first came to Dalston, it was rough, with drug couriers on bikes outside the betting shop and prostitutes in the abandoned houses. Now there were fountains in the square by the library and they'd even done up the kebab shop with red leather banquettes. The bar opposite the station was jammed, with more people outside, smoking. Bailey could hear live music, something folky.

The workmen's barriers by the station made the pavement too narrow and everyone walking past was jostling him. He moved just inside the entrance, where he could still see both bus stops.

38, 242, 277. Bus after bus pulled up. People poured into the bars and around Bailey, into the station. He checked the time. It was just past nine. Maybe it was a joke. He couldn't be sure it was Indigo who messaged him. Austin was probably crouched down in the kebab shop filming Bailey's stress. Another bus, a 56, stopped across the road. Bailey moved out of the station. Was that Indigo, standing in the aisle? It was hard to see. The bus pulled away and he waited for the mass of people to clear. God, it was Indigo. It was like his heart gulped. She looked amazing. She was wearing a white dress with matching high-heeled sandals and a black leather jacket. Her hair was backcombed and rolled up, with a few strands hanging down her neck.

She spotted him and waved. He weaved his way through the queuing traffic, towards her.

He said, 'You look good.'

She smiled. Her eyeshadow made her eyes more copper, like in the common room that time. Eyes just like her granddad's. Bailey had to shove that – JJ, his parents, all of it – to the back of his thoughts. Just for the minute. Just until he worked it all out.

He said, 'What do you fancy doing?'

'I have a plan.'

'Cool.' Because he didn't. Even if there'd been one, it would have collapsed into a muddle as soon as he saw her. She opened a sparkly shoulder bag. 'I brought something.'

He looked inside. 'Tequila?'

A small bottle of it, complete with a bright yellow label decorated with a cartoon donkey in a sombrero.

She said, 'Do you like it?'

'I've never had it. Last year, there was a party and Saskia had so many shots she ended up in hospital for the night. It put me off.'

'Yeah, anything to do with Saskia would put me off too.' He laughed. 'Where did you get it?'

'The first shop that didn't ask for ID.'

'How many shops did you go to?'

'Just one.'

Their eyes met and she laughed. 'Next time I might buy the banana cream rum or the melon liqueur.' She shifted closer to him to let a woman with a trolley pass. Bailey smelled perfume, something sweet and heavy.

She said, 'You ever played London Bingo?'

'No. What happens?'

'Not quite sure, but I was on a coach once, coming back from a camping trip. Some kid called Zac had a bag full of those miniature bottles, brandy and stuff. We all had a list of different things, cow, tractor, whatever. If you saw one, you had to have a drink.'

'Didn't the staff notice?'

Indigo laughed. 'They were too knackered after a week with us lot! They only woke up when Zac's twin brother vommed. So you up for it?'

'Do you have a list of London stuff?'

'I'm gonna trust you to tell me. I haven't lived in London much.'

'And it's a shot every time we see somewhere famous?'

Indigo rummaged in her bag and brought out two egg cups. One was shaped like Humpty Dumpty, the other one was plain white. 'My foster mum doesn't drink. It was the best I could do. Classy, right?'

He laughed. 'Completely.'

Indigo hooked her arm through his. 'I reckon we should take the first bus and change after each shot.'

'Why?'

'Just to make it more interesting.'

Indigo's leather jacket was brushing against his arm and for a second, her hip bumped his. Sorry, Austin. Even the Black Widow in her skin-tight leggings couldn't be better than this.

A 56 came first, heading towards St Bart's Hospital. 'Come on,' Indigo said. 'Upstairs. That's the best view.' The seats at the very front were taken. Indigo clicked towards the back and sat in the corner by a window. She patted the seat next to her. 'Hurry up! We might miss something.'

Her dress sprawled across the gap between the seats, bright white against the blue checks. She pulled it over her lap to give him more room. When she leaned forward, he could see their reflections in the window, faces cheek to cheek.

The bus headed across the traffic lights at the junction and down towards Essex Road.

Bailey said, 'See that?'

'The big church?'

'I went to nursery there.'

Indigo handed Bailey the Humpty Dumpty egg cup. She fiddled around in her bag and brought out the tequila. 'New rule. If it's a landmark to you, it counts.'

She poured a shot and grinned at him. He smiled back. His throat had to be like a letterbox – click open, click shut. Down in one. He breathed in. His nostrils smouldered and – whoosh – it hit his belly.

Indigo gave him an approving look. 'Excellent work.'

Had she done this before? Not just with kids on a coach, but with other guys? Maybe Bailey had to pass some kind of test. A couple of African women came and sat bang in front of them. It was like he and Indigo were cut off from the rest of the bus.

'Look!' Indigo tapped the window. 'This one's mine!'

They were passing the old bingo hall. A sign said that it now belonged to a church. 'You? In there with all the old grannies?'

'No! One of my foster mums was a proper bingo addict, though. She kept coming home with toasters.'

'When was that?'

'Can't remember. It's a bit of a blur, sometimes.' She poured herself a shot and knocked it back quickly. She blinked. 'That's rough, man.'

'No wonder the guy in the shop was happy to get rid of it.'

She wiped her lips. 'Yeah. Best off without it.' She rang the bell. 'Come on.'

'Where?'

'We're supposed to change buses. We should have got off at the church.'

Bailey was still holding his egg cup. He shoved it in his jacket pocket and followed Indigo downstairs and off the bus. A 38 pulled up straight away. That would take them past Sadler's Wells. And Finsbury Town Hall. Four landmarks in and he wouldn't be able to speak.

'Hurry up!' She took his hand and led him up the stairs, her dress swishing round her hips and legs. She'd played it all casual, but Bailey could feel his heartbeat thud as their palms touched.

The top deck was busy. They had to sit separately across the aisle from each other until they reached Angel tube station. Then virtually everyone got off and they moved to the front. Indigo took off her jacket and leaned forward against the rail. The dress was sleeveless, with thin shoulder straps and cut in a V at the front, gaping as she moved. He looked away.

They passed Sadler's Wells. Bailey kept quiet. Finsbury Town Hall. They passed that one safely too.

Indigo shifted in the seat so her thigh rubbed against his. He nearly pressed back. Not yet, though.

'Bailey?'

'Yeah.'

'There's something I have to ask you.'

You knew about Horatio all along. You sent JJ to test me. I did plan to tell you. He turned towards her.

She said, 'Did your mum say anything about me?'

He nearly blew out his cheeks, right in front of her. 'She said she recognised you.'

'What did she say?'

'She remembered doing art stuff with you at a PRU in Medway.'

'Is that it?'

She told me your life history. She warned me away. 'More or less.'

'I was in a special unit. I got put there because . . . because I used to fly off the handle.' Indigo was staring out at the road. He had to lean in close to hear her. 'They said it was like I'd go a bit mad.'

He said, 'Is that what happened at school?'

Her cheeks were starting to redden. Should he put his arm round her? Or would she think he was just feeling sorry for her? The bus was passing a long stretch of high wall with a garden behind it.

He said, 'That's Gray's Inn, famous barristers' chambers.'

He took Humpty out of his pocket and offered it to her. She unwrapped the bottle and sloshed in more alcohol. It slid down his throat like greasy bleach.

Indigo replaced the bottle. 'I might have yelled at your mum. I was a bit hyper, then.'

'She's used to people yelling at her.'

'Like who?'

'Kids at school. Parents. Even a couple of teachers, when she's had to tell them about something they've done wrong.'

'Have you ever yelled at her?'

'Not that I can remember. Maybe when I was little.'

She was staring out of the window again. No landmarks, just buses and taxis and the hi-vis cyclists. Suddenly, she twisted around to face him. 'It's from him.'

'What is?'

'The thing inside me, the thing that makes me blow my top. You know like when kids have a tantrum?'

'Yeah.'

'It's like that. The counsellors reckon it's taken longer for me to deal with the anger. But it's not that. My dad had it. A thing. He passed it on to me. It waits until there's a trigger and then it goes mental and I'm not there anymore, it's just the thing.'

He reached across for her hand. She let him take it. He should tell her that he knew there was more to her. There was the Indigo who'd laughed in his kitchen. The Indigo whose face lit up when he said he liked Blondie too. It was all these things about her that made him want to be here now. But his mouth was a mush of words. A few of them could be the right ones, but how would he know? He could keep holding her hand, though, tight in his.

He said, 'Do you remember the first time it happened?'

'Sort of. I think I was about four or five. I was doing a painting at the kitchen table and I had it in my head that I was going to send it to my mum, even though I knew I couldn't.' She frowned. 'There was a really fat, grey cat and it jumped up and knocked water all over my picture. And then … it felt like there was a snake inside my stomach. Something big, like a python. The stupid cat had woken it up and I could feel it untwisting itself and stretching. And the weird thing is, it was horrible and nice at the same time. It was like, before that, I was just empty and I didn't know. The thing sort of made me feel full. And then it burst out.

After that it's a bit blank. I'd torn up my painting. And I'd thrown the jar of water against a wall. There was glass and painty water everywhere. I wasn't very popular.'

Bailey said, 'I can imagine you weren't.'

She gave him a little smile, then turned to the window. Shit. He had said the wrong thing. He'd known it as soon as he heard himself. She'd poured all that out to him and that's what he gave back. I can imagine you weren't. A bit jokey, a bit too light. Something one of his old aunties would say. No wonder she turned away from him.

He said, 'I'm sorry. It must have been pretty scary when you realised what happened.'

'Yeah.' He'd got that right, at least, because she shifted back towards him. 'It was. I was sent to a counsellor but I didn't want to talk about it in case it happened again. I got moved on too. But I think that's because I painted the cat's ears red.'

She slid her hand out of his and rested it on his knee. 'Where are we?'

'Coming up to Shaftesbury Avenue. If we get off now, we can walk to Covent Garden.'

'That's famous,' she said. 'Very famous.'

Indigo hooked her arm back through Bailey's as soon as they were off the bus. He liked that, she could tell, and she could feel his body move with every step.

from Indigo Donut *(2017)*

A POLITICAL PASSENGER

Michael Foot on the No 24 bus

I used to see Michael Foot of a morning when catching the No 24 bus to Westminster in the late 1980s. An elderly man then, he appeared to a watchful acolyte new to London as a compelling blend of apparent fragility and prehensile strength. I imagined him having braved the vertical steps to the upper desk with their wicked twist in the well, clasping his walking stick and hauling himself up the handrail like a mountaineer as the bus careered down the road. He would sit bundled up in the frontmost seat, right in the corner and see out the journey to Parliament. It was the most see-saw seat on the bus and I was never sure whether he sat there for privacy or the discomfort suited him.

Comment posted on the BBC News website, 3 March 2010

My other lasting memory of Foot came from his final months as a serving MP, then in his 70s. At the end of the day, MPs would cluster around the member's entrance of the House of Commons — some to climb into government cars, others into their own big cars, and still others waiting for a taxi. But rain or shine, Michael Foot would politely refuse all offers of a lift and stomp off in a serviceable coat waving his stick — off to catch the No 24 bus to Hampstead.

Diane Abbott, as part of her tribute to the former Labour leader on her website

A young Joe Kerr, Bethnal Green, 1980

HOW LONG'S THE NEXT ONE?

Or, from on the back to up front

Joe Kerr

The bus conductor yells out 'Two on the top only'. He counts off the lucky couple and shepherds them towards the stairs, then stretches both arms square across the edge of the platform, denying access to any more of the desperate crowd swarming around his bus. He rings the bell three times to tell the driver they're full up, and not to stop again until he gets another bell, and they edge away from the stop, leaving swarms of frustrated would-be passengers behind.

A despairing voice cries out: 'How long's the next one?', and the conductor gleefully hurls back the appropriate response, designed to further enrage the seething public: '27 feet and 6 inches, just like this one!' In all of my years of using this response I was only bettered once, when one sharp soul came straight back at me with the reply: 'And does it have a shithouse on it like this one?'

Such ripostes may not be the most humorous ever, but they were deeply cherished by my former profession; it was the birthright of conductors, who were gifted few chances to wreak revenge on a hostile public, to trot out their set of stock responses on such occasions. Another favourite was deployed when the conductor yelled out 'Last Stop, All Change!' and some despairing passenger complained: 'It said Aldgate on the front!'. To which the inevitable reply was: 'Well it says India on the tyres, but we're not going there either!'.

But that answer of '27 feet and six inches' — the length of a standard Routemaster Bus, incidentally — also neatly describes the progress that my career as a busman has made over the years: my first proper job as a youngster was as a bus conductor, or *on the back* in bus parlance, and now decades later I work as a bus driver, or *up front* as we once used to say. OK, so a modern bus is a bit longer than that — up to 36 feet and 10 inches for the new Boris Buses — but please allow the conceit, for it gives a useful frame for this essay.

Black Lives Matter placards adorn a No 243 bus at a vigil for Rashan Charles, who died after a violent encounter with police in 2018

On the Back, Route 243

As the long drought summer of 1976 drew to a close I finally escaped from my remote rural village and made it to London. A recent report claimed that year to be the happiest ever for the British, but it certainly wasn't for me. I was an ill-educated, misinformed and immature 18-year-old, with no sense of a viable future, and I was entering adulthood in a country that seemed to be falling apart at the seams. Fortunately, the buses gave me a short and sharp education in the ways of the world, and I remain grateful for that.

My interview was short and sweet, as my former school had written a reference that suggested such a lowly trade was beneath the dignity of its pupils, an attitude that so enraged the London Transport recruitment officer that he offered me the job on the spot. A short time afterwards, I presented myself at the legendary Chiswick Works, where bus crews were trained. To pass through the gates there was to enter a bygone age, already an anachronism then, and now wholly disappeared. It was the spiritual home of London Transport, that great paternal corporation which had spent more than 40 years serving the public and had a total self-belief in its particular way of doing things. Raw recruits such as myself were signing on for a way of life and not merely a job, in which provision was made for every social and cultural need that 'The Transport' could imagine: garage football teams organised into a competitive league; staff excursions (on a bus naturally) to such exotic destinations as Brighton or Calais; snooker rooms; home sales of own-brand Griffin foodstuffs, most memorably enormous sacks of teabags; and even a flying club where staff could gain their wings.

After a week of fairly easy training in tickets and money, of the 'Johnny and Jenny get on the bus with 20p' type, our final exercise was to commandeer an old RT bus and then set off down the road, all of us in full uniform and each equipped with a Gibson ticket machine, every trainee taking it turn to issue tickets, whilst the rest acted as passengers. I remember the shock on the face of an old lady jumping on the bus at traffic lights, only to be confronted with 20-odd bus conductors and no passengers! This was also my first experience of Londoners' propensity to jump on anything large and red without ever thinking to check either number or destination, and then to complain loudly when neither suited.

And then at last to my garage, Stamford Hill in north London (garage code SF), a former London County Council tram shed that had only lost its trolleybuses 14 years earlier. I came to regret working there eventually, as trolleybuses never really went into central London, so their replacement routes, which by and large simply replicated their predecessors, were never as glamorous as the legendary old central bus routes that I idolised. However at the time I loved talking to the former trolleybus crews, many of whom had still not got over the loss of their much-loved vehicles, and had never really taken to the new-fangled Routemasters. My first week was spent in the care of a wonderful old crew, Cyril and Rosy, who had worked together forever and regaled me with tales of trying to hook themselves back onto the overhead wire with the long wooden pole slung on the side of the bus, whilst in the midst of a dense London smog. Individual bus crews, it should be noted, worked together on a permanent basis: the official term was that you were 'married', which wasn't so far from the truth given the 40 or more hours a week you spent together.

I have vivid memories of my first day working by myself on the back. It was a Saturday late shift on route 149, and the first journey just after 4pm was to go up to a little-used terminus point called Tottenham Snells Park, and then turn round and enter service. I soon found out why as we pulled up outside White Hart Lane stadium just after a quarter to five. I grew up rapidly in the next few minutes as I tried to load my bus properly, and then collect the fares, largely failing in both tasks in the face of a full-blooded football crowd of 1970s vintage. During that first rather lonely winter on the buses, this green-behind-the-ears country boy was handed out plenty of life lessons. Imagine for instance my surprise and dismay at encountering a busload of senior citizens – or Wombles as we rather insultingly dubbed them – shrouded in many thick woollen layers and wielding fully laden and potentially deadly shopping trolleys, physically fighting each other in order to board my bus outside the teeming Ridley Road street market. I learnt a new respect for, and mistrust of, that tough old generation who had lived through two world wars and many years of hardship and austerity. I learnt that bus conductors were public enemy number one for many Londoners, the ambassadors of a crumbling public service, and often the first person encountered by someone after opening the electricity bill or arguing with family. On the other hand, most people still queued, and most still said please and thank you when purchasing tickets. We of course gave as good as we got, and I was wholly capable of a hot-headed or officious response to some perceived offence from my passengers.

I was too curious and full of the joys of London for the bus garage to be the entire centre of my life, unlike some crews, but I really did relish the camaraderie that came with the job. After you had worked there for a certain time everyone knew your name, and people were genuinely friendly, but there were certain unwritten social rules that had to be learnt and obeyed. The canteen was a convivial and lively place, but of the three rows of tables that organised the space, those on the left were where white crews sat, those on the right were occupied by Black and Asian crews, whilst the middle row was a neutral zone. There was little overt hostility, and mostly we were all more than happy to work and talk together, but there were also open supporters of the fascist National Front to be found, and a very few drivers remained in their cabs at the end of the route rather than lounging on the long seats with a young white conductor. In that London of my youth racial tension was palpable, and racist attacks on bus crews were all too frequent – something that I certainly experienced. Drunken and aggressive Teddy Boys on a Friday night in Bishopsgate were a potential threat for minority ethnic crews (and for me as well when I later became a punk), whilst white crews used to fear late Sunday duties on the 243s to Wood Green on account of the plethora of reggae clubs *en route*.

Of the various routes that I worked on, the 243 was far from my favourite, but I remember it as a quintessentially London route because of the manner in which it cut a cross section through the growth rings of the city. Starting way out in bleak, suburban Wood Green, it traversed the vast LCC cottage estate of White Hart Lane, before bustling through the older communities of Tottenham, Stoke Newington and Dalston, strung out like rather distressed pearls on the necklace of the A10 (aka the dead-straight Roman Ermine Street); places that were now home to every conceivable immigrant group. There were pubs like the Swan in Tottenham and the Three Crowns in Stoke Newington that were exclusively frequented by men from the Caribbean, and from where the sound of dominoes being crashed down on pub tables startled many a passer-by; there was Stamford Hill, home to the Hasidic Jews who would catch the bus down to work in Hatton Garden, and whose heavy, dark clothing seemed ill-suited to traveling on a hot, crowded bus; and there was Ridley Road market which had long ago driven out the blackshirts who had once infested it, and where everyone was now welcome.

Purim in Stamford Hill, 2014

Eventually the bus reached the ancient community of Shoreditch, where it turned sharp right along Old Street. Of all the areas of London that I have known over the course of my adult life, this is the one that has perhaps changed the most – at least not its physical fabric but rather its inhabitants. Clustered around the High Street its traditional trades of shoe selling and furniture making still clung on, and its old-fashioned pursuits of boxing and stripping were still very visible, but the dirty, unloved Victorian warehouses that spoke of a dynamic industrial past were in large part empty and abandoned; at night the whole district was deserted and we rushed through it without being troubled by passengers. The skilled trades of printing and watchmaking that had once populated the road through to Clerkenwell had only lately succumbed to technological change, and the area was to lie dormant for another two decades before succumbing to spectacular gentrification.

But the pace picked up again as the 243 came closer to its final destination, especially at night, as it dropped off print workers for the now defunct presses of Fleet Street and posties for the enormous

Mount Pleasant sorting office. At last it arrived at Holborn Circus, close by Smithfield meat market, whose (exclusively white and often racist) workforce it deposited in the evening, and then picked up again in the morning rush hour, by this time uproariously drunk on account of the early opening hours kept by their various local boozers.

I'm glad that I knew that dirty, dishevelled London that had still not recovered from the ravages of the War, but it wasn't a happy place. I learnt my picketing duties in the infamous Winter of Discontent of 1978–79, that last outpouring of anger against the grinding decline in public services, before the Thatcherite revolution that began just a few months later swept them away entirely. London Transport itself was to disappear eventually, and with it all of that benign corporate culture into which I had been inducted. Gone, not forgotten, but not wholly lamented either.

―――

Postscript: Up Front on the 19s

―――

The Routemaster bus was only designed to have a maximum 17-year working life, but it eventually ran in service on London's streets for nearly 50 years. It even outlasted many of the buses bought in to replace it, and also survived the privatisation of London Transport. But by 2005 a combination of age and politics had caught up with it, and the last few routes were facing conversion to One Person Operation and the demise of my former trade of bus conductor.

I was by now a bus driver, and I had the privilege of driving RMs on the last days of several grand old routes, including the 19s, the 22s and my own route the 38s. They were bittersweet occasions, giving bus crews their few minutes of fame as they cautiously steered their way through throngs of well-wishers and press, whilst also driving towards an uncertain future. For many it was the end of their careers on the buses, and one of the saddest occasions I ever attended was the farewell party for the conductors on the 38s. As the very last crew route north of the Thames, many conductors had transferred onto the 38s as their own routes went OPO, but this was the end of the line for them, and a grand old London tradition was coming to an end after 175 years.

I now drive on the 19s, a route that epitomises my fascination with the unique history and development of London's bus network; on the one hand it is a modern high-frequency route providing a vital service for today's Londoners, but on the other hand it is merely repeating a journey that has been undertaken scores of times a day for well over a century.

It never ceases to amaze me that I am driving an ultra-modern diesel-electric hybrid bus down the very same streets that my predecessors of the London Motor Bus Company negotiated with primitive Daimler petrol buses in 1906.

Life on the buses has changed markedly with the end of crew operations. Garages are far quieter places without conductors, and drivers lead a fairly solitary existence. The privatisation of the buses themselves has led not merely to a fragmentation of operation but of identity also: we no longer all work for one monolithic corporation, driving the same buses and wearing the same uniform, and I think something has been lost in the relationship London has with its buses as a consequence of that. Money is no longer taken on London buses, and most fares are paid for with plastic; consequently, there is virtually no social interaction between driver and passengers, and the traditional etiquette of please and thank you, or even just eye contact, has largely disappeared.

On the other hand, buses in London have enjoyed a golden age in the early 21st century, with passenger numbers rising to levels not seen since before the advent of mass car ownership. The introduction of congestion charging coupled with a modern digital system of control has resulted in greater punctuality and reliability. Personally, I'm still acutely aware of my tiny but essential role in the provision of a vital public service. I am merely one small cog in a vast and complex machine that daily keeps London on the move, and I'm proud of that.

There are uncertain times ahead, with passenger numbers now starting to drop after years of growth, and traffic speeds are slowing as London rebuilds itself at an unprecedented rate, recently dropping below the 8 miles per hour in central London that horse-drawn carriages were estimated to travel at in 1900. Bus services are being trimmed back, and no doubt investment will be curtailed as well. But it would be premature to write off the London bus too quickly; I hope to be driving a red double-decker from Finsbury Park to Battersea for a long time yet, before I hand over to another generation to perform the same basic task that London's men and women have managed unceasingly for the last 190 years.

For as our city's current public service provider Transport for London is fond of saying, 'Every Journey Matters'.

TO VENUS AND BACK
ON THE NUMBER 8

Rowena Macdonald

Back in the mid-90s when I was at Sussex University, which was full of
Metropolitan kids who spoke in Mockney accents, my friend Liz and I —
both provincialites, from Southampton and Wolverhampton respectively
— privately sniggered about the fact our London friends bonded over bus
routes in the capital — 'Oh, the 38, yeah, know it well, mate,' — 'The 134
to North Finchley — yeah, used to go on that bus every single day, get on
at Archway up to Muswell Hill'. It was yet another example of Londoners'
boastfulness and smug assumption that the world inside the M25 was
intrinsically more fascinating than the world beyond.

Fast forward to 2001. I had moved to London and now realised that
London bestowed a glamour on mundanities such as bus routes. Only
locals knew bus routes, not tourists, so it was insider knowledge. At that
point, lodging in the basement of a single mother's flat in Camden and so
poor I couldn't afford the tube, I got to know the No 24 very well and it
was more exciting than the 501 from Wolves town centre. I caught it from
Mornington Crescent Station, opposite the old Black Cat cigarette factory,
and it trundled down Tottenham Court Road, Charing Cross Road, around
Trafalgar Square, down Whitehall and past the House of Commons, where
I got off for work. An iconic journey from start to stop, freighted with the
weight of history and world-famous places on postcards.

Fast forward another six years and I had moved to the East End. It took
too long to commute to Westminster via bus and I could now afford the
tube. For a long time I rarely got buses.

Last January I was diagnosed with bowel cancer. I am now in remission
but, almost exactly a year ago, I started treatment. It began with six weeks
of radiotherapy at Barts Hospital every weekday. I went on sick leave.
Cancer became my new job. Every morning for those first six weeks I put
on a carefully composed outfit and full make up and waited at the bus
stop on Roman Road for the No 8 bus to take me to through the City
to St Paul's, where I would alight and descend to the basement of the
hospital to the radiotherapy unit. The unit was like a semi-boutique hotel.
A reception desk with flowers and charming lipsticked women. A lounge
with magazines like *Harper's Bazaar* and artwork by Turner Prize nominees.
Low lighting from lamps on coffee tables. Comfortable sofas. Amazingly, it

was NHS. I felt lucky to be having treatment at what was clearly a flagship radiotherapy unit. I also felt lucky that Barts was in an upliftingly posh and historical area – near the site of Bartholomew Fair of Ben Jonson fame, opposite Smithfield Market, surrounded by all the ancient guilds and churches of the City. I even passed the Bank of England on my way there. I was not being treated in any old hospital, I was being treated in the oldest hospital in Britain still on its original site. It had been there since 1123, since the reign of Henry I. A hospital with an ancient London pedigree, although the consultant told me they had the newest and best radiotherapy machine in the country. The machines were in rooms assigned with planet names: 'You're going to Venus today, Miss Macdonald.' I went most often to Venus.

During one appointment, I asked the consultant if Venus definitely had the best machine, as I wanted to make sure that I was absolutely on the best machine. He burst out laughing: 'All the rooms have the same machines.'

'OK, but it's just you said before you had "the best machine" in the country – "machine" singular.'

'No, they're all the same.'

'You definitely haven't palmed me off with a lesser machine?'

'No, you are definitely on one of the best machines. Did you think you'd been given one with only half a battery or something?'

During my first appointment with him, my consultant told me I would be cured. The terror of death lifted immediately and although the year of treatment ahead was a harrowing prospect, I was able to view it as an unpleasant job with a time limit. I dressed up each day for this job because I refused to be a shuffling invalid clad in comfortable but unflattering invalid garments. I admired the woman I met in the radiotherapy unit who wore a different, stylish outfit each day. She had throat cancer. 'I used to be a TV director,' she said, 'And now look where I am. This isn't me, you know.' I knew. We had entered the parallel world of the seriously ill. I'd entered it far earlier than was fair. She'd entered at a more appropriate age but she still didn't want illness to overwhelm her identity.

The best medics see beyond the illness to the real person. The consultant was one of these. He asked about my forthcoming novel, my job and my daughter. I was so grateful for his kindness and expertise that I considered asking him to my book launch, until a physio friend explained it would be against his professional ethics to socialise with patients.

It also seemed important to maintain high standards of grooming because the No 8 passed through the City, past ultra-soignée women marching along Cheapside with garish health drinks and auras of success.

London has always kept me on my mettle when it comes to clothes and it wasn't going to stop now I was ill. The women's magazines were right: you had to put on your war paint before you went to battle. It was a form of control when life was unsteady. Luckily, bowel cancer chemo does not cause hair loss, so I didn't look like a cancer victim. Actually, I did not look ill at all. Friends exclaimed how well I looked, clearly expecting me to be like a memento mori. Strangers were never going to give up their seats on the No 8 for me. Often I did feel ill though. Nauseous and weak. Particularly on the way home. Radiotherapy, coupled with chemo pills, was exhausting. I had to sleep for several hours every afternoon. The effort of the half-hour bus journey was sometimes like walking up a steep hill in horizontal rain. I couldn't afford taxis though and with my depleted immune system I didn't want to go on the tube. The bus – probably spuriously – seemed cleaner because it was above ground with a throughflow of air. Plus it took me practically door to door. Also, now I had nothing else to do but be ill, I had time to enjoy the journey. Roman Road into Bethnal Green Road, E Pellici, established 1900, the market stalls selling vegetables and clothes, barrows, actual barrow boys, the Bangladeshi grocery where I'd been given a cute red plastic basket, which had once held lychees and now held my daughter's toy tea-set, Shoreditch, hipster zone, the TEA building, once an actual tea warehouse, now a bar/café/creative whatever, Boxpark, shipping container shops selling £5 doughnuts and £500 trainers – were we in the end of days? – kids hoping to be stopped by style bloggers, the homeless sleeping under the railway bridge as the bus turned into Norton Folgate, masters of the universe on the sharp corner of the RBS HQ smoking and vaping, the office block with the enormous tank of tropical fish behind the reception desk. Who had the job of feeding the fish and cleaning the tank? Did the firm employ a dedicated fish wrangler or was there such a job as a freelance fish wrangler especially for offices with enormous fish tanks? We really were in the end of days, although I would take Leah there to look at the fish as it would be cheaper than the London Aquarium and she would appreciate the fish more than the office bods.

If there were no seats left on the No 8 I asked healthy-looking people to give up theirs. I took a perverse pleasure in explaining why. 'I've got bowel cancer and I'm going through chemotherapy.' The pleasure came from shocking people out of their complacent wellness. Death is in your midst. Despite my apparent health and relative youth, I am diseased. Cancer is happening right here on the No 8 bus. In the midst of mundanity – even mundanity glossed with London glamour – is suffering.

In reality, the real suffering came later. Those six weeks travelling back and forth to Barts in the spring sunshine came to seem like halcyon days compared to the later real horror of intravenous chemotherapy and major bowel surgery in the less rarefied surroundings of the Royal London in Whitechapel but, at the time, I was cocky. I was doing cancer really well, turning up to my new job on time every day with a positive attitude. I was brave. Everyone kept telling me so, which was an ego boost. And I hadn't succumbed to wearing tracksuit bottoms.

'For many people cancer will be the hardest battle of their life,' warned the Macmillan leaflets in the radiotherapy unit. At the time I thought, pah! many people are clearly wimps – if this is my life's hardest battle, bring it on.

TIME AND RELATIVE DIMENSIONS IN SW3

Ali Catterall

Of the handful of bus routes that rumble down the King's Road, Chelsea, some are rather more *Kings Roady* than others. Yes, the 49 also ambles through this incredibly diverse patch of West London – yet it's not a true believer. It's not True Blue. Slinking down from South Kensington, it merely joins the swinging mile halfway, like a cheating marathon runner, before, like the No 19, veering sharply into Beaufort Street and over Battersea Bridge towards South London proper. There've been some Johnny-Come-Latelys too in recent years, the 211 and 319, but let us never speak of them again.

It's the good old 22 and the 11, then, that most encapsulate the spirit and plurality of the King's Road, trundling cheerfully down the length of the high street from haughty Sloane Square to the less salubrious World's End, from SW3 to SW10 and back again, crossing postcodes and demographics. And importantly, these two buses *cross the Twilight Zone.*

All the locals know about the Zone. It's our own Bermuda Triangle; our little equator; the zone within the zone. About a quarter of the way up (or, alternatively, three-quarters of the way down) there's an odd and rather pronounced bend or kink in the Road. For centuries, and even today, that curl, situated roughly between Terence Conran and Vivienne Westwood, marks an invisible but very real border between the upper-middles and the working classes. In the 17th century, randy Sloanes clip-clopped through the kink in search of mistresses. Later, Punks and Teds clashed here at weekends before straggling east to hunch on the wall outside the Chelsea Barracks, practicing nihilism. Once, a fellow 10-year-old suggested we take a 22 up there to 'beat up the Punks'. (I think his dad or uncle was a Ted.) I can only imagine how that would have played out. 'Come on punks, let's 'ave ya!' 'Ah, go ahead kids. There's no future in my life. Fruit pastille?' 'Cheers mister. Can I have a black one?' 'Everything's black, son.'

And fittingly, it's in this mysterious liminal space, as the psychogeographers say, that I first met a time-and-space-travelling Doctor on a No 11 Routemaster. Actually, both my meetings with the benevolent alien have taken place in this exact same 20-yard stretch. The fact that this is where a pub called The Man in the Moon once stood is possibly no coincidence at all.

It's 1977, the Chinese Year of the Fendahl, and while sitting on one of the buses' long seats, a seven-year-old boy with a bowl-head haircut to relating to his mum in elaborate detail a dream he'd had that morning about being chased through a medieval castle at night by cannibals. Gradually, we become aware of a presence close by – a tall, imposing figure, standing in the packed aisle, leaning over us... listening in. 'And they had grass skirts, and skull necklaces, and...' I trail off, as I look up to meet the stranger's gaze. His eyes, impossibly huge, infinitely kind, shine like headlamps under an unruly mop of giddy brown curls. He is grinning, wildly. And swaying slightly. He is unmistakably himself. Time ceases. I stare at him, as planets revolve, age and die. He gazes back, his eyes growing larger and larger, filling my entire field of vision, until nothing else exists but the purr of the bus and those two enormous blue orbs. He reaches up and tugs the yellow cord to sound the bell; the spell is broken. The Doctor (Who) alights – but turns, as he steps off the platform, to wave goodbye. Bye bye, spaceman. Bye bye, spaced-boy.

I met the long-scarved one again again a couple of years later while on a map-reading exercise with my fellow cub scouts. Needing directions, we stumbled into the Man in the Moon (publican: *Grange Hill*'s Pogo Patterson's dad) and found him there; not so much propping up the bar as conjugally tied to it. 'Doctor, we're lost!' we cried. 'HELLO BOYS!' he beamed. 'Have a pound.' And so saying, handed over the readies. We doffed our caps gratefully, and backed out in terror and delight. Then spent it all on Curly-Wurlys and blue pop.

COLOMBIA ROAD
FLOWER MARKET

Jo Roach

On Sunday mornings, spring comes in
on the 149

the bus fills with petunias, geraniums
there's a Kumquat tree under the stairs

a tray of wallflowers on the seat
the aisle crowds with marigolds

the leaves of an apple sapling
tickle the ceiling.

ROUTE RIDERS

Peter Watts

Sometimes, it feels like there are few slower ways of getting round London than by public transport. And the bus – so often a victim of roadworks and burst water mains – can be the slowest of all. But for some, that slowness is part of the attraction. Jo Hunt (67), Mary Rees (68) and Linda Smither (64) are 'ladies who bus'. Since March 2009, they have been taking all of London's buses in numerical order, starting at No 1, travelling each route from one end to the other, and then writing about it on their blog. As a way to pass the time, it is a distinctively London thing to do. There are, after all, over 500 routes in London; more if you include those that start with letters, like the A10 or X68.

'It began when I retired from my last job,' says Jo, the head buskateer and a former teacher. 'People asked what I was going to do. I said I'd just loll about or play computer games, but then I decided I'd get every bus in London.'

From that moment of whimsy came a plan, which became a blog and has now evolved into something like a mission. Jo, Mary and Linda have acquired matching sweatshirts with their blog address on it – these proved to be handy in winter when one bus's central heating was broken – and they have printed business cards to hand to drivers at the end of journeys to explain what they are up to. Online, they have built up a following among London nerds and bus enthusiasts.

Jo got the idea when she got on a bus and saw it was terminating at Ponder's End. 'I thought, "Where's Ponder's End?" and elected to find out. Then I thought if I was going to do one, I should do them all, and if I was going to do them all, I should do them in the right order.' Linda and Mary were both ready for retirement as well, so – armed with their Freedom Passes – they agreed to come along. Jo's son created a blog, and 200 buses later we are now travelling by bus from Brixton to Mitcham on one of the hottest days of the year.

And here I must make a confession. I also spent a couple of years on the buses, writing a weekly column for *Time Out* about exactly this topic – taking every bus in London in numerical order, from end to end. Well, it started as a weekly column, but soon lethargy took over, the column became fortnightly and then monthly and in the end I never made it further than the low 60s. Jo, Linda and Mary have persevered, resolve stiffened by each other's company – and by Jo's determination to complete the task. 'Jo is the leader,' confesses Mary. Jo plans each route a week in advance, working out how they are going to get to and from the stops that bookend the route, and she and Linda take turns writing them up on the blog.

But they are clearly enjoying themselves as well. There is much to appreciate about a lazy morning spent taking a bus for no other reason than the sheer fun of travel, watching London knit together while everybody outside rushes about their daily business without time to stop and absorb the city around them. As we slip languidly through south London streets, the trio note familiar landmarks and reminisce about other routes that have passed this way. They are also able to recall what an area was like 5, 10, 20, even 40 years previously. 'It's evocative,' says Linda of the experience of revisiting old haunts. She also comments on how they have watched London change in the two-and-a-half years they've been doing the routes. When they began, the Strata Tower at Elephant & Castle was a building site – now it's one of the tallest buildings in London. A rapid transformation, observed at leisure.

They are fascinated by London's arcane history – such as the Balham estate we pass that was reported to be Hitler's choice for a home if he successfully invaded Britain – but also by the present, especially in Tooting, as South Indian restaurants slowly give way to West African clothes shops and Mary contemplates hopping off to pick up three crates of mangoes for £10.

London as seen by bus is a city of delights and surprises. 'I've been surprised at how good the drivers are,' says Jo. 'I've really enjoyed being able to understand how London ties together. And sometimes you'll be bumbling along and then suddenly you are in the country, surrounded by green. It's like you've reached the end of the world.' Or the end of London, which sometimes feels like much the same thing

originally published in Completely London *in 2011*

ON THE WAY

Linda Mannheim

She rides the bus because she can't afford the Underground – a pound for all journeys to all zones, while the Underground charges more for taking you to the centre from the cheaper neighbourhoods. She can see how people are sifted by this system now she had lived here for a while; the bus has children, the disabled, people who work in shops and carry their lunch with them. There are more black people on the bus. On the occasions she rides the Underground, she notes the suits and briefcases, the pressed clothing and pursed lips, the lack of conversation and eye contact; it is silent except for the roar of the wheels against the tracks. The Underground never seems, to her, especially crowded – no packed bodies, no shoves, no shouting to move down like there are back home. People laugh at her when she says she does not find the Underground crowded. 'What are you used to?' she's asked.

She was used to the packed anger of New York City subways, the bodies pressed up against one another, the shoves against shoves, crotches against backs, the need to keep hands near a pocket or a bag. She was used to occasional eruptions of fury, shouts either challenged or ignored. She was used to changing trains in stations that looked derelict when they were not, the damp and grimy concrete and white tiles, the rats skittering along the rails until they slipped into shadow and disappeared in the dark. She was used to waiting for the delayed connection, the honk of an AP system with sound so distorted, no one ever knew what was announced. She was used to the train still not coming even though, by then, it should have to come. She was used to dismay when the platform filled with people and then more people, because the train still hadn't come, and those were going to be the people you would fight for a seat when the train did arrive. She was used to leaning over to see if the light in the tunnel was coming closer, as if she could will the train into the station by seeing it before anyone else. She was used to train roaring towards them finally, relief and then an irrational fear of falling onto the tracks. She was used to entering the train before the other passengers came out, looking desperately for a seat and then, once none can be found, at least a good place to stand or to lean. And she was used to other people shoving in until she was unable to move again, stuck there, trying to free her arms, trying to grab onto something so that she would not fall against someone else when the train pulled out.

Story book images of London are easily evoked for her – *Mary Poppins* illustrations, Sarah Crewe sketches, the city returned to by children in *Peter Pan* – and she still gets a thrill from seeing the red double-deckers make their way through the congested streets. And when she climbs the steps to the top level of the bus and looks out over the grimy Victorian buildings repurposed for another century, she feels as if she has realised a childhood hope, escaped a bad ending, jumped a ship that was going down. She grew up in a part of New York where even desire to move to another part of town would be called unrealistic. Getting out was her first and most significant accomplishment; landing on the other side of the world made her feel as if she'd successfully robbed a bank. The provincialism of big city neighbourhoods is something that she ran from and ran to. When the schoolchildren get on the bus in their blue uniforms, screaming at one another in a tone between threat and joy, laughing and roaring insults into the air, she recognises the city they live in, feels at home again.

The bus takes over an hour to deliver her from the house she shares with annoying acquaintances to the claustrophobic office where every worker is miserable, where she watches the clock and secretly searches for another job. She reads a newspaper during her journey, but there are places she wants to see every day: the street that seems too narrow for a bus to go down, the sagging brick school that all the students cluster in front of, the housing estate where everyone on the street seems to be wearing the anachronistic clothing of the ultra-orthodox. Her hands are always streaked with ink that's rubbed off the newspaper when she arrives. Sometimes, she has smudges all over her face because she rubbed her eyes while she was reading the newspaper. Once, she even finds streaks of ink across her white t-shirt, has to cover it with a cardigan when she thinks someone else in the office might spot it.

She likes to leave late, begin the commute back after everyone else, when there is less traffic on the way, and sometimes she walks part of the way so she can have some time outside, walk during the time when everyone seems pleased to be outside: the workday done, a drink waiting at the pub, or maybe just getting home for dinner. Still, if someone is walking behind her, a reflex kicks in: she stops to look in a shop window or she stops to take something out of her bag. She waits to see if the person behind her will move ahead; she wants to be sure she is not being followed.

She came to London from a country undergoing a transition: South Africa during the Truth and Reconciliation Commission hearings. She thought about the testimony she had been studying often; she thought about it when she tried not to think of it. She thought about the witnesses who described interrogations, solitary confinement, beatings, bombing of activist's homes, the destruction of body parts. She even thought about the perpetrators' testimony; she especially thought about the perpetrators' testimony: their attempts to explain. They said they were doing it for their country, and there was a war on though one had not been declared. They said they were afraid that the country would be plunged into violence; they were afraid that everything they held dear would be destroyed and this place that they loved would descend into chaos.

Cape Town seemed unreal, with crystal blue skies and a strangely flattened mountain in the centre of it and that blue blue ocean with a ring of foamy surf lapping upon the shore. She felt suspicious of cities this pretty. And of course, there was a catch: the violence that people spoke of from the past; the violence that reshaped itself for the new era. Her friend who'd done struggle-work showed her the back paths of the mountain when she'd arrived, showed her how to spot the townships ringing the white areas, showed her where the smoke had risen and flames had torched during the 1980s uprising. All that violence had to go somewhere, said her friend looking into the distance, and now, at the exact moment when we should be celebrating our liberation, it is everywhere – the rapes in the informal settlements and car-jackings that end with brutal deaths, the beatings during burglaries and gunblasts even when someone hands over money during a street mugging.

In Cape Town, she was told never to walk alone, was advised to drive everywhere, was instructed to look out onto the street before leaving the house – first left, then right. She was told to look into her car before getting in, keep the key ring panic button in her palm so she could press it if she felt threatened, hire a private security firm that would arrived within minutes of when the button was pushed, because God knew the cops wouldn't. And the townships that she was advised to avoid felt like a better fit than these suburban houses with their big fences and their driveways. The dusty streets lined with postage stamp houses and shacks, and the overstuffed minibus taxis that pulled through the unpaved streets felt more comfortable than the wealthier districts. People walked there. But she was advised not to walk there, not to visit unless she was with someone who was from there. She was told never to go out alone in the dark, to stay in, get picked up, get brought somewhere by someone with a car who could drive her. She missed the night sky, the smell of the city at the end of the day, the unpredictability of walking in darkness.

She walks down Seven Sisters Road. And it is nearly night now in this cramped, overbuilt city. She walks from bus stop to bus stop so that, if the bus pulls over, she can get on it. She does this also so that she will not get lost; she will follow the route of the bus on foot. And the sky is darkening, and light seeps from storefronts. Children wearing blue backpacks run and hide behind a lamppost, a mailbox, a car until they are found by their mother who's wearing a hijab and pushing a pram and the schoolchildren laugh and run again. A big-bellied man walks out of a news agent's carrying a litre of milk. Teenage boys stand on the street corner, speaking to one another with fake American accents. The traffic is thinning, and she spots the bus, sees it pull over on the side a street ahead of her. She runs for it and climbs on and pays her pound to the bus driver.

From the top of the bus, she looks out at the flats above the storefronts; yellow light seeps from the windows at dusk. Sometimes light from a TV beats against the walls in a dark room, appearing and disappearing in a way that's unearthly. Sometimes she can see into someone's kitchen in an upper floor flat, watch a woman open a pot and let out a cloud of steam, oblivious to an audience. Sometimes she spots a family walking out of a shop with groceries in a blue plastic bags, toddlers nearly wandering but held by a hand, a mother checking to make sure she has everything she should have with her. Sometimes she can see a pub and, outside the pub, tables where men and women sit even when it does not seem warm enough to sit outside. They knock back pints, move their hands when they speak, smoke, laugh, carry on like normal. She wonders if she will want to do what they are doing one day; she wonders if she will ever feel normal.

She thinks of the stories she recorded for the book: the beatings and solitary, the disinterment of hastily buried bodies. She thinks of secret imprisonment and of executions carried out in the silence of early morning. She cannot help it; she thinks of these things.

Camden Town always reassures her — the canal, and the boats, and the old-fashioned market shut at night. The first bus route ends here, and she walks again for a little while, alongside the tourists and the leather-jacketed suburban kids who've come here to score. The bright blue-and-gold lattice lock, the glistening dark water beneath it, takes her breath away every time. She dreams of getting on one of the sightseeing barges; she will never get on one of the sightseeing barges. But this is the moment when she is between places, when she does not have to account for anything, when no one knows precisely where she is. She catches the buzz of voices as she passes a pub, a fug of cigarette smoke, a whiff of beer. These are all people who live their lives without thinking about the shifting of dirt, the discovery of bruised bodies. These are people who talk about football games, shopping, and holidays. They take turns buying drinks for one another.

She sometimes stops in the Sainsbury's here: she buys a small head of lettuce, a few tomatoes, a plastic container of soup. She keeps the food on her shelf in the shared fridge in the shared house. She buys plastic trays of single-serving lasagne with a sheet of clear plastic sealed across the top, and when she gets home, she pops holes in the plastic with a fork and she puts the tray in the microwave until its humming stops. She tries to do this when the others won't be in the kitchen. Sometimes, instead, she stops for something to eat along the way, but always something she can eat while she walks, or something that she herself can bring to a small table: a kebab, a cone of chips, a plate of cheap fried noodles eaten at a picnic table. That way, she does not have to engage in the ritual of making conversation over a meal. She does not have to deal with a waiter asking: just you? And she does not spend much this way. She cannot afford to spend more than a few quid on each meal.

She walks along the route of the 31 bus, up Camden High Road, past the Roundhouse and Chalk Farm, and then diverts down to Primrose Hill. And there, she looks at the city, the lights beyond the green. And this too is reassuring. There's the London that she used to imagine living in, just over the hill, when she'd stop off here to break up the journey between New York and Cape Town. She used to wonder what it would be like to stay here for a while during those quick trips, imagine these quiet streets and this quiet neighbourhood with Georgian houses lining the leafy streets and middle-aged women wearing Barbour jackets walking their happy Labradors.

She walks back to Adelaide Road, past the low blocks of flats that would have been modern in the 1960s, the aqua coloured panels in above the windows streaked with soot from the buses. The cars slip by and *fwap* the air. And then she hears the low rumble from a bus and she turns around and sees a 31 pull over. She runs for it, watches the dark outlines of the passengers alighting, hopes they will take long enough so that she can make it there. She makes it just in time. She climbs up the steps, and she drops down another pound coin, and she takes the ticket in her hand. People are moving down with their shopping bags, shifting slowly, edging towards the back. She goes to the upper deck, spots a window seat, settles back. She looks out over the traffic, the trees, the tower blocks.

The manuscript is with a publisher now; the stories she collected fact-checked and copy-edited. When they are out in the world, will she stop seeing the images that keep appearing?

The bus, with its bubble of light in the dark, is perfect and safe and gliding slowly. The driver downstairs keeps track of everyone, notes what's happening without saying a word. Around her, people read their newspapers, play games on their phones, speak to one another in languages she doesn't understand.

She wishes she could keep riding.

244

Anna Maconochie

If you say run
I'll run for you.
If you say wait
I'll wait for you.
There's no other bus
I'd do that for.
Although you ignore me,
Too full to stop for me
You're the bus I adore.
The Two. Four. Four.

In dreams I wait
At Bus Stop J
But I'm too late again.
I've missed my chance with you.
And still I wait, I pray
As hope has me in her jaw,
Dreaming of every 244
That will never come.
Walking the half-mile home, I think
'What a metaphor.'
The Two. Four. Four.

Other buses I could hail
Other routes, by wheel or rail
But no one leads me to my door
Quite like you, the 244.

13 THE BORIS BUS

A new generation of red double-decker bus, with folding doors that allow passengers to hop on and off, and backed by the Conservative Mayor of London Boris Johnson, was launched in 2012. Billed at the New Routemaster and styled by Thomas Heatherwick, the 'Boris bus' as they became known came at the cost of around £350,000 each, with TfL making an initial purchase of 1,000 of them. In December 2016, Sadiq Khan, Johnson's Labour successor, announced that there would be no further orders of the bus, citing their expense and the need to move to greener, fully electric vehicles in the longer term.

ROLL UP FOR
THE BORIS BUS

Peter Watts

At Victoria bus station, a heaving mass of grey hair and boom poles spills on to the road as bus nerds and journalists fight to catch a glimpse of the New Bus For London as it completes its maiden voyage on the No 38 route. The bus may be 45 minutes late, having comically broken down while being chased by a Routemaster filled with anti-Boris protestors at Angel, but it's finally arrived: the crowd readies to board and ride it back to Hackney.

As the bus pulls into the garage to muted cheers, a woman in a wheelchair eases her way to the front. She hopes to be the first wheelchair user to try the new bus. The doors open, the passengers disembark, and the crowd at Victoria hums with expectation. This is the moment they have waited for since Boris Johnson caught the public mood by insisting he would return the Routemaster to London during his 2008 electoral campaign. Only one is currently in service (there will be eight by summer and a fleet within a year) and there have been delays, controversies and much sniping, but it's finally here.

Then the doors slam shut in our faces and the bus pulls off, empty, parking 100m round the corner for an hour while men with screwdrivers scratch their heads and try to fix a broken rear door. Passers-by queue up to take photographs of the static bus, while at the bus station, the transport nerds are reduced to discussing the new rail stock recently introduced on the Metropolitan Line. The woman in a wheelchair heads home, disconsolate. The bus finally leaves Victoria two hours behind schedule. The nerds pile on board excitedly.

It is, in many ways, classic Boris. A bus has been delivered at great expense (£11.3m), broken down twice, is two hours late, doesn't really do what was promised in terms of rear-loading and conductors, but people still love it. It's almost impossible to find anybody – outside of those with vested political interests – with a bad word to say about the Boris Bus. Edward Hammond, 89, thinks it is 'lovely'; Ian Smith, 71, admits 'it's a lot of money, but that's what things cost these days', while Mark Gale, 37, who won a competition with LBC to be the first person on the bus, reckons it's 'nice, a good use of money'. As we watch it being fixed, a man (they are all men, notes a bemused Dutch female journalist) joins the admiring throng. Is he impressed? 'It's great to have the Routemaster back,' he says, 'they're much better for fare dodging.'

He's kidding, I think, but has a point. The key element of the new bus – the one that has people calling it a Routemaster – is the rear open platform for ease of access. This will close in the evening, but during the day is manned by a conductor, who cannot take fares or check Oyster cards and is basically there to enforce health and safety regulations – precisely the sort of non-job Boris groupies usually rage against but now find themselves awkwardly condoning. The new bus is supposed to replace the bendy bus, partly because Boris insisted the middle doors made fare evasion so easy: the new bus also has a set of inviting middle doors. Boris supporters have decided to blame these inconveniences on TfL rather than the Mayor's office.

Rarely has a bus been so politically divisive. Left-wingers say that during a time of recession and rising fares it is sheer vanity to spend a fortune on a bus that has a lower capacity than the one it is replacing, that it isn't really a Routemaster and even if it was, Routemasters were rubbish anyway. Right-wingers argue this is an almost uniquely terrific use of public money, defend the employment of a conductor (a combined cost of £500k a year) and insist good design trumps expense.

And it certainly looks striking. As we roll through London, heads turn and people scamper into the road to snatch a photo of the passing bus. The design – by Thomas Heatherwick – is a blend of old and new, inspired by the Routemaster but without looking dated. The bus, like many in

London, has a hybrid diesel-electric engine, so is much quieter than the rattling old Routie. On the downside, while it is 1m longer than most buses, it's also a couple of feet shorter, meaning tall people are likely to bump their head on the top deck. But rightly or wrongly, these quibbles and the exorbitant cost can be easily dismissed given the overwhelmingly positive public reaction. As I jump from the rear platform, alighting between stops for the first time in years, a passer-by coos admiringly. 'Isn't it marvellous,' he says. 'It's great to have them back.' Strike one to Boris.

originally published in Time Out, *2012*

BUS

Penny Pepper

On the bus
Boris bus
dirty bumpy
horrid bus.

There's a trolley in the crip space —
see the child, snotty faced —
bullish buggy hellish mummy
disposition far from sunny.

On the bus
double decker
smelly shaky
bony wrecker.

There's a suitcase in the crip space
nervous girl who grips in haste,
snarling hoodie chomping burger
Doesn't he know that meat is murder?

On the bus
Boris bus
dirty bumpy
horrid bus.

Another journey, ramp is broken,
access just an empty token?
Public selfish, my dismay,
while driver grunts and looks away.

On the bus
double decker
smelly bumpy
bony wrecker.

In my slot a man with doggy —
by my shoulder youth who's groggy
armpits foul, hair is stinking
smells of vomit, and binge drinking.

On the bus
Boris bus
dirty bumpy
horrid bus.

There we were such humble cripples,
fought the system sent out ripples —
now to take a London bus
with the throng to push to fuss —

On the bus
Boris bus
dirty bumpy
Tory bus
any bus
big or small
dirty rough
crowded empty
loud and surly…

Scarcely,
Just a London
Bus.
Not
Much
fucking
Use to us.

NEW BUS FOR LONDON

Douglas Murphy

In an early scene in Patrick Keiller's *fin-de-siècle* portrait of British capitalism, *Robinson in Space* (1997), the narrator visits the eponymous hero, who at this point has moved from London to Reading:

> Robinson had been living in a single room in a house in the northern suburbs. His job was poorly paid and insecure. He did not eat well, he seemed to know no-one in the town, and he had no telephone. His only reassurance was the presence of eighteen undeniably utopian Routemaster buses, operated by enthusiasts in a deregulated market.

Ten years later, Boris Johnson, quiz show celebrity and MP for Henley-on-Thames, while campaigning to be elected mayor of London, told a hustings:

> We should on day one, act one, scene one, hold a competition to get rid of the bendy bus. [...] It's not beyond the wit of man to design a new Routemaster which will stand as an icon of this city.

Sure enough, in early 2012 a brand new bus, the New Routemaster, entered service in London, replacing the fleet of reviled articulated buses. But by the end of 2017, production of the New Routemasters had come to an end after the delivery of only 1,000 vehicles, less than half the run of its namesake. In this five-year period the new bus was heavily criticised for functional failure and waste, and for being one of a series of whimsical additions to the London environment Johnson made the public pay for.

But what does it mean that a leftist artist such as Keiller could see the Routemaster as something progressive, utopian even, while the conservative Johnson could utilise it as an aesthetic weapon from the nostalgic right? How does one particular design of public transport come to signify so heavily in two different directions? Looking for answers suggests a fundamental gap in understandings of the city.

Original Routemasters can still occasionally be found on the streets of London, operating on heritage routes and on special chartered journeys.

But beyond the pure recognition factor that forms the bedrock of their iconic-ness, they appear somewhat strange. Notably smaller than contemporary buses, their seats are narrow, the ceilings are low. Formally, the famous 'hop-on-hop-off' opening at the back, so familiar as a global symbol of London, is balanced against a cutaway hood at the front, which means that the entire form is top-heavy, giving it compositional dynamism.

This energetic quality is made more clear by the story of the Routemaster, an example of technology transfer from wartime. Making use of aluminium technology developed for the Halifax bomber in World War II, the Routemaster in its day appeared as a sparkling example of advanced manufacturing in a time of austerity, with its folded corners and riveted seams, and the isolated cab that almost resembles the cockpit of an aircraft.

It is partly these qualities that allow the Routemaster to be understood part of a narrative of the progressive history of the UK, alongside the 'white heat of technology' and the radical design that eventually became the global success of British High Tech architecture. This is a parallel vision of Britain that would not experience a Thatcherite reaction, a more egalitarian society, less individualistic, more comfortable with modernity.

Keiller, in his earlier film *London* (1994) highlighted this progressive memory of the Routemaster with the following lament, spoken from the dying years of Thatcherism, that London was:

> *...a city under siege from a suburban government which uses homelessness, pollution, crime, and the most expensive and run-down public transport system of any metropolitan city in Europe as weapons against Londoners' lingering desire for the freedoms of city life.*

The London that Johnson was appealing to be allowed to run was a very different city to that of the early 1990s. Most significantly, in 2000 its metropolitan authority had been resurrected in the form of the London Assembly after the destruction of the Greater London Council in 1986, voting former GLC head Ken Livingstone in as an initially independent mayor.

Furthermore, the establishment attitude to the inner city had markedly changed. One of New Labour's key urban strategies was to adopt the recommendations of Lord Rogers and the Urban Task Force, and their recommendations in *Towards an Urban Renaissance* (1999) to learn from European city culture, 'regenerating' areas with street life and mixed-use development. Livingstone also poured energy and money into public transport, meaning that by 2008, Keiller's lament was to a certain extent moot.

But in this context, what did Johnson's appeal to the Routemaster really mean? In a period where the Great Recession had yet to kick in, and where the collapse of New Labour was not yet inevitable, various policy appeals and suggestions were made about how Conservatives could 'take' a left-voting city like London. One of these was what became known as the 'zone 6 strategy', the idea being that urban voters were a lost cause, but if peripheral suburban voters could be convinced to come out on the day, then victory was possible. This was a common tactic of strategist Lynton Crosby, who ran Johnson's 2008 campaign, and in practice often meant stoking paranoid fears of the inner city (something that easily degenerated into the unsuccessful, racially charged campaign of Zac Goldsmith in 2016).

But as well as appealing to suburban prejudices, appeals to suburbanites could be posed 'positively'. For example, in 2005, the influential Conservative think tank Policy Exchange published a pamphlet entitled 'Replacing the Routemaster', featuring contributions from Simon Jenkins, Andrew Gilligan (who would become one of Johnson's most vocal supporters at the *Evening Standard*), and Goldsmith. This document argued that Livingstone's decision to phase out the buses was evidence of a 'group-rights agenda' (otherwise known as 'PC gone mad'), and that disability rights groups were trampling all over the enjoyment of ordinary members of the public.

Furthermore, the document argued that the Routemaster represented something that was in danger of being stamped out by the statist health-and-safety brigade: *freedom*. The argument was that the 'hop-on-hop-off' open back of the Routemaster allowed for personal choice in embarking or disembarking, personal choice that was being systematically removed by unaccountable politicians and mandarins.

Sure enough, Johnson would lift the attitude and language from the Policy Exchange document wholesale, later claiming of the open platform: 'It is, as far as I know, one of the few recent examples of a public policy that actually gives back, to sentient and responsible adults, the chance to take an extra risk in return for a specific reward.' The strategy was simple – the new articulated buses were unpopular, and the Routemaster was an icon, like the pointed police hat, that spoke to a certain crude British nostalgia.

Johnson's suburban strategy duly paid off, and some of his first policies enacted were the quintessentially anti-public, motorist-friendly ones of abolishing the western Congestion Charge extension and banning the consumption of alcohol on public transport. But making the Routemaster rise again wouldn't just happen overnight; indeed, it was clear that any new bus would take years to roll out.

The first stage, as promised in the manifesto, was a design competition soon after the election. A study was published in *Autocar* magazine to kickstart ideas, and hundreds of entries came in. Joint winners were published, one by CAPOCO, taking clear styling cues from the original, and one that was a collaboration between Aston Martin and architects Foster and Partners, which featured details such as bug-eyed LED headlamps and ostentatiously rounded wrap-around windows throughout.

The next stage was a competitive tender, out of which emerged a completely new team; that of Northern Ireland-based Wrightbus (allowing Johnson to be proud of awarding the contract to a UK company) in collaboration with designer Thomas Heatherwick, who would find himself attached to a number of controversial design projects over the course of Johnson's mayorship, including the later Garden Bridge fiasco.

The 'New Bus for London', as it was known at that time, was an odd beast. The most unconventional thing about it was the addition of a door at the rear for the much-discussed open platform. This was in addition to the front and middle doors common on a contemporary bus, compared to just the single rear door on a Routemaster. This new door at the back also meant an additional staircase to add to the standard one near the front, which overall meant that the bus was more than 11 metres long, compared to just 8.5 for an original Routemaster. The additional circulation meant that the bus had a lower capacity than a comparable contemporary model, a double sacrifice in performance.

Visually, the bus was reminiscent of the AM/Foster's design, although more pragmatically designed. The main feature was the use of double-curved glazing panels that wrapped around the rear of the bus, following the curve of the second staircase, while a flat window swooped up to follow the normal staircase. The front of the bus had a deliberately asymmetric design, pairing the circular LED headlamps with a black stripe that swept down towards the front entrance. Inside, the Heatherwick styling attempted to give a certain class to the conventions of transport design, eliminating the 'Hi-Vis' pastel colours so common to the type in favour of brasses and burgundies.

It wasn't long after the New Routemasters were introduced that the shine started to wear off. The elaborate windows, attractive from the street, were surprisingly small from the inside, and their swoops meant that passengers couldn't look out the back to see when to change buses. Furthermore, the original stock had unopenable windows which, combined with teething troubles in their air cooling systems, meant that when summer came around, the internal conditions were frequently unbearable – leading to the nickname 'Roastmaster'.

Other problems include bumped heads due to the curved ceilings, and a disappointing tendency for the hybrid diesel/electric engines to shut down and require regular restarting throughout a journey, eliminating the energy savings the hybrids were supposed to achieve. And while the buses originally had a workforce of conductors to staff the open platform, they were soon phased out to save costs, meaning the door at the rear became just an additional, and rather superfluous, standard entry. The overall impression was that the bus made for some attractive street decoration, but at the cost of any actual usefulness.

***

After the production of the New Routemaster was halted by Sadiq Khan, the genuinely positive characteristic of the bus are being transferred onto more conventional models, with Wrightbus now producing New Routemaster bodywork to fit onto a standard 2-door Volvo chassis. With this in mind, the 'Boris Bus' becomes little more than an expensive gimmick, one paid for from the Transport for London budget rather than private operators, a budget that comes largely from the public in the form of fares and government subsidy.

This shows a remarkable lack of democratic accountability, precisely what was lamented in the original calls to replace the Routemaster, and indeed this was a recurring theme in Johnson's interventions in the built environment, from the ArcelorMittal Orbit sculpture and the Emirates Air Line to the Garden Bridge. Considered against these other projects, the New Routemaster takes its place as a very specific 21st century vanity project, one specifically tied into an electoral cycle, and thus comparable to a very expensive piece of physical marketing for Johnson himself.

Furthermore, what is clear is that the New Routemaster was simply not created for bus users in London, who were, in terms of performance, far better served by the articulated buses that were phased out. No, the New Routemaster was for looking at, not riding in; it was designed to appear in TV clips and advertising images signifying 'London'; it was to be made into toys; it was to be seen from the window of the car. It was not a utopian image of quotidian ingenuity and modernity, but rather a ready-made picture postcard image of a city whose needs are rather more complex than just looking nice on your day trip into town.

TASTY TRANSPORT

The Stockwell Bus Garage canteen

Will Self

The sweet pork with savoury rice (or potatoes) at £3.40 doesn't seem so bad to me, especially when it's perfectly tasty and comes piping hot on a damp, autumn day. I could've had spaghetti bolognese for the same price or spicy chicken and special rice for 10p less. I could even have gone for the more Dickensian lamb's liver, mash, steamed cabbage and onion gravy – a snip at £3. And there were several healthy options, including a cheese or ham salad with a jacket potato and coleslaw, weighing in at £3.16.

The combination of low prices and the slightly quirky price points – there are other dishes costing such non-commercial amounts as £2.09 and even £3.01 – should alert you to where we are this week, namely a works canteen.

Time was, I suppose, when the great majority of the British workforce had access to a subsidised works canteen of some kind – it was part of the great postwar settlement, together with such nostrums as full employment and a welfare system. Nowadays, we have no need of such frivolities – we have Starbucks and Bupa and sub-sub-subcontractors, for such is the way of progress. True, Go Ahead London is a private business but as Colin Opher, general manager of Stockwell bus garage, assures me, as we sit in the tiled canteen, there's still some of the old London Transport ethos.

When it comes to food, at any rate. The canteen is open from 7am to 10pm every day (with last orders at 9.30pm), serving a full hot menu to drivers, mechanics and other staff. You can mosey in in the morning and Theresa, the canteen manager, and her staff will plunk down grilled kipper fillets and brown toast in front of you for a mere £1.75, the menu card noting that this healthy fare comprises 418 calories.

Colin tells me that the canteen is fullest on Fridays, the day after staff receive their weekly payslips. There may no longer be any physical pay day, but there is still the anticipation of the weekly wage going into the account; this engenders collectivism in the workforce.

My impression of the bus garage – which I walk past every day – is that it's a happy enough place. In the late 1940s, the West Indian immigrants who arrived on the SS *Empire Windrush* were quartered up the road from here, deep underground in a giant air-raid shelter. A half-century on, Colin has drivers on his books who are second- and even third-generation African-Caribbean employees. He tells me that the African and African-Caribbean staff get on well together – unusual for this neck of the woods – and there are also sizeable Portuguese and British Asian contingents. The staff dispersed around the canteen seem relaxed, their high-vis jackets lending Fauvist intensity to the light-green tiling on the walls. There's a game of dominoes clacking on at one table; at another, newspapers are being read intently. A couple of huge fruit machines wink in the corner.

It helps that the canteen is well lit by high windows. They're difficult to replace, Colin tells me, as they're the original Crittall ones. That's the downside of having a Grade II-listed garage.

On sunny days, the drivers cluster by the main gates, smoking and drinking mugs of tea, while the mechanics have created a sort of 'peace garden' that runs along the flank of the building, complete with its own makeshift shelter. I don't want to overstate what a happy, extended family inhabits Stockwell bus garage, but if the truism that the heart of any home is its kitchen holds good, the sight of Theresa and her colleagues dishing up jerk chicken – Friday is jerk chicken day – must be perennially warming.

Time was when most bus garages had their own canteen, but now only seven or so of the bigger garages in London do. Drivers who have waiting periods at Euston usually eat at the University College Hospital canteen, which is also open to the public, while those waiting at the stand by Clapham Junction have recourse to Asda.

As I chase grains of rice about my plate, Colin casts an eye around to see if Lena, his oldest driver, is in. She's been with the company since 1978 and, at 71, shows no sign of retiring. Even before the recent legislation, there was no mandatory retirement policy at London General. So long as they pass their medicals, Colin says, the last thing the company wants is to lose its older employees – it's a job that benefits from the application of wisdom. Still, if drivers want to stay on the road, they'd better give the 'London General Special' a swerve – a full English breakfast of artery-busting proportions – and pay attention to Theresa's laminated card by the till: 'KICK THE SUGAR'.

New Statesman, 7 *November 2011*

Stoke Newington Common, 1978

A Bus Pass for people who don't want to pay London prices.⊖

106

FREEDOM OF THE CITY

Richard Boon

In an interview with Irish academic and journalist Paul McDermott for an oral history project about the (mostly) Irish band Microdisney's historic Rough Trade album, *The Clock Goes Down The Stairs*, I remarked that, apart from the music, I loved the title: 'We all get old, we fall down stairs and that's our clock ticking.'

And the bus pass reminds one how true that is. Over the years, I seem to have gathered a reputation for rarely leaving my northeast London neighbourhood of Stoke Newington, which – of course – I refute. With no tube lines, Stoke Newington has a village characteristic. Most amenities are local: grocers, restaurants, fishmongers, locksmiths, Post Offices, a park, schools, places of worship for a variety of faiths, music venues among its plentiful pubs, a library and more. It's easy to rarely leave. But, despite my reputation (even among my family), of course, I do.

It was once the Oyster Card that helped, as long as one remembered to top it up at the local newsagent. When I lived in West London and worked at Rough Trade near King's Cross, the magisterial Routemaster bus, No 73, with a long route from there to Stamford Hill (now broken into different routes and other buses) worked for me. As it does now, albeit from the eastern direction. No longer the much-fetishised Routemaster, alas. Then come the notifications: 'You now qualify for the 60+ Oyster Card bus pass.' And the clock goes 'Tick.'

This didn't particularly alter my bus travel habits (or tube use, for that matter), but at least I didn't have to remember to top-up at the local newsagent. Going forward, I probably employed and enjoyed its use more frequently, accessing other London sites and neighbourhoods more often than previously.

Time passes, inexorably, and the notifications come again: 'Your 60+ card is due to expire; please renew.' One tried and one failed. It seems someone technical had made an error regarding my age and date of birth. Someone who would never cut it as a Maternity Nurse, obviously. After several emails and phone calls, they 'fessed up: 'We made a mistake over your expiry date.' Just as well. 'We're moving you to the Freedom Pass, slightly earlier.' OK, but in the interim I was back at the newsagent, using a regular Oyster Card, remembering to top-up...

The Freedom Pass finally arrived, still with its younger image of me from previous 60+ card. Fewer wrinkles, like an airbrushed or Photoshop portrait. And it works in various places outside London, to boot. It hasn't changed much of any public transits I may make (it expires, naturally, hopefully before I do likewise), but it's a reminder: the clock also goes 'Tock.'

PUBLIC TRANSPORTS: 38 STOPS

Gareth Evans

Disclaimer: These notes are the product of a deeply London-centric, double-decked view of omnibus reality. Your correspondent cannot really apologise for that, however, as bus travel is, without doubt, a completely subjective experience seeded entirely (as it should be) out of lived encounter. Distanced observation of what it means to 'take the bus' fails in almost all criteria of assessment. The 'busness' of buses, their daily business of stop-start, sometimes veering, sometimes jeering passage through the polis is what demands multi-sensory, embodied reportage. Let's be clear, this is not to claim we are in the realms of volatile dispatch, of broadcast under fire from the blasted frontline; but in terms of transport transmissions, the story of the bus *is* divisive, often generates more heat than light, and has seen many get off a stop or two early, to avoid the argument degenerating.

1 / In the opening line of the alleged 'fiction' *Downriver*, his decade-divining live anatomisation of Thatcherism, Iain Sinclair has a character ask, 'and what is the *opposite* of a dog?' While the answer is clearly not feline (and nor is the prompt barking), the question is well put. The canine cannibalism of the free-market almost pre-supposes (at least to itself in its blood-stained mirror-bowl) no opposition, no alternative, no 'other' to its top-dog dominance, its neo-liberal end-of-history triumphalism. This was, after all, the age of the preacher, of the woman more alpha than the males around her, who derided the warm and gentle ties of human(e) association in favour of 'no such thing as society' (tellingly, and poignantly, the late Angela Carter's contemporaneous review of the novel in the *London Review of Books* was titled 'Adventures at the End of Time'). The erectile self, gender irrelevant, standing proud over its wasted dominions, was the epitome of arrival at the gates. And to reach the said golden portal, the last means of transport you would take, unless you were a 'failure', would be a bus (which is what makes the Thatcherite moment and legacy so pernicious – its hatred, despite PR to the contrary, of the 'common person').

2 / That being said, the wheels on the privatised bus did continue to go round and round as the 1980s also saw the deregulation (amongst many

other structures and services) of the sector, and the emergence into national and then global market dominance of the romantically monikered Stagecoach. From its brother and sister origins as a driving/sandwich combo to its corporate behemoth status, the operation has named itself, perhaps understandably, after a vehicular mode that suggests certain historical and topographic possibilities not so easily to be found in the monosyllabic and altogether more reduced appellation 'bus'.

3 / The etymology (omnibus) shouts it loud: carriage or conveyance *for all*. Buses don't have classes. They are banal in the founding sense of the word – open to every/body. There's no first and standard. Yes, there's sitting and standing. But this is often a preference, not prescribed.

4 / True, no bus should have a seat facing backwards (as certain of the new model London double-deckers have). Such an arrangement and the attached journey it is part of, suggestive of flight from difficult scenarios, of a past being shed as the distance from the start point increases, requires either a surface it is difficult at once to return across (the wake, in every sense, of water via a ferry), a scale of undertaking (certain US trains with a rear viewing gallery of the desert infinitude) or a speed it is reckless to consider countering (childhood finger insults out of the back window of a motorway car on the way to a mouldy caravan surrounded by a growing vacancy). The wake of a bus offers normally a glimpse of cyclists trying to stay alive in the toxic torrent of the road. A bus should – and does – offer an unarguably forward-looking proposal.

5 / Regardless, at the same time, of location in the vehicle, lower or upper deck, front or back, the *fact* of a bus is inescapable. A bus undeniably *is*. It is heavy matter moving relatively slowly through generally dense arenas of softer matter. If double-floored, it feels inherently *unlikely* even before the engine turns over (how will it corner, surely it might even be blown over). It's inevitably hard to generate the escape velocity and the *jouissance* that often comes with other forms of transport (that's not to say it can't be found or felt and, when it does come with a bus route, it's that bit more remarkable, and feels somehow more *earned*).

6 / However, as has become clear over three decades of travelling upon them, buses and their peregrinations are not so much about leaving – in a final, ecstatic or catastrophic sense – as about entering more fully into the parameters of one's own life, and finding what has perhaps been latent there, and nurturing it, through steady mileage, into the light, into greater prominence and priority (more on this to come at a stop a little further on).

7 / The bus then, while appearing at once both design-improbable *and* danger-unlikely, does of course contain within and without a number of risks. Admittedly sometimes a paid-up participant in the left-turning cycle assault zeitgeist, a bus's external kill-mode is considerably less common than the likelihood of interior upset. My father, on an extremely rare recent visit to the city for which he spent 30 years in home-counties servitude, broke several ribs in collision with the railing at the top of the stairs of a 38 after a sudden halt. The dangers of hands-free descent of said *escalier* are not to be understated. The 'throw' on stopping can be something to behold, with potentially fatal distortions to one's body arrangement and generally amenable working limb layout.

8 / I've seen a bus wing mirror take a stationary police officer's helmet off, knocking him to the pavement and severely blooding him. The fortunately casualty-light but undeniably dramatic occasions of what might be termed 'top floor tree slice' – a particularly strong bough entering the deck and refusing to leave (a little like certain night bus pilgrims) without its newfound friend, ie. the top deck – have unfortunately not been witnessed directly by the eyes of the person currently typing.

9 / It is not the remit of this offering to dwell on the fluctuating fears – and fortune – of the last bus home (or out, as it might often be more accurately termed), suffice to say that menace, mystery, mediocre mayhem and moments of terror and joy all mingle, all jostle for space on the back row. What does stay in the mind, so many years later, however, lies way down the threat scale*, below yellow even, but somewhat reminiscent of that hue: the one seat unoccupied on an otherwise crammed route; the sitting down on it, the discovering why such a vacancy remained, as the odorous damp soaks swiftly into your clothing...

10 / We measure out our lives in Prufockian bus rides, since the purpose of most journeys, those driving dailies, is to commute, with whatever destination intended. Is this why some people hate buses so much, because all they engender is the feeling of losing your one precious existence to the Man for so much of the waking day or night-shift hours? I know a person who doesn't ever take buses; he despises them that intently. He'd rather tread great swathes of the cityscape (a pleasure of course, but often impractical) if no viable rail-based option presents itself. His loathing is based not so much on the journey potential or lack thereof that a bus offers. His bile seems stirred by something far more existential, something darkly active, like a still flailing body in drowning water, pressing up at us from under the ice of normal existence.

11 / The main 'problem' of buses (especially in unjust relation to trains) is of course *other* traffic (road-works don't help but, however ubiquitous and ceaseless they might feel, they remain the exception) and, by this, I mean cars. It's cards on the table time: I despise private vehicles. I reserve my small reservoir of undiluted hatred almost exclusively for them. Here is not the place to rant against their vast contribution to resource depletion, mortality both human and animal, sonic and atmospheric disturbance, ecological devastation, individual and general physical, emotional and mental ill-health, and much, *much* more.

12 / Let's focus instead on their blatant transport inefficiency, area domination and privatised stratification of what should be the commonly held street, experienced and even enjoyed more or less equally. As Mrs Thatcher astutely observed — and desired — the separateness of a car removes conversation, a meeting with the 'other' and a bodily feeling for the implications of one's own actions that is disastrous for social cohesion and shared development. While I accept that some people find solace from domestic difficulties or pressures in the mobile space of their own four wheels, the situation has become so grave that in this case the majority needs must rule. And, regardless of the fact that a majority *here* might drive, I mean an even greater majority, that of the *global* human and cross-species population.

13 / Just as a key US commentator, when asked for the one change he would make towards the establishment of a better world, said that he would remove all titles, at a stroke instituting a non-hierarchical linguistic nomenclature, the ramifications of which one can easily and pleasurably begin to conjure ('Mister President' being a half-way hybrid of this possibility), so my version of this would be the erasure of all private cars. An enormous expansion of public transport would follow, structured alongside a system of smaller hire vehicles and municipally owned taxis with full disability access. I'm not interested in whether this is economically sensible or not. We have larger concerns here (a strong eco/nomy being meaningless without a strong eco/logy).

14 / Merely on the level of effective use of space, the car fails so profoundly as to be laughable if its offer were to be made now for the first time, in our present tense. The masturbatory solitude of the vehicular interior — with music, temperature and (greater or) lesser awareness of the world beyond all at the whim of the privileged driver — needs urgently to give way to a far more open sense of how one's own body in motion should interact with other vessels similarly underway.

15 / Clearly I don't drive, the roots of this grounded perhaps deep in ancient childhood memories of nauseous half-hours driving out on Sundays to a dismal, probably dogging car park in scrubby woodland (driving to walk is absurd, first off); the stuffy back seat, the sink when the engine stopped, the loaded silent pause before the door creaked open. The stroll was never the problem, but the means was so much worse than the end.

16 / Just now, in the park, I saw a remote-controlled car squeaking along through the slush of the snow days' fade. The model vehicle moved a few metres and then the mother controlling it had to kick it a little. The distinction here was two-fold: the car had a living child in it, and the motion came with a soundtrack not dissimilar to that of the fairground, a pumping bass that blasted the early blossom buds. It was modelled on a sports car, but how much more distinctive it might have been to have a micro double-decker working the playground collection points. Underneath the dodgem roar, there tinkled a little ring of toddler attention: I am here beneath the blare. In the context, it sounded more like the fabled coffin-bells of the Victorian period: still alive beneath the loam, dig up the box, and fast.

17 / As ever, it is about perception. Some will say that the bus imposes such a monoculture on its passengers, such a numbing intonation, a repetitive stalling, dulling, or ponderous judder, that the self is broken beneath it. But mood is and can be fluid, and *fluent*, generative of its own demands. Attention, if activated, can find fascination in the smallest details as well as the bigger picture, and this applies no less to a bus than anywhere else. In fact, such a potential arguably (needs to) exist more in the environment of the bus than in most repeatedly encountered spaces, both inside and out.

18 / Yes, the 242 seems to require a change of drivers so often it defies timetabling logic. But would you really want to risk driver tiredness, even if it's over-anticipated, and why not use the short pause of the switch to take a moment oneself to consider whether the life you're leading could not itself benefit from subtle transitions, or even major alterations.

19 / Yes, the increasing volume and frequency of announcements can be perceived as a kind of sound-driven oppression of all that is gentle and kind, but there is a rhythm in such mantras that can also be claimed, and used, as an accompaniment to the progress of the journey. And, while the order to 'hold on, the bus is about to move' can come across as unnecessary as the commandment to keep breathing, imagine if you're

sight-challenged, or wrangling so many toddlers you have to count their heads second by second, like the daytime alt-sheep *against* sleep that they are.

20 / Yes, a single London bus now carries more CCTV cameras than most small countries, but why not position yourself near to the multi-screen monitor, scatter friends across the seating areas and construct complex, interlinked frame-by-frame narratives of comic cause and effect, much in the spirit of the Surrealist game Exquisite Corpse. Successful online careers have been based on considerably less.

21 / Yes, travelling in a new London bus can often feel like you're inside a particularly large, distended and mercantile condom, sheathed as the entire vehicle might be in a single diaphanous commercial. But, like Jonah in the belly of the whale, this passage will pass and, if you undertake small subversions on the way, perhaps stickering politically on the seat-backs, ostentatiously reading a copy of a left-leaning weekly or, while pretending to speak loudly hands-free, declaiming found lines from insurgent tracts, you can legitimately say that you've been trying to change the system from within.

22 / And who can deny the found poetry of ticket options and pass names, past and present? Freedom pass, day riders, wayfarers, rovers and more: sometimes it's hard not to conjure that with a simple purchase one is involved in a civil rites struggle, a marine exploration or some kind of troubadour undertaking, the mythos of grail quest, simply by jumping on the 73 to a midweek afternoon screening at Vue Islington.

23 / All this, of course, before we've even looked outside. It was Richard Thompson, wasn't it, he of golden-age Fairport Convention and solo Sufi insight, who said he secured most of his lyrics from top deck watching of the way. Sit at the front and you have almost 270 degree sightlines; you can stare into the future, you can gaze slant as poet Emily Dickinson advocated, through the side windows; you can peer into the half-drawn curtains of flats over shops for whatever your voyeur vision might wish to find, and most of the time you'll be moving again before you're noticed (top tip: there's been some pretty major action on the first floor at the corner of Lower Clapton Road, just past the sports centre).

24 / And the stop/start of bus movement can inform, not only hinder as might be the case, a particularly contemporary form of thinking. Unlike the general smoothness of train passage, where the land appears to scroll cinematically beyond the glass, the view through the perhaps grimy pane

of a bus is closer in its mosaic of divergent and juxtaposed textures to our perceptual experience online, to our sense of hyperlinks and net trawling. Its constantly distracting associations give us a template of time and place a little like Kurt Schwitters' modest but magnificent collages of the city and its tempo, from ticket stubs to newsprint and magazine grabs. With my son Tom I've found video screens on the roofs of bus shelters, counted magic mushrooms sprouting from numerous concealed ledges, spotted graffiti you can only see from such an elevation, to name only three visual visitations. It's a glitched, liminal form of beauty most of us live within, a scratch-street of found fascinations, and it's important to celebrate it, not discount it.

25 / My own childhood was not bus-defined in any way. Recall only brings two journeys to mind, along the valley floor, once in each direction, to Luton and St Albans, both about five miles hence. The town was reduced in area and aspiration; it was all about walking, and cycling out to the fields behind the house, along the former rail-bed, between the experimental crops of Rothamsted testing station. I associate bus travel almost exclusively with London.

26 / Navigating rural services — where they exist — is of course rarely positive. The dependence on the car that finance capitalism forces on the countryside only compounds the frustrations felt and described above. In this way it unsurprisingly resembles the inequalities, the uneven spread of resources known across human activity and infrastructure. Journeys between scattered villages often require you to return before you've set out, risking limb and life at a stick stop on a high-hedged racetrack completely free of pedestrian consideration. One memorable exception was the sunset ride back to Eastbourne from Birling Gap. It shines with its almost-singularity.

27 / What might lift non-urban public waiting into the sphere of secular bliss would be the range of Soviet bus shelters revealed in several volumes of note published in the last few years. Normally, however, foreign travel is not measured in bus trips, city or coastal, mountain or metropolitan.

28 / At least one significant bus journey should end in death; not of anyone on board or in the road, but literally, at the gates of the final stop, on the necropolis run to an edge-land cemetery, as many European cities so structure their terminal arrangements. Routes are all; describing and defining the potential of the polis. The whole-city crossways lie like lines of the hand on the map, both of the lives we actually occupy and those we might never pursue, Robert Frost's 'road not taken'.

29 / And yet, and yet, we are moving inexorably to the core of the proposal.

30 / The bus is often used as a unit of measurement, like Wales or Belgium, for weight or length or height, for matches as varied as skyscrapers, whales, motorcycle jumps or the Angel of the North. Why employ a bus as comparison? Because it is public and it is shared, I would hazard. It establishes a common currency and appreciation. It is common *ground*, of and for the *commons*, in the best sense of the word, in the original meaning.

31 / One of the great pleasures of bus rides is what we could call the unlikelihood of the overheard, possible because the space is contained and therefore audible. Just this week, three young Americans, one of whom I should declare looked a lot like the hugely endearing actor Parker Posey, first noticed hazing younger students in *Dazed and Confused*. I was a little too far back for major audio intervention but I did catch this, which has stayed with me: 'curiously isolated, the viaduct stands aloof'. It does, it really does.

32 / The bus offers a model of democratic co-operation, evidence of negotiations between inevitable differences, towards the common good and goal of onward mobility. Ramps slide out and down for wheelchair access. Pushchairs, prams, dogs, schoolchildren, the elderly — all of them citizens often rejected or prohibited by intention or material design from other so called 'public' arenas — find an accommodation within. Yes, there have been lines drawn over buggy access to the disability space, arguments over the top-deck canine count and, by some margin the most extended, often drink or drug-fuelled solo passenger showdowns with the driver about payment refusal, Oyster card glitches or, more appealingly, pleading weather and fatigue scenarios. These are exceptions, however, to the general sense, love it or loathe, of finding ways to co-exist within fixed frames of shared necessity.

33 / To adapt an observation by poet and essayist Eileen Myles, they reveal to us a form of 'collective self'. Even if we do not do so much of it, we still talk more, to those we know and are travelling with, and to strangers, than we do on other forms of transport (and this *before* a challenge, such as that of trains stranded in a blizzard-bound 'nowhere', with the attendant sleeping in luggage racks and rationing of the buffet car provisions as if we were in a Michael Bay picture). This strange mode of public intimacy — even the ridiculous proclamations of excessive phone volume — reveals

a form of accepted accommodation that tolerates human variety, from marginalised sleepers to boisterous school runners.

34 / Time on the bus can generate both a hatred or euphorium of co-existence; mundane moments of actual (dis)grace. It is a framed world, a country of all nations even. It is (part of) the world, constantly in flux and shift. All transports offer distinctive pleasures — train, tram, plane, ferry, foot, cruise ship, even car I am sure — but the bus is where we are most regularly tested and blessed, sometimes just minutes from the door.

35 / Finally, like almost all of communal life, perhaps we have the bus service, journey and system that we deserve. However, regardless of the material infrastructure, personnel, frequency (or not) of provision, ticket cost or fuel used, a bus is not ultimately a *vehicle*. It is a way of being in the world. This might change on a daily basis. We might get diverted from our destination, we might have to change in mid-flow, might even have to get off early and walk as it returns to the depot or turns around to regulate the timetable, but the bus in us remains, a perennial possibility of collaborative belonging. An actual commonwealth, tolerance on wheels, the bus stands for a form of achievable and enduring civilisation, a humble civility and mobile proof that there *is* such a thing as society.

***

36 / Gareth Evans has recently stepped into the decade-long waiting room for a Freedom Pass. Eyes on the prize...

37 / Portions of this essay have been written on a bus seat, but not one currently on a bus. We possess a vintage double, covered in orange checked moquette, and fitted across the UK network throughout the 1980s. You can take the person out of a bus, but...

38 / *Although somewhat off-piste, but not unrelated given the events of 7 July 2005 in London, it feels important to relay, gleaned from extensive research, that Britain and the US used to operate colour-coded levels of security alert (both countries have now abandoned these in favour of simple descriptors). The UK system in place prior to this was called 'bikini state', initiated on the 19th May 1970. The word 'bikini' was apparently *randomly selected by computer*. Or was it? Given the eponymous atoll was a key site of bombs testing in the 1940s and '50s, and the term describes a form of swimwear that can dramatically unsettle certain zones of the simpler straight male brain, it appears less coincidental in retrospect.

14 HOLD ON , SLEEP TIGHT, GOOD NIGHT BUS

If described by one interviewee in the *Evening Standard* in 2014 as 'most definitely the worst part of a London night out', the London night bus is a blessing to the commuting late or earlier shift worker and those wishing to burn their candles in capital until well after dark, alike.

BUS STOP H
AND THE GHOST

George Pringle

It is a dark night in Kennington, down in the Oval. When the lights in the local authority blocks are out, the park is closed and all that's illuminated on the horizon is the Strata building with its motionless fans, silently razoring the night sky.

You know you're closing late when even the chicken shop has thundered its shutters to the pavement. Straws and napkins swim with leaves lost since autumn and sweet wrappers from schoolchildren move like algae in the bottom of a tank. How do I know this? Because I have policed this strip, as a barmaid, protecting my door from outlaws and the many pieces of wanton trash, blown by buses like ticker tape in our solemn, southern parade.

The top end of Brixton Road is a peculiar place. I think of it as a Bermuda triangle. A space where lost souls convene, floundering in its temperate waters. If you are to head south, you will go all the way to Brixton, if you steer east, it will lead to Camberwell and Peckham. At Oval, people drift up or downstream, alive but sometimes, outright crazy. Magnetically drawn up the Brixton Road towards darker and leafier Kennington. This route ends at Bedlam.

The bar is by a bus stop. Bus Stop H, next to the 'Lucky Day' takeaway. Often I have watched passengers waiting here, as long as the day itself. From behind the coffee machine, whose steam creates mirages... beyond the plate glass, people purposefully stroll or amble with strange gaits, stopping to peer at you, in the gloom. Women fleetingly catch themselves in your mirror. They pull their best face.

A bus stop is a strange metaphysical place, not altogether real, with its apparitions.

The morning people come from the office block across the way. They wear expensive brogues and backpacks, like overgrown Bauhaus children. They sip on artisanal coffee in rubbery, sustainable cups and flick with thumbs on their phones. Little old ladies with shopping trollies squint, tearily into the wind. And in the afternoon, at 4, teenagers leave school and go to the chicken shop next-door. They lean with their bags on the glass. They scuffle and shout, running back and forth from the frame and the first drunk shakes his leg, to start his sparring with the shop owner, to our left. The street is part owned by a Sri Lankan family. They own multiple businesses. Both chicken shop and corner shop are theirs.

Bus stop H heads uptown to Trafalgar Square and Marble Arch, apart from the 415 which heads across to the Elephant. There's the 3 and the N3, the 133, the N133 and then, the N109. There's the 159 and her younger sister, the 59. How funny it is, in London, these routes... similar but different.

Bus stop H captures a strange period in my life. Back in 2014 I worked winter nights here, alone.

I sat in this dark, empty bar, illuminated by candles. Like a Medium, awaiting her spirit, often, it felt that way... like waiting for stray ghostly faces to wander in off the street.

These haunted evenings merge, demarcated only by subtly unnerving incidents that differ in tone and intensity.

THERE BUT FOR THE GRACE OF BAUHAUS

Tim Wells

The beige vomit
trailed down her front
sits vivid
against the black
of her coat.
Nightbuses
are indeed
a fantasy world.
The spatters
on her faux fur collar
smize.
Though she is fierce,
unrepentant
and glorious,
in her drunkenness
the puke in her hair
makes it difficult
to commit.
The stranger
sat next to me
must think the same.
For she smiles
and we both laugh.
I stand for my stop
and she whispers
'get home safe.'
The goth
heaves into a newspaper.
David Cameron's face
looks appalled.

NIGHT BUS FACEBOOK UPDATES

Julius Beltrame

 Friday, 4 April 2014 at 03:20 UTC+01

Unwisely I removed my earphones just now on the nightbus.
I was thrown into a silence so miserable I considered asking the bus driver to stop so I could get off early. Unusually grim quiet on the bus home tonight...

 Saturday, 26 October 2013 at 01:36 UTC+01

As the nightbus pulls out from under East Finchley station, and passed Cherry Tree Woods where my late Brother Alex and I played as children (it's going to take a while getting used to calling him that), it strikes me that for better or worse, entropy entails necessarily the accretion of memories in place of heat: of people parted and passed away, of moments otherwise insignificant to anyone else, haunting familiar places like forlorn ghosts nobody else can see.

 Monday, 19 August 2013 at 01:43 UTC+01

Ah yes the Night Bus. The only zoo I know where I can sit next to the animals. Where else could I see a furious candy crush casualty and an extra from Game of Thrones IN THE SAME MILLENNIUM (Eeuw stop scratching dude, you'll have no arm left when you finish at this rate)?
AM I THE ONLY SANE PERSON ON THIS CIGAR?

 Friday, 29 March 2013 at 04:11 UTC

An amusing straw poll (and believe me, I've amused myself for otherwise wasted hours so polling) for understanding the deep seat of our economic problem in Britain is to ask anyone who, at 3am is loudly blaming the bus driver — rather than whoever is responsible for running the service — for running late, exactly how much money they'd accept to be the bus driver picking up a hoard of drunks like us and take us home at this hour on a Friday night. To date nobody has said they'd do it for less than a king's ransom, if at all.

After some slow 40 minutes, the bus has only just passed Baker St. I shall save my anger and relish the sparkling lights of the West End from the top deck. LISTENING TO: Gerry Rafferty's Baker Street, accordingly.

In darkest South London on a bus heading in, in order to take a bus that heads back out, to the darkest edges of North London. Will gratefully be stopping for refreshment in Soho in between.

Hit me up if you're near and fancy some drunken late night Soho nonsense...

Grooving to Sonny Rollins' 'Alfie' soundtrack album on the bus home. Would be SO much better to be strolling in Soho to this soundtrack.

I first met (local character) Horace of Finchley walking to Tally Ho bus station after school in the year of our lord 1859 (or a similarly long time ago). After a few failed attempts to pronounce my surname, I thought of the first surname beginning with 'B' and told Horace my name was in fact Mr Bassett. Every day for the next several years on the way home from school I'd be greeted by his signature call across the street 'Best of luck Mr Bassett, the best of luck' always said with such gusto. Sad to hear he's died so young, he made so many people smile each day.

Exhausted after an intense but successful few days' shooting around Iceland.

Coming home late and sitting on the top deck of the bus as it bumbles through a huge city for an hour brings feelings of satisfied elation, dulled at times with the acknowledgement that sadly life must return to 'normal' tomorrow — empty of the kind of absorption that makes days feel like weeks and moments stretch into hours, or the kind of purpose that throws whatever vicissitudes may be hovering in the background blissfully out of focus, and delays their sharp return. So the bus bumbles on and one sits buzzing, hopeful for a next time soon but without any idea when the opportunity may come.

Thursday, 26 July 2012 at 23:47 UTC+01

'Fuck off Boris you oaf' I think, every time I get on a bus and hear his stupid posh voice making its announcement about London2012.

I suppose those announcements are one way of ensuring Londoners don't travel into town much during the Olympics.

Monday, 27 February 2012 at 15:24 UTC

There used to be (and maybe there still is) an apocryphal 'fact' about the Greek Railways that seemed to illustrate for those so inclined, their public sector inefficiency: it would be cheaper, the saying goes, to send every Greek rail passenger on the same journey in a taxi, than for them to take the train. And how smug we were in our northern cities, with our privatised (but still heavily subsidised), 'efficient' transport systems. Until now that is. Because Boris' new purchase of his vanity buses reputedly cost £1.4m each. EACH. Compared to £190k for a 'normal' double-decker. With 62 seats on each new bus, that works out that for each seat we could buy a 3-series BMW. Well done Boris, thanks for the shiny new bus but I'd rather you paid for a few taxi rides yeah?

Friday, 23 December 2011 at 04:36 UTC

I felt broadly melancholic, there was a girl on the N20 who kept glancing my way but neither of us dared speak across the silence, before walking our damp suburban streets home.

Wednesday, 19 October 2011 at 01:05 UTC+01

Although quicker and more comfortable, the last tube home seems less inspiring than the night bus. Perhaps comfort and speed are antithetical to inspiration, unless one designs jet planes. Or Bentleys perhaps.

Tuesday, 12 July 2011 at 02:46 UTC+01

I like sitting at a bus stop, at night. Especially I like it when a bus I don't want pulls in, stops and pulls put again. At Euston so many buses are just a stop from terminating I think the passengers must forget the window they're sat next to is but a frame for us pavement dwellers. It's especially entertaining when they unwittingly pick their nose too...

Friday, 6 May 2011 at 04:06 UTC+01

On the night bus. The chap sitting next to me, in his mid-20s, his hand a bit scratched but swollen with clench, pressed his fist into the seat in front of him all the way from Camden Town to Finchley Central, in some grinding frustration or thinly repressed show of strength. Rare to sit so close to someone so silent yet emotionally active.

I wonder what was bothering him?

Friday, 6 May 2011 at 03:02 UTC+01

Tonight's unforgettable moment was being sprayed in a verbal shower of nonsensical expletives, from the drunk 20-year-old girl who took offence at an admittedly facetious question about her littering, and the observation that throwing her fried chicken box on the floor of the bus stop differs only in scale to the morality of BP's Deep Horizon...

Embarrassed looks ensued from her friend, who although unsure if I was joking or not, knew exactly what I meant.

Last week it was a similar scene with a few young men of undergraduate age, who thought wrongly they were in safe company at the bus stop to throw around some gross misogyny, instead of fried chicken boxes.

My first intervention as a 'man of responsible age' and it went better than tonight's second attempt, really.

I won't put it down to a generational lapse though, so much as the random bad luck of the draw for whom one will share this wait at Camden Town in the small hours.

Thankfully after a wonderful evening I didn't feel obliged to make any new friends tonight, or any night at this recent rate. And you know, I'd miss all this excitement if I took taxis everywhere...

Sunday, 3 April 2011 at 07:03 UTC+01

OMFG I've never seen a 7am bus. It's full of African Christians looking at me like I'm a looney. I suppose it's understandable, I am after all only just going home after a night out, when they're all on their way to church in Sunday best.

Friday, 1 April 2011 at 19:00 UTC+01

It's a sunny Friday evening, we wrapped on time after a day in a green screen studio. Bus ride home has to be a top deck for the sunset view. Happy April! Happy Spring!

Tonight began with a friend wishing every bar had a barmaid who looks like Audrey Hepburn, and ended with my wry observation that if one drinks as much as we did, every bar does.

Now it's 5am and I'm standing at this cold, drizzle-soaked bus stop.

Monday, 27 December 2010 at 14:11 UTC

3 little words I hate on a bank holiday? 'Replacement Bus Service'

Saturday, 4 September 2010 at 02:37 UTC+01

Oh bus of the night, will you ever cease to surprise me?

Tonight in 'North London Night Bus Freaks', the zoo continues: we were all loudly informed thanks to half a mobile phone conversation that a box of chocolates absolved an erstwhile boyfriend of apparently heinous emotional crimes (the news was spreading fast around that group of friends), several crimes against fashion were witnessed, and too many sins, both grammatical and culinary, to deal with in one update...

Tuesday, 6 July 2010 at 13:28 UTC+01

Looking aimlessly out of the upper deck bus window and who should I see across the street?! My god I lost touch with her ten years ago when I missed a chance to swap numbers! Haven't seen her whatsoever since. What are the chances?! And there she is, Erica G*******, looking just as lovely now, just across the street! Blimey. Then the bus jolts me from my daze, pulls away and whisks me in the opposite direction. All I can do is look back.

Gone again. Sigh.

Tuesday, 22 December 2009 at 19:21 UTC

I hate shopping and doubly so, Christmas shopping with its crowds even madder than usual. Feeling weary and sorry for myself, I look out the window of the 73 bus travelling slowly in the traffic up Tottenham Court Road. An ambulance crawls passed slowly on our right — sirens howling. Inside I can see all manner of gadgets and devices solely for the purpose of preserving life, a life. Paramedic staff in front and back wearing green overalls. Someone isn't though, instead she sits quietly and stares out the window in my direction but not at me, more through me, gazing elsewhere, or nowhere perhaps. It's not an expression I've seen before. She looks a bit bewildered... She's not ill I reason, sitting and staring, so what's she doing there? In the moving din of the sirens barely a moment passes and the ambulance goes ahead in a gap through the traffic. As it does I glimpse what looks like an incubator in the back.

I know what my Christmas wish will be now.

Turnpike Lane
Bus Station at
night, 1982

APPENDIX: TRANSPORT TERMS
AND
LONDON BUS TIMELINE

A BUNCH OF BUSES

Andrew Martin

You Wait Ages For a Bus And Then Three of Them Arrive at Once.
Transport for London says that this hardly ever happens, a position
somewhat undermined by the fact that it has an official name for the
phenomenon: bunching.

Insofar as it admits that it occurs, TfL attributes bunching to heavy
traffic – a bus get delayed; by the time it arrives at the stop a lot of people
want to get on, and it must wait while they do so, causing the ones behind
to catch up. But public have always put bunching down to bus drivers
conspiring so that only one out of any given three has to do any work –
this arrangement being a leitmotif of the so-called comedy series, *On
the Buses*.

TfL says this can't be right because there are people in bus depots
whose job it is to ensure that buses leave at the proper intervals, and not
in convoys. As for bad traffic, TfL points out that the greatest number of
buses in London and the congestion charge have reduced the number of
cars, making it easier for operators to fulfil the regulators' top requirement:
keeping buses evenly spaced.

Talk of the Town, The Independent on Sunday, *13 April 2003*

A BUS GLOSSARY

Joe Kerr

Any self-respecting profession that has been in existence for a couple of centuries, and which has its own specific procedures and ways of working, will develop a rich internal language. Bus driving is no exception to this and the industry uses many words and phrases that are understood by staff, but which would be meaningless or inexplicable to the general public. Below is a list of such terms, some now obsolete, but many in current usage amongst London's bus workers. Possessing and understanding such a vocabulary is one of the ways in which people identify with their profession and enact a valuable kind of camaraderie with their fellow workers. This is by no means a comprehensive list but represents a particular kind of linguistic depiction of the London Bus that, to the best of our knowledge, has not been archived or presented publicly before.

Blinds. The route number and destination carried on the front of a bus (and to a lesser extent on the nearside and rear) are displayed on adjustable rolls known as blinds. Traditionally made from linen-backed paper (now just paper), they are yet to be replaced by digital displays, making them a surprising survival of older technology. Historically they displayed more information, particularly intermediate stops, but now only the route number and final destination are shown to aid visibility. One driver will indicate to another that they have forgotten to change their destination blind by making a gesture imitating the turning of the handle that operates the blinds, although handles have largely been replaced by electronic selectors. There is a lucrative market for framed destination blinds displaying familiar London places.

Booked/knocked off. to be caught by an official and put on report for an alleged misdemeanour.

Bonnet Number. Every bus of a particular type, for instance Routemaster, is given a unique identifying number, officially known as its Fleet Number. This number was traditionally displayed on the side of the bonnet on **Half Cab** types, hence the common name of Bonnet Number, a term that still persists long after buses have ceased to have bonnets at all.

Budget Key (T Key). The traditional key carried at all times by drivers, conductors and engineers that gives access to lockers, cab doors, **Blinds,**

etc. and is therefore essential to bus operation. The key is roughly T-shaped, hence the alternative name.

Bunching. A self-explanatory term for when several buses on the same route start running together, much to the annoyance of the public and of officials alike. It is an even more unpopular occurrence today as bus operators are penalised financially for not maintaining **Headway.**

Bus Stop. Whilst the meaning of this term might seem patently obvious, it's worth remembering that fixed bus stops didn't exist for the first 90 years or so of bus operation – prior to that buses stopped on request, initially on either side of the street. The first experiments with fixed stops happen immediately after World War I, and introduce the particular London distinction between red Request Stops – where the bus only stops when a passenger 'requests' either by ringing the bell on the bus or sticking their arm out when on the stop – and white Compulsory Stops when in theory all buses must stop regardless. In recent years this distinction has been abandoned by TfL, and all buses are expected to stop at stops, but that is patently not observed on quiet stretches of route.

Clippie. The traditional term for women conductors. It's not clear why this only applied to women, as all conductors used to 'clip' tickets prior to the introduction of the **Gibson** ticket machines, but if mistakenly used by a member of the public to address a male conductor was deemed to cause offence.

Coming Off/ Handing Over. This is when a driver has finished either the first part or the whole of their duty and is replaced in service at an official changeover point by another driver – the slight delay this causes often leads to passengers jumping off and onto another bus behind, but it's rare that this results in any time advantage for them.

Controllers, (who used to be called inspectors), are responsible for supervising and controlling all buses on the streets of London. Traditionally Controllers/Inspectors stood by the side of the road at key points on bus routes to supervise the services, but are increasingly being replaced by remote, centralised controllers using the digital ibus system.

Decker/ Low Decker. These are the traditional London busmen's names for double-decker and single-decker buses respectively

Dolly Stop. This is the name used by bus staff for the ubiquitous temporary stops, used when a permanent bus stop is closed or obstructed, or for diversion routes. They are lollipop-like to look at, with a round concrete base, a thin metal pole, and then a large, round, flat head, painted either as a compulsory stop or as a request stop. They were first introduced during World War II in response to the need to divert buses due to bomb damage.

Drive. Whilst the public say 'Driver' as the formal term of address for a bus driver (when not using more colourful descriptions), the traditional variant used internally by inspectors and controllers is **Drive,** as in 'Morning, Drive'. To say this identifies one as being on the job.

Duty. A bus driver's daily job is described as a Duty. Every route has multiple duties numbered consecutively, and divided into Early, Middle and Late shifts or 'turns', as they are known colloquially. Each duty signs on at a precise time, precise as in 04.23, or 16.34. Traditionally drivers worked a different shift each week on a long rota, but it is now common for them to work exclusively Early or Late turns. Night bus drivers work on their own rotas. Drivers are normally allocated to one route exclusively.

Duty Card/ Time Card. This small laminated card, which can normally be seen inserted into the top of the driver's ticket machine, describes in detail the whole of the driver's duty for that day. It has precise departure times for every journey made, and precise times for a range of intermediate points. It is probable that the public imagines that buses just randomly drive from end to end, but in fact they are timed to the minute, and every effort is made to keep to those very exact timings.

Engineer. The mechanics who maintain London's bus fleet have always been known by the superior designation of Engineer. The historic slang term was a Ginger, as in Ginger Beer, but from the 1970s that came to mean something very different indeed and was subsequently not used in this context.

Garage. In London buses live in bus garages, and most definitely not in depots as is often the case elsewhere. The only occasional variation to the word garage is 'Shed', which may well date back to tram and trolleybus days, and is consequently heard less often today.

Garage Code. All bus garages in London are assigned an identifying one or two letter garage code which is traditionally displayed alongside the **Running Number** on each side of the bus, a practice that is still common but not now universal. Some single letter codes go back over a century to the early days of motor buses (eg N for Norwood Garage, built by the LGOC in 1909), whilst others are identifiable as belonging to a former tram or trolleybus shed (eg SF for Stamford Hill, originally opened for trams in 1907).

Gibson. The legendary Gibson ticket machine was originally designed for London Transport by their Ticket Machine Superintendent George Gibson. It was introduced in 1952 and used by conductors for over 40 years. The metallic whirring noise made when a ticket was issued was one of the iconic sounds of London. By tradition if the four digits of the ticket number added up to 21 then one possessed a lucky ticket, although the potential rewards of this were never specified.

Going Round. This describes the action of a bus overtaking the one in front, a manoeuvre normally undertaken in order to share the workload. When two or more buses continue to pass each other in this way it is described as 'working the road'. This was a more common practice when crew buses were involved, as they were quicker at serving bus stops. It interferes with the maintenance of **Headway,** and so is officially frowned upon. It is evidently the opposite of **Scratching.**

Gold Top /Silver Top. These were slang terms (derived from old-fashioned milk bottle tops) for bus inspectors, who wore either silver or gold cap badges to denote their rank. Bus inspectors no longer exist, having been replaced by **Controllers.**

Hail and Ride. On certain routes operated by **Low Deckers** predominantly through suburban residential streets, certain stretches are designated as **Hail and Ride** which means that there are no fixed bus stops, and passengers hail the bus at certain points, normally street corners. How these certain points – essentially invisible bus stops – are agreed upon, and how passengers learn what and where they are, is one of London's minor mysteries, perhaps resembling the process of Hefting by which herds of hill sheep pass on knowledge of paths and pasture from generation to generation.

Half Cab. The term used to describe traditional front-engined motor buses, where the driver sat in a cab half the width of the bus situated alongside the engine, as with the famous Routemaster bus.

Headway. This is one of the most important terms in bus operation. It describes the timed interval between buses on regular timetabled services and can vary from 3 minutes on a high frequency route such as the 38, to 90 minutes on the 375, possibly London's lowest frequency route. Bus operating companies are penalised for failure to maintain headway and it is the job of route **Controllers** to sort this out, by getting buses to leave their terminus points late, or to instruct them to 'hold back' for a minute or two when necessary. The term was celebrated in bus-driving author Miles Mills' *The Maintenance of Headway* (2009).

ibus, (all lower case), is the automatic vehicle location system that is linked to all of London's 8,000 buses, allowing controllers to monitor and communicate with bus drivers, and drivers to see their headway is relation to the bus in front. It also announces each stop, visually and verbally, for the benefit of passengers. The system also provides a series of recorded announcements of the kind designed to strike fear and despondency into the hearts of passengers, eg: *The Next Bus Stop is Closed;* or *This bus is on diversion. Please listen for further announcements;* and the worst of all, *The driver has been instructed to wait at this bus stop for a short time to help* *even out the service.* This latter announcement often sparks a mass exodus amongst passengers.

Jumper. An archaic term for a ticket inspector. It dates back to the very early days of motor buses, when inspectors would jump onto buses as they slowed down for corners, in order to catch the conductor unawares. However, once bus drivers became accustomed to this ploy they would deliberately accelerate or brake sharply, hoping to injure the unfortunate inspector, and the practice was abolished, although the name survived until at least the 1970s, but is no longer in use.

Leader. The term used for the bus in front, as in 'your leader is running late/missing', or occasionally and counter-intuitively 'your leader is behind you'.

Log Card. Every driver carries a log card on which each individual journey from one end of the route to the other is recorded by hand, giving precise arrival and departure times. It also records any variations to their scheduled **Duty,** as for instance when they are given a **Turn,** or when they go **Mechanical.**

Mechanical. The shorthand term for a mechanical fault, particularly when a bus has broken down or is mechanically unfit to enter or continue in service. It is often used as an adjective, as in 'I'm Mechanical', one of those terms that seems perfectly normal in an internal context but might sound bizarre to the outside world.

NSB (NBA). An acronym for No Serviceable Bus (or No Bus Available), indicating that there is not a bus available that is in a fit condition to enter service, the cause of considerable happiness for whichever lucky driver has no bus allocated to them. Most common on a Monday morning when maintenance issues have built up over the weekend. The letters are written on the driver's **Log Card** to explain why they didn't leave the garage on time and hence didn't complete their full duty. It is used as an adjective, as in 'I was NSB'.

On the Couch. An old term for a conductor lazing on the long rear seat on the lower deck.

On the Roof. An old conductor's term for the Upper Deck – as in 'we're full up inside, seats on the roof only'.

OPO. Is the acronym for One Person Operation, now the universal mode of operation with the demise of bus conductors. The original term from the 1960s was OMO – One Man Operation – as there were no women drivers before 1974.

Peak. The proper term used to describe what the public would call the 'rush hour', which of course lasts a lot longer than an hour. There is a Morning Peak and an Evening Peak.

Relief/ Late Relief. Relief is the official term for one driver replacing another when a bus is in service. Bus drivers themselves use the term 'taking over' when they are relieving another driver. When this is a bus that is in service it is called 'taking over on the road'. Late relief refers to a deferred meal break when a driver has finished late on the first part of his duty late, meaning they won't return for their next bus at the scheduled time. This leads to the term 'warning up', when a message is sent to the driver of a bus that there won't be a driver waiting at the relief point, and so the bus must terminate there. It is unlawful to take less than a minimum break of 40 minutes.

Road. An old interchangeable term for Route as in 'What Road are you on today?'. It is possibly a survival from tram days. **Road** is more commonly used to mean that a bus is very busy, as in 'I've got a hell of a road on'.

Rounder. A very important term meaning a complete journey over a whole route in both directions, measured to and from the point that the journey commences. A day's duty is often described as 'two rounders', 'three rounders' etc., or perhaps 'two and a half rounders'. Drivers indicate to each other the amount of driving they still have left by saying eg 'I've only got a rounder to do on my second half'.

Route Learning. All drivers have to 'learn' a route before they can drive it, and new drivers will often start by learning all of the routes that run out of their garage. This normally involves observing an experienced driver over a whole **Rounder**, and then taking over the driving for another rounder whilst being observed by the scheduled driver, who will normally point out where **Turns** are located, which lane to select at a particular junction, and other local knowledge specific to that route .

Running Light. The common term for running out of service, ie driving without passengers, and with the destination blinds blank or displaying 'Out of Service'. This is normally done either to the point where a bus commences service operation or from the point at which it finishes in service and drives back to the garage.

Running Number. Each bus is allocated a unique number each day in the garage which corresponds with a number on each driver's **Duty Card**, telling them exactly which bus they are driving out of the garage, or which bus they will be **Taking Over.** Traditionally the number is displayed next to the **Garage Code** on each side of the bus. The running number is also used for radio communications, as in '238, are you receiving?'.

Running Shift. In bus garages one can find a range of **Engineers** employed in differing specialist functions. Those whose specific task it is to ensure that the buses needed for the day are fit for service and that sufficient buses are allocated to cover all of the scheduled duties are known as the

Running Shift. When a driver discovers a fault on a bus it is the Running Shift that they report it to.

Scratching. This is the MORTAL SIN of bus driving! (Although the derivation is unclear). It means to drive slowly, hanging back and lingering on bus stops, in order to let the bus in front do all of the work, often with the consequence of running late and thereby getting an overtime docket or a Turn. A 'scratcher' usually gets a garage-wide reputation for avoiding hard work. An alternative term is Punching Up, although it has been argued that this is not exactly equivalent, and instead means following rather more closely behind the bus in front, and then not passing them as one is ethically obliged to do, which is a rather more blatant way of letting others do your work for you!

Slaughtered. A bus term for being extremely busy, with too many people waiting at stops and trying to board, as in 'I was slaughtered coming out of Waterloo.'

Spare. A spare driver has not been allocated a place on the rota, either because they are new, or because they only work part-time. This means they are allocated duties arbitrarily on any and every route that their garage operates. Once they are given a rota place they normally work exclusively on one route, day in day out.

Spot. A Plain clothes inspector who does not make themselves known but is watching the behaviour of a conductor or OPO driver suspected of embezzling, drinking on duty, or some other serious misdemeanour. This term was already in use at the beginning of the last century and is still current. In the 19th century respectable-looking women were commonly employed in this role. Also formerly known as a 'wrong'un'.

Spreadover. A particular shift pattern common on busy, high frequency routes, whereby the driver works several hours during the morning Peak, then has several hours off, then returns to work during the evening Peak — and is paid for the total number of hours from start to finish. It is commonly shortened to Spread, as in 'I'm doing a spread today'.

Spreadover Bus. On busy routes extra buses will often be on the road in the morning and evening Peaks but will sit in the garage in between — these are known as spreadover buses, and are often commandeered if another bus goes Mechanical.

Stand. Short for Bus Stand, an officially designated parking areas where buses can 'stand' — ie stop for a while — when they have reached their terminus point. A common instruction to drivers is to 'put it on the Stand', meaning to leave their bus on a particular stand when they are Coming Off.

Sticky. An old term for a staff pass. Apparently in the past the two sections of the pass were glued back to back, but the name survived long after that ceased to happen. It is now obsolete.

Straight In and Out. An instruction issued by controllers to drivers not to stand on arrival at their destination, but to return straight away regardless of time card information, normally used if the bus is needed to plug a gap in the service.

Thank you. An old-fashioned term that was apparently once used by passengers to address bus crews. It has now dropped out of use entirely.

Turn. A term much beloved of bus drivers, describing an authorised curtailment from their scheduled destination, normally issued in order to get a late running bus back on time. A controller normally gives a driver a turn by saying eg 'Show Camden' thereby instructing the driver to change the blind to show Camden Town as the new destination. 'Show Camden on the way back' would be called to indicate that a bus should curtail on its next trip back. Turning a bus generates much annoyance and confusion amongst passengers.

Turns. These are the designated places where buses may be turned short on any route. A driver has to learn every Turn as each involves a different dropping off point for passengers, a manoeuvre to get the bus facing back in the right direction, a bus **Stand** where a bus can wait until its scheduled departure time, and a picking up point for passengers on the subsequent journey.

Twirlies. The old and largely affectionate term for senior citizens, whose free bus passes were at one time only valid at off-peak times: as that time approached they would stand at bus stops and ask 'Is it too early?', which became contracted to 'Twirly'. Another term used for the elderly in the 1970s was '**Wombles**', probably a visual reference to the many layers of clothing these fictional creatures wore in the popular children's television show. It is not meant to be taken literally to say that these are both dying out.

Up Front/ On the Back. These are the old terms used by bus crews to describe drivers and conductors, as in 'Who have you got up front?' or 'I've got Bill on the back today'. They remained in use until the end of crew operations in 2005.

WTI. One of the many acronyms that may be entered on a driver's **Log card.** This one, an abbreviation of Working to Instruction, is used when a driver has been told to ignore their scheduled time as recorded on their **Duty** Card, and to follow new instructions – 'leave 3 early please, **Drive**', usually issued to regulate **Headway.**

LONDON BUS TIMELINE

4 July 1829 The first two Shillibeer omnibuses run from the Yorkshire Stingo, Paddington, along the New Road to the Bank

1832 The Stage-Coach Act permits omnibuses to pick up and set down passengers in the street and introduces licences for buses

1833 The 'Era' and the 'Autopsy' steam omnibuses are introduced

1838 An Act of Parliament establishes the Office of the Register Of Metropolitan Public Carriages to licence omnibuses and their drivers and conductors. All buses are required to display the number of passengers they are licenced to carry, and all drivers and conductors are to wear numbered badges in order to identify them

1846 Advertisements first appear on a London omnibus

1847 Adams & Co of Fairfield Works, Bow builds the world's first double-decker bus for the Economic Conveyance Company of London

1850 Licencing of omnibus passes to the Metropolitan Police

1851 The first 'knife-board' omnibus is introduced

1851 The first meeting of omnibus proprietors is held at the Duke of Wellington, Argyle Square, to devise and to work new bus routes in cooperation rather than in direct competition, with agreed times and fares

1851 Thomas Tilling runs his first Omnibus

1855 The London General Omnibus Company (LGOC) is established in Paris

7 January 1856 the LGOC commences its first operations on the routes of some older companies that it had acquired. Within a year it owns 600 of London's 810 omnibuses

1867 The Metropolitan Streets Act required buses to stop on the nearside of the road only, whereas previously they had pulled over to whichever side the passenger wished to alight. This simplified bus design as it only required access to the platform on one side

1869 An LGOC 'City-Atlas' omnibus is the first vehicle to cross the new Holborn Viaduct

1880 The London Road Car Company is formed, eventually becoming London's second largest horse bus operator. It introduces the first bus with garden seats on the roof. It is also the first operator to introduce bus tickets

1891 The LGOC adopts the bus ticket system, prompting a week-long, London-wide strike of bus crews, settled by a substantial wage increase and a reduction in hours worked

1892 Bells are introduced to alert the driver to stop the bus

1899 The first petrol engine bus is introduced by the Motor Traction Company, operating on a short-lived service between Kensington and Victoria

1899–1902 Hundreds of London's omnibus horses are requisitioned to serve in the Second Boer War

1900 The number of horse buses in London peaks at 3,736

1902 The LGOC introduces its first motor buses

1904 Thomas Tilling starts using motor buses on the Peckham to Oxford Circus Route

1905 The London Motor Omnibus Company is founded as the first purely motor bus operator

1906 The first bus route numbers are introduced by the London Motor Omnibus Company, which names all of its buses Vanguard, and then adds a number 1 to 5 for their five routes, rising to 12 by 1908. Several modern routes owe a direct lineage to these Vanguard routes, including routes 2 and 19

1907 The LGOC paints its buses red, the colour that is eventually adopted by London Transport for all London buses

15 July 1907 The London Electrobus Company commences operating electric buses between Victoria and Liverpool Street Stations, eventually operating a fleet of 20 buses. The company tests the first double-decker bus In London with a roof on the upper deck, but the police refuse to licence it. The company is liquidated in 1910 amid allegations of fraud. It is more than a century later that London next sees electric double-deckers

1908 The LGOC merges with the London Road Car Company and the Vanguard Company, establishing a virtual monopoly of London's buses, and the first methodical route numbering system is introduced. Of these, routes 1, 2, 3, 6, 7, 8, 9, 11, 14, 16 and 19 are still running today on at least part of their 1908 route. There are more than 100 numbered routes by 1914

August 1909 The LGOC starts manufacturing its own motor buses, at the former Vanguard works in Walthamstow, commencing with the X-type, of which 60 are built by December

1910 The LGOC's legendary 34-seat B-type bus is introduced, the first reliable mass-produced bus. More than 3,000 are eventually built

1910 Joe Clough becomes London's first black bus driver, driving B-type buses on Route 11

1910 The LGOC produces the first free guide to London's bus routes

25 October 1911 the LGOC retires its last horse bus

1912 The Underground Group purchases the LGOC

1912 Bus route 24, introduced in 1910 to run from Hampstead Heath to Victoria Station, is extended to Pimlico, making it the oldest bus route in London to still run in its entirety

1913 Headlights are introduced on the B-Type bus. It had previously been thought that the interior lights (electric since 1912) would illuminate the bus sufficiently at night

1912 The Associated Equipment Company (AEC) is established as a subsidiary of the LGOC to manufacture London's buses, becoming the main supplier of the capital's buses until the 1960s

1913 The first night bus service commences

1913 The LGOC begins experiments with fixed bus stops

4 August 1914 London's last horse bus is retired by Thomas Tilling

1914–18 1,300 LGOC buses, including 954 B-Types, nearly one third of London's entire fleet, are sent to serve on the Western Front. In 1918 there were 2,277 buses running on London's streets, compared with 3,057 in 1914

February 1915 21 per cent of men employed on London's buses and trams have enlisted, leading to severe staff shortages. In total around 9,500 busmen leave London for the battlefields

1 November 1915 Mrs G Duncan becomes London's first 'clippie' (or 'Hurry-Along girl') with Thomas Tilling on route 37

24 February 1916 The LGOC employs its first clippie. They would eventually employ 3,500 women conductors. Women were not permitted to drive, and all had lost their jobs by 1919

1916 Rationing of petrol is introduced. Standing inside buses is allowed due to the scarcity of vehicles

1916 The production of buses by AEC ceases in favour of military vehicles

15 August 1918 Women bus and tram workers go on strike to demand equal pay with men

21 November 1919 The last women bus conductors, Mrs T Petty and Ellen Bullfield, are discharged by the LGOC

1919 The 46-seat K-Type bus introduced; 1,050 are manufactured by 1926. By placing the driver next to the engine rather than behind it, the influence of horse buses on motor bus layout is ended and capacity is increased significantly

1919 Fixed bus stops at the busiest locations are introduced by the LGOC, but buses still have to stop elsewhere when requested

1921 The famous Chiswick Works are opened by the LGOC, as a centralised bus overhaul facility, the first of its kind

1923 The innovative NS bus type is introduced with upholstered seats and a lowered chassis, which allowed for a lower platform for easier boarding, and a covered roof – although the licencing authorities did not allow this until 1925. More than 2,400 were built, the last being withdrawn in 1937

1923 For the first time buses carry more passengers than either trams or the Underground

1924 London Traffic Act restricts independent 'pirate' bus operators in favour of the large monopoly operators. The Metropolitan Police are given authority to allocate compulsory route numbers under the Bossom Scheme, by which LGOC routes were numbered 1 to 199, and authorised independent routes from 200 to 299 plus 509 to 599

1925 The first pneumatic tyred bus is introduced. By 1928 all new buses have pneumatic tyres

1929 The revolutionary prototype ST bus is introduced with an enclosed platform and staircase, front windscreen and roller destination blinds at front and back

1930 Enclosed cabs are introduced for bus drivers

1930 The Road Traffic Act establishes the Commissioner of the Metropolitan Police as Traffic Commissioner for London

13 April 1933 The London Passenger Transport Act establishes the London Passenger Transport Board (LPTB), which is given a monopoly over all bus services within its area, an approximate 30-mile radius from Charing Cross. All services are branded as London Transport (LT)

October 1934 LT introduces a new numbering system with 1–199 for central double-decker routes, 200–289 for central single-decker routes, 290–299 for central night bus routes, 300–399 for country area (north) routes, and 400–499 for country area (south) routes

1935 LT introduces an experimental scheme of fixed bus stops along an entire route from Euston Road to Tottenham. By the late 1940s the entire LT network has bus stops

1939 The prototype of the classic 56-seat AEC RT bus type is introduced. Only 150 are built before wartime production is halted in 1940, as some parts are sourced from Germany. Some 7,000 RT buses are eventually built after 1946, replacing all other double-decker bus types. They run in service until 1979

September 1939 London Transport vehicles spearhead the mass evacuation of 550,000 children, expectant mothers and hospital patients over 4 days

1940 The LPTB starts to recruit women bus conductors again. They also work on bus maintenance and as garage shunters but are not allowed to drive in service

1940 Over 800 buses are withdrawn to save on petrol

1940 470 buses are loaned to London from provincial fleets to cover for war damage. Later in the war the LTPB was to loan 330 buses to other operators whose fleets had been depleted by the war

1940–44 150 London buses are converted to run on gas produced by injecting water into burning coal in a trailer unit towed behind the bus. They can only operate on flatter routes requiring less power

June 1946 Two RT buses in wartime livery take part in a Victory Parade in the Mall attended by the King and Queen

1947 The Transport Act nationalises public transport and establishes the London Transport Executive (LTE) to replace the LTPB, under the control of the British Transport Commission

1949 The first 8-foot-wide RTW type bus is introduced

1950 The last petrol engine bus is withdrawn

1952 London buses are carrying 8 million passengers a day, but numbers will decline steadily for the next four decades

1952 The Gibson ticket machine is introduced to replace bell punch ticket machines. It is used on all LT crew-operated buses until 1993

September 1954 The AEC Routemaster (RM) bus is introduced, becoming London's most famous and loved bus type. More than 2,700 are built for London Transport

1956 The Aldenham bus overhaul works for bus bodies and frames is opened. The strict maintenance regime operated there is later credited with the extraordinary longevity that the RT and RM bus types achieve

8 February 1956 The prototype Routemaster RM1 enters service on Route 2

1956 London Transports begins to recruit staff directly from the Caribbean via a recruitment office established in Bridgetown, Barbados. The scheme operates until 1970

1958 London Transport advertises in the Republic of Ireland for single women over the age of 20 to work as bus conductors

5 May–20 June 1959 A bus strike leads to the complete withdrawal of all of London's buses. The strike is later blamed for a serious long-term decline in passenger numbers, leading to the withdrawal of a number of routes and the closure of some bus garages

1961 The 72-seat, 30-foot-long Routemaster (RML) is introduced, serving first on route 104

1962 The Transport Act replaces the LTE with the London Transport Board, which is directly accountable to the Ministry of Transport

1962 The 57-seat Green Line coach version of the Routemaster (RMC) is introduced

1965 London Transport recruit a small number of bus drivers directly from Malta, seen as suitable as vehicles drive on the left-hand side of the road there

1965 The last 27 feet 6 inch standard-length Routemaster, RM2217, is built

1965 The first experimental front entrance, rear engined, buses are introduced; the 72 seat, 30 feet long Leyland Atlantean (XA) and Daimler Fleetline (XF) types

1967 The experimental front-entrance, rear-engine Routemaster (FRM) enters service on Route 76

March 1968 The last Routemaster, RML 2760, enters service

18 April 1966 The first Red Arrow service is launched, intended to operate between busy hubs with single-decker AEC Merlin buses catering for more standing passengers than conventional services

14 September 1968 The Bus Reshaping Plan drawn up by the London Transport Board paves the way for what was then called One Man Operation (OMO, later renamed One Person Operation or OPO). It also introduces shorter routes to improve reliability and flat fares on new bus routes centred on such suburban hubs as Wood Green and Walthamstow

26 October 1968 The first single-decker OMO buses are introduced in southeast London

1968 Women conductors demonstrate in demand of equal pay

November 1969 Route 233 serving the Croydon area become the first route to be operated by OMO double-decker XA class Leyland Atlanteans

1969 Transport (London) Act transfers responsibility for London's public transport to the Greater London Council (GLC). Bus services outside the GLC area are passed to the new London Country Bus Services

1970 The first buses with two-way radios enter service on routes 74 and 74B

2 January 1971 The first Daimler Fleetline (DMS) OMO double-decker buses are introduced on routes 95 and 220. London Transport eventually purchase 2,646 of this class. Following adverse public reactions to OMO, the original plan to phase out crew-operated Routemasters by 1975 is abandoned

1971 The last conductors on single-decker services are withdrawn from route 236

1974 Jill Viner becomes London's first female bus driver, aged 22

Jill Viner posing in the cab of an RT-type bus for a picture taken to commemorate her becoming London's first woman bus driver, 1974

1977 The last AEC Merlin buses are replaced with Leyland National buses

1978 The Leyland Titan is the last bus type with a significant design input from London Transport to be built in London

1981 The Greater London Council (GLC) under the leadership of Ken Livingstone introduces the Fares Fair policy of subsidising public transport, leading to a reduction of approximately one third of fares. The legality of the policy was challenged by the Conservative leader of Bromley Council, and after the House of Lords found in his favour, the policy was abandoned

1982 The 'Can't Pay, Won't Pay' campaign is launched against rising public transport fares and the scrapping of the Fares Fair policy

1984 The London Regional Transport Act established London Regional Transport (LRT) to run Greater London's public transport network under the direct control of the Secretary of State for Transport, as a preliminary to privatisation

1985 London Buses Limited is formed to manage the bus network. The Tendered Bus Division is set up in order to begin the process of competitive tendering

1985 The first London bus services are put out to competitive tender

1988 Following trials of competing designs, all OPO buses in London are fitted with Wayfarer 2 electronic ticket machines

1 April 1989 London Buses is divided into 13 geographical subsidiary units in preparation for privatisation

1992 The government announces the sale of the 13 subsidiary units into the private sector

1992–3 Trials of electronic smartcard ticket are conducted on route 212, extended to a far larger trial on routes in the Harrow area in 1994–95

1994 the privatisation of London Buses Limited is complete

29 January 1994 Route 120 becomes the first route to be operated entirely with low floor wheelchair accessible buses with the introduction of 10 Dennis Lance SLF single-deckers

1998 Route 242 becomes the first double-decker route to be operated by low floor buses, using DLA type Alexander ALX400 bodied DAF buses

2 July 1999 The Greater London Authority Act establishes Transport for London to replace LRT as an agency of the newly created Greater London Authority, bringing London's transport system back under local government control

October 2001 The first six of the articulated buses, popularly known as 'bendy buses' enter service on bus route 207, introduced by Mayor Ken Livingstone. They eventually operate on 11 central London routes, but are all withdrawn by December 2011, following an election promise by Mayor Boris Johnson

2002 TfL introduces the first 'spider' maps; these are single bus route maps designed in the schematic style of Harry Beck's famous Underground Map

30 June 2003 The Oyster Card electronic ticketing system is launched. By 2012 over 80 per cent of journeys on London's public transport system are made using the card

January 2004 The first two zero emission hydrogen fuel cell buses are trialled on route 25

7 July 2005 52 people are killed in bomb attacks on three Underground trains and a route 30 bus

9 December 2005 The last crew-operated Routemaster buses are withdrawn from service on bus route 159, ending 49 years of RM operation, and marking the end of conductors on London's buses after 175 years. All of London's buses are now wheelchair accessible low floor types

2006 The first hybrid electric buses are introduced on single-decker route 360. They use an electric battery pack in combination with a diesel engine, reducing emissions by 40 per cent

February 2007 The world's first hybrid electric double-decker bus enters service on route 141

2012 Bus passenger journeys have reached their highest level since 1959. Between 1999/00 and 2011/12, bus passenger kilometres have increased by 80 per cent while bus journey stages have increased by 64 per cent

February 2012 The first LT or 'Boris Bus' enters service

2014 Bus passenger numbers start to decline for the first time in a decade, falling by 6 per cent over the next two years, but remains at over 2 billion passenger journeys a year, roughly double that of the London Underground

July 2014 Cash fares are no longer accepted on London's buses after 185 years. Contactless payment cards can now be used to pay for fares alongside Oyster Cards. TfL are the first transport authority in the world to accept payment in this way

2015 Route RV1 becomes the first to be operated entirely by fuel cell buses

2016 Planned expansion of London's bus services is halted for at least five years in response to declining passenger numbers, having grown by 35 per cent to almost 500 million kilometres a year since 2000

April 2016 The world's first electric double-decker buses (at least in this century, and excluding trolleybuses) are introduced on route 98. They are built by Chinese company BYD and can travel 180 miles on a single charge

September 2016 Mayor Sadiq Khan announces that single-decker central London routes 507 and 521 will be the first routes to be operated entirely by electric buses

30 November 2016 The world's first double-decker hydrogen fuel cell bus manufactured by UK company Wrightbus is unveiled outside London's City Hall. London's Transport Commissioner Mike Brown commits to making London's transport system 'one of the cleanest in the world'

2017 The London Assembly Transport Committee proposes a redistribution of buses from central to suburban London in response to changing demand and a decline in overall passenger numbers

March 2017 The first Low Emission Bus Zone is introduced along Putney High Street, followed in December by Brixton Road and Streatham Road. Only buses with engines and exhaust systems that meet or exceed Euro VI emission standards can be used in these zones. 12 zones in total are due to be introduced by 2019

December 2017 The last of 1,000 LT buses is delivered after Mayor Sadiq Khan cancels further orders

2018 TfL intends to cease buying diesel-only double-decker buses completely. All central London double-deckers are planned to be hybrid by 2019

February 2018 There were 174.9 million passenger journeys made in the past year, a slight increase on the previous year

BIBLIOGRAPHY AND ACKNOWLEDGEMENTS

Various authors, individuals, publishers, and estates have generously given their permission for pieces and extracts from copyrighted work to be reproduced in this book.

Every reasonable effort has been made to secure permissions before this book went to print. Anyone who we have not been able to reach is invited to contact the publisher so that a full acknowledgement may be given in subsequent editions.

Agate, James, *Ego, 8 vols* (London: Harrap, 1935–1947)

Barbellion, W N P, *Journal of a Disappointed Man*, (London: Chatto & Windus, 1919)

Beltrame, Julius, 'Night Bus Facebook Updates 2014-2009', reproduced here by generous permission of the author

Bennett, Arnold, *The Journals of Arnold Bennett 1921–1928, vol 3,* edited by Newman Flower (London: Cassell, 1933)

Blumenfeld, R D, *R.D.B.'s diary, 1887-1914* (London: Heinemann, 1930)

Boon, Richard, *Freedom of the City*, previously unpublished piece, reproduced by kind permission of the author who retains copyright

Bownes, David, The Way to London's Country: LGOC country area posters, 1912–1932 (2018), previously unpublished piece by the museum curator, copyright with the author

Braithwaite, E R, *To Sir With Love* (London: Bodley Head 1959) © The Estate of E R Braithwaite and David Higham Associates

Brown, Matt, 'Why Are London Buses Red?' and 'Lost in the Thames' from articles originally published on the Londonist website, permission generously granted by the author

Catterall, Ali, 'Time and Relative Dimensions in SW3' (2018), previously unpublished piece, copyright the author

Crawford, Marion, *The Little Princesses* (London: Odhams Press Limited, 1952) © Orion Publishing Group, London

Cunningham, Peter, 'Omnibus Information' from *A Handbook for London, past and present* (London: John Murray, 1850)

Curtis, Barry, 'Red Bus, Silver Screen' (2018), previously unpublished piece by the academic and film historian, copyright the author

Dennis, Richard, Picturing the London Bus (2018), previously unpublished piece, copyright the author

Dickens, Charles, Omnibuses, Street Sketches No 1 in the *Morning Chronicle*, 26 September 1834

Dickens, Charles, *All Year Round*, Issue 30, 12 June 1869

Dirix, Emmanuelle, 'The Lure of the Omnibus: Hurry-Along Girls and World War I', previously unpublished piece, copyright the author

Edwards, Dickon, online diary (2002), republished with permission of Dickon Edwards

Elborough, Travis, 'The Bus That Didn't Stop' from *Tower Bridge: A Guide* (London: Scala Arts & Heritage 2016) © Tower Bridge, City of London Corporation

Evans, Gareth, 'Public Transports: 38 stops' (2018), previously unpublished piece by the writer, editor and curator, copyright the author

Ford, Ford Madox, *The Soul of London* (London: Duckworth & Co, 1911)

Games, Naomi, 'Poster Masters and Routemasters' (2018), previously unpublished piece, copyright the author

Gordon, W J, *The Horse World of London*, (London: The Religious Tract Society, 1893)

Gregg, C F, *Murder on the Bus* (London: Hutchinson & Co, 1930)

Green, Oliver, Buses During the Blitz (2018), previously unpublished piece, copyright the author

Greenwood, James, *The Seven Curses of London*, (London: Stanley Rivers and co, 1869)

Grindrod, John, Fellow Travellers: Tracing the parallel journeys of the Green Line and the green belt (2018) previously unpublished piece by the author of *Concretopia*, copyright the author

Grossmith, George & Weedon, *The Diary of a Nobody* (London: Hutchinson & Co, 1935)

Hadfield, Mark, 'The Reasoning Behind the Numbers of the Routes' email exchange originally published on That Gormandizer Man blog 12 March 2009, reproduced here by the generous permission of the author

Hardy, Thomas, *The Life of Thomas Hardy*, edited by Florence Emily Hardy (London: Macmillan, 1933)

Hulme, James, 'Green Line and Country Area Services: Taking modern design into the countryside' (2018) previously unpublished piece, copyright the author

Jack, Ian, 'End of the Line', first published in *The Guardian* 29 October 2005, reproduced here by generous permission of the author

Jane, Fred, 'The Romance of a London Omnibus', From *The English Illustrated Magazine* V11, 1894

Kerr, Joe, 'A Bus Glossary' (2018), previously unpublished piece, copyright the author

Kerr, Joe, 'London Bus Timeline' (2018), previously unpublished piece, copyright the author

Kerr, Joe, 'On the Back to Up Front' (2018), previously unpublished piece, copyright the author

Kipling, Rudyard, 'In Partibus', *The Civil and Military Gazette*, 23 December 1889

Krupskaya, N K, *Reminiscenses of Lenin* (New York: International Publishers, 1970), permission granted by Gary Bono for International Publishers

Lawrence, Patrice, 'Sightseeing Drinking Game' extract from *Indigo Donut* (London: Hodder Children's Books, 2017) © Patrice Lawrence, permissions Hachette Children's Group and Patrice Lawrence

Levy, Amy, 'Ballade Of An Omnibus' from *A London plane-tree and other verse* (London: T Fisher Unwin, 1889)

Lockwood, F T, extracts from diaries published online, https://aghs.jimdo.com/acocks-green-s-vulnerability/extracts- from-the-wartime-diaries-of-frank-taylor-lockwood/ Permissions the Lockwood Family and the Acocks Green History Society

London General Omnibus Co, *One Hundred Years of the London Omnibus, 1829–1929* (London: London General Omnibus Co, 1929)

MacDonagh, Michael, *In London During the Great War: The Diary of a Journalist* (London: Eyre & Spottiswoode, 1935)

Macdonald, Rowena, To Venus and Back on the Number 8 (2018), previously unpublished piece by the novelist, copyright the author

Maconochie, Anna, '244' (2018), previously unpublished poem, copyright the author

Manby Smith, Charles, *Curiosities of London Life; or, phases, physiological and social, of the great metropolis* (London, 1853)

Mannheim, Linda, 'The Commute' (2018), previously unpublished story, copyright the author

Mannheim, Linda, 'On the Way' (2018), previously unpublished story, copyright the author

Martin, Andrew 'A Bunch of Buses', originally published in Talk of the Town, *The Independent on Sunday* 13 April 2003, reproduced here by the generous permission of the author

Martin, Andrew, 'Death of the Routemaster', originally published *Daily Telegraph*, 1 January 2005, reproduced here by the generous permission of the author

Mayhew, Henry, *London Labour and the London Poor* (London: Cassell, 1861–62)

Mills, Roger, 'Glimpses Through the Window of a Number 73 Bus' (2018), previously unpublished piece, copyright the author

Mills, Magnus, 'Standing Orders', *The Independent*, Monday 27 June 1994, reproduced here by the generous permission of the author

Monro, Michele, *The Singer's Singer: The Life and Music of Matt Monro* (London: Titan 2010) © Michele Monro, permission generously granted by the author, www.mattmonro.com

Moore, Henry Charles, extract from 'Tram 'Bus and Cab London' published in *Living London* periodical (1905)

Morton, H V *Our Fellow Men* (London: Metheun, 1936) permissions Methuen and the estate of H V Morton

Mullins, Sam, 'The Bus During World War I', previously unpublished piece by the Director of the London Transport Museum, copyright the author

Murphy, Douglas, 'New Bus for London' (2018), previously unpublished piece, copyright the author

Nicholson, Geoff, 'The Bastards on the Bus' 2018, previously unpublished piece by the novelist, flâneur and connoisseur of urban ruins, copyright the author

Pepper, Penny, 'Bus' (2018), previously unpublished poem by the performance poet, singer and disability activist, copyright the author

Pringle, George, 'Bus Stop H and The Ghost' (2018), previously unpublished piece, copyright the author

Rennison, Nick, previously unpublished piece by the author and critic, copyright the author

Reynolds, Z Nia, *When I came to England: An Oral History of Life in 1950s & 1960s Britain* by Black Stock Books (2001) permissions granted by Black Stock Books

Roach, Jo, 'Colombia Road Flower Market' 2018, previously unpublished poem, copyright the author

Self, Will, 'My Paean to London's Most Important Building', originally published in the *Evening Standard*, 14 March 2011, reproduced here by generous permission of the author

Self, Will, 'Tasty Transport: The Stockwell Bus Garage Canteen' originally published as 'Real Meals' in *New Statesman*, 2011, reproduced here by generous permission of the author

Selvon, Samuel, 'Working the Transport', first published in *Ways of Sunlight* (London: Macgibbon & Kee, 1957) permission courtesy of the Estate of Sam Selvon

Shahani, Ranjee, *The Amazing English* (London: Adam and Charles Black 1948)

Sinclair, Iain, 'Queen of the Road' from *Hackney, That Rose-Red Empire: A Confidential Report* (London ; New York : Hamish Hamilton, 2009) reproduced here by the generous permission of the author

Slate, Ruth, *Dear girl: the diaries and letters of two working women* (1897–1917), edited by Tierl Thompson (London: Women's Press, 1987)

Sommerfield, Vernon, *London's Buses: The Story of a Hundred Years 1829–1929* (London: The St Catherine Press, 1933)

Thomas, Ian, 'Joe Clough The first Black Bus Driver' originally published on 18 August 2015 on www.blackhistorymonth.org.uk, reproduced here by generous permission of the author, who retains copyright

Unsworth, Cathi, 'To the World's End' (2006), reproduced here by generous permission of the author

Votolato, Greg, 'Designing London's Buses' (2018), previously unpublished piece, copyright the author

Watts, Peter, 'Roll Up for the Boris Bus', originally published in *Time Out*, 2012, reproduced here by generous permission of the author

Watts, Peter, 'Route Riders', originally published in *Completely London* in 2011, reproduced here by the generous permission of the author

Wells, Tim, 'There but for the Grace of Bauhaus' (2013), poem reproduced by generous permission of the author, once described by the *Guardian* as 'the Suedehead bard of N16'

Williams, Kenneth, *The Kenneth Williams Diaries*, edited by Russell Davies (London: HarperCollins, 1994) © HarperCollins, permission granted HarperCollins and the estate of Kenneth Williams

Wilson, Elizabeth, 'Ahmed on the 274' (2018), previously unpublished piece by the novelist and critic, copyright the author

Wolmar, Christian, 'Hold Tight on the Clapham Omnibus: Next Stop, Privatisation', *The Independent*, Monday 14 September 1992 reproduced, along with a further piece reflecting on the subsequent 25 years, by the generous permission of the author

Woolf, Virginia, *Jacob's Room* (London: Hogarth Press, 1922)

Woolf, Virginia, *Mrs Dalloway* (London: Hogarth Press, 1929)

Additional content from various archive newspapers, journals and magazines, credit as per extract.

IMAGE CREDITS

The Automobile Association would like to thank the following photographers, companies and picture libraries for their assistance in the preparation of this book.